A Rock Fell on the Moon

A Rock Fell on the Moon

Dad and the Great Yukon Silver Ore Heist

Alicia Priest

Lost Moose is an imprint of Harbour Publishing Co. Ltd.
P.O. Box 219, Madeira Park, BC, V0N 2H0
www.harbourpublishing.com

Front jacket, main image: Helen Priest, centre, with daughters Alicia, left, and Vona, 1958; Gerald Priest photo. Front inset: Gerald Priest, right, poses with friend George Esterer outside an abandoned Yukon homestead; Rob Stodard photo. Back jacket: Looking toward the Moon Claim, 1963; photo from author's collection. Page ii: Left to right, Gerald, Helen, Alicia (holding Mitzi), Vona and Omi near their Elsa home *c.* 1960.

The poetry selections at the chapter openings all come from *The Best of Robert Service* (McGraw-Hill Ryerson Ltd., 1953) and *Songs of a Sourdough* (McGraw-Hill Ryerson Ltd., 1957).

Edited by Pam Robertson
Indexed by Brianna Cerkiewicz
Map, text and jacket design by Peggy Issenman
Printed and bound in Canada

BRITISH COLUMBIA ARTS COUNCIL

Canada Council Conseil des arts
for the Arts du Canada

Harbour Publishing acknowledges financial support from the Government of Canada through the Canada Book Fund and the Canada Council for the Arts, and from the Province of British Columbia through the BC Arts Council and the Book Publishing Tax Credit.

Cataloguing data available from Library and Archives Canada
978-1-55017-672-8 (cloth)
978-1-55017-673-5 (ebook)

FOR BEN AND CHARLOTTE

Gerry, around 1951, early on in the employ of United Keno Hill Mines.

Contents

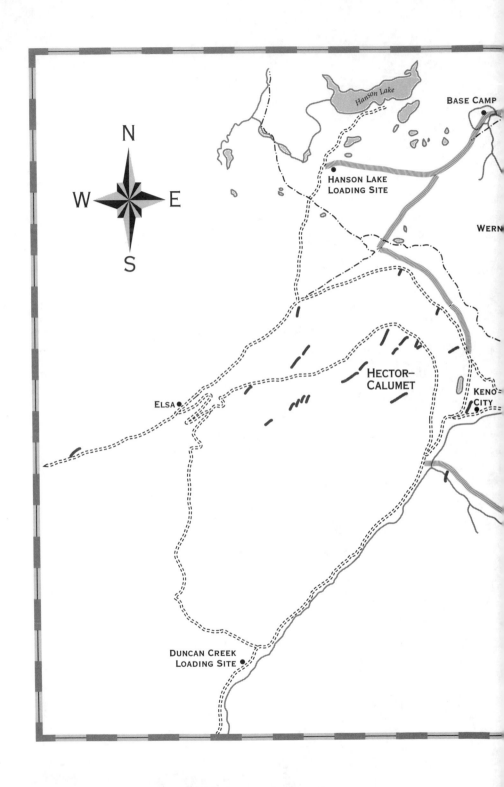

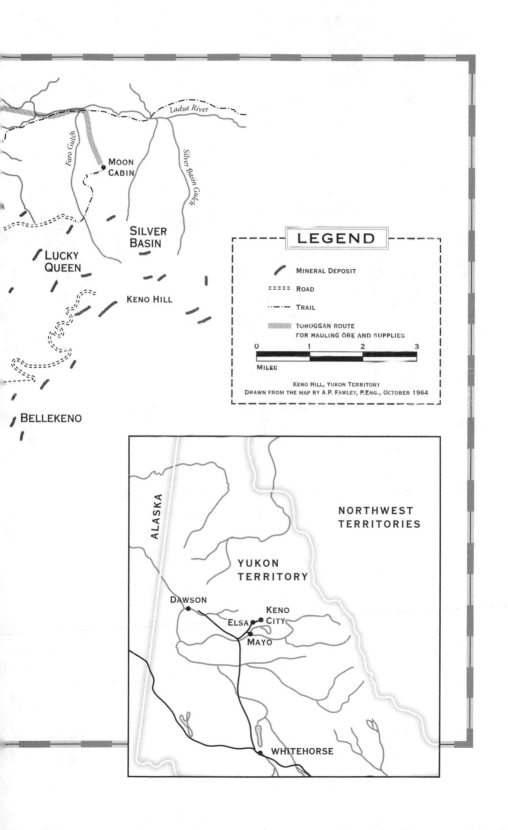

Ladue River

Faro Gulch

MOON CABIN

Silver Basin Gulch

SILVER BASIN

LUCKY QUEEN

KENO HILL

BELLEKENO

LEGEND

Mineral Deposit

===== Road

—··—·· Trail

||||||||| Toboggan Route
For Hauling Ore and Supplies

0   1   2   3

MILES

Keno Hill, Yukon Territory
Drawn from the map by A.P. Fawley, P.Eng., October 1964

ALASKA

NORTHWEST TERRITORIES

YUKON TERRITORY

DAWSON

KENO CITY

ELSA

MAYO

WHITEHORSE

My, what big teeth you have! Caesar and Alicia, age six.

Things Go South

Alas! the road to Anywhere is pitfalled with disaster.

IT IS SO BAD NOW BECAUSE BEFORE IT WAS SO GOOD. I've been kidnapped and taken far, far away, and the worst thing is, my own parents did it. Yesterday, August 29, 1963, I turned ten. Crouched in a shady spot under a shrub in the sun-baked backyard, I scrawl in my diary, writing out a scheme to run away from the cramped, dank East Vancouver basement suite I find myself living in with my grandmother, mother, older sister and one dog. I will return to my real home, a log house in Elsa, a remote Yukon settlement 300 miles north of Whitehorse. I'm not running *away* from home. I'm running *to* home. Where I have a real dad, caring friends, a cheerful school, the best dog in the world and my own room. Here, I'm not only sharing a bedroom with my sister, I'm sharing a bed. And where is Dad?

I'll take any money I find in the house (so far $12.41), get to the airport and fly to Mayo where I'll ask our friend Herb Zollweg to pick me up, drive me to Elsa and build me my own log cabin. I scribble another few words: "Miserable. Life sad." Earlier, I found Mom's ten-cent Hilary notebook, where she'd penned: "Bad news! Still on radio."

I was born in the Yukon, and having lived in Elsa all my life I know that home is more than a house and the people in it.

More than two months have passed since my abduction but all day, every day, I think only of my lost home. Elsa is so small and so nowhere it doesn't make it onto most Canadian maps, but to my sister and me it is Grand Central Shangri-La. In Elsa, I'm free to wander, secure without being smothered, and experience the serene excitement of tramping alone through the tamed wilderness outside my doorstep. I know someday I'll have to leave—our school only goes to grade seven—but until then, Elsa and I are inseparable. Shortly before the end of grade four, though, Dad announces we're moving. Next week. Vancouver will be a temporary stop, he says, but then our lives will dramatically change for the better. Better? We're gathered round the kitchen table—the hub of our northern home, where we eat together, play board games and have all manner of discussions and philosophical debates. It's after supper and the well-worn wooden surface is clean and clear when Dad brings out an 8 × 10 black and white photograph of a sprawling two-storey house with a wide filigree porch spanning the long front side. The photo is taken from the air, capturing not only the house but sky-brushing full-leaf trees, forever lawns and flower and food gardens that stretch past the picture's border.

"Feast your eyes on our new home, my dears. In the rolling foothills of Alberta, ranching country but close enough to a city to keep your mother amused." He pitches her a wink. We're dumbstruck, except Mom, who smiles reassuringly and strokes our heads and lets out a soft laugh. "And this," he continues, pointing to a tiny window on the second storey, "will be your bedroom, Vona. Over here, on the other side, will be yours, Alice."

I stare at a grainy square speck on the photo, unable to speak. But Vona manages to blurt out the question closest to her heart.

"Can I have a horse?"

"A horse?" he says. "Of course. But why only one!"

Vona beams. For the moment, the promise of having her very own steed (or three) has upstaged everything. The reality of leaving Elsa will hit her later.

Not me. I find my voice and shaky as it is I plead to please, please let us stay. At least until we finish grade six or seven. "Do we have to move now? Why? What's the big hurry?"

A scowl darkens Dad's face and then suddenly he brightens and sweetens the deal. Before we move to our grand new residence on acres of our own land, he will whisk me to Disneyland, an unheard-of fantasy vacation for a young girl in the 1960s, especially a Yukon girl. And Dad will take Vona on her dream trip—a horseback trek through the Rockies, a venture he has made three times before. We can't finish the school year. We have one week to collect our school records, say goodbye to friends and pack one suitcase with clothes and essential treasures. Dad will stay behind to pack our belongings, find a good home for our tabby Mitzi and then join us with our long-haired, large and loyal to the point of death Belgian shepherd, Caesar. I have an enormous dog chart covering one bedroom wall with pictures of all the breeds. Although Caesar looks like an extra large and shaggy German shepherd, I am thankful he is a Tervuren Belgian shepherd because in the world we live in anything German is evil.

Dad carries me to bed, where Mom sits on the edge massaging my leg until I sink into sleep. In the morning, I wake with a twisted knot in my stomach. Something isn't right, and then yesterday surges back. Unwilling to rise or open my eyes, I hear a nameless bird sing three long, single notes outside my open window: *Twoo-dee-doo. Twoo-dee-doo.* "Do not leave. Do not leave," it chants. Later, when packing, I stuff that birdcall into a zippered pocket.

In three days, far less than the week we were promised, my mother, sister and I are thousands of miles away from everything familiar and holed up semi-below ground at 348 East Fortieth Avenue. At one end of the block cars race along a highway called Main Street. At the other end, a vast and alluring graveyard where shaved trees stand like soldiers spreads for blocks. I am repeatedly told not to venture there even though it's the closet and largest green space around. Omi, my German-speaking grandmother, has tight connections in her Mennonite community, and one good friend, Mrs. Krause, a Russian-born war widow with impeccable Christian manners, takes us in. Dad arrives, two weeks later, but he's left Caesar, our fully loaded Alsatian—another euphemism for German shepherd—who's never known life on a leash, with his parents in Revelstoke. Caesar's absence is a gaping gash in our family unit.

Dad is chipper, joking and affectionate, and flirts with Mom more than usual. Kisses to the back of her fawn-like neck. Love-slaps on her shapely bottom. But within days he's gone again, saying only that he has "some trouble" to settle. He returns soon enough and once again promises that our fractured family will soon be whole. "Fretting is verboten," he says airily. "The day will never dawn when I allow the fruit of my loins to become city slickers."

But as summer slips into fall and we reluctantly start at a strange new school, it seems more and more as if he's brought "trouble" back with him. My parents' usual banter and coquettish, easy laughter has evaporated. They wear masks of hope but speak in low tones, glance at each other sideways and hold hands across the kitchen table late into the night, long after we're in bed. Dad's erratic comings and goings continue. And Mom frequently sits staring out the window or retreats to her room and closes the door for "a rest."

In an attempt to stop our whining for Caesar, a friend of Omi's gives us a white toy poodle puppy. We name him Pierre. We love animals, knowing they are individuals like people, only better. But the new dog isn't a true dog and while I will grow to adore him, right now he doesn't matter to me all that much. Pierre isn't part of who we are and he never can be. The small knife-edge in my stomach that makes all food tasteless nestles deeper. As the days drag on, Mom's explanations of what's happening, where our new home is and when we will move grow weaker and finally peter out. Our home, our school, our neighbourhood, everything is still "temporary," Mom says, but our dreams of paradise are gone.

Then stories begin to appear in the *Vancouver Sun* newspaper—one on the front page headlined "Mystery Shipment of Silver Probed." Another declares "Silver Mystery 'International,'" referring to an Elsa mine that is the economic bedrock of the Yukon. The following week the *Sun* runs a story announcing that the RCMP are looking for a man in Vancouver in connection with the mystery shipment. The man is "Gerald Henry Priest, 35, of Elsa, Y.T."

Ten-year-olds don't read newspapers but similar reports are on the radio. The week I start grade five at Van Horne Elementary School on the west side of Main Street, a boy in my class asks if that "Yukon guy in the news" is my dad. No, we just happen to have the same last name. It is the first of countless lies I tell for years. When asked what Dad does for a living, I say he is a chemist and works for the government. When asked why he is never home, I explain he is a geologist and is up north exploring for diamonds. Or, one year, he is an engineer in Mexico helping set up a big manufacturing plant. Then in Toronto, consulting for an important company—he only comes home on holidays. When summer arrives and he still doesn't show, I declare he's riding cross the Rockies on horseback.

The truth—that one late summer afternoon, two men knock on our back door and I see Mom and Dad cling to each other before the men take Dad away; that over the next year and a half Dad is home one week and gone the next as he flies back and forth to the Yukon for a preliminary hearing and then a trial and then another trial; and that, subsequently, he is behind bars—is too disgraceful to reveal. Shame covers me like a shroud and my lips are sealed.

It is years before any of us know the facts, or at least a select few, about how Dad came heartbreakingly close to masterminding a massive silver heist from under the nose of one of the biggest mining companies in the country.

This is the story of what he says he did, what he appeared to do and how he most likely did it. It is also the story of what happened to us, his family, in the meantime.

CHAPTER 1

Stopping for Smokes

No man can be a failure if he thinks he's a success.

THE MORNING OF JUNE 21, 1963, a Friday, Al Pike glanced out his office window and spotted a fully loaded flatbed truck parked in front of the Elsa Cookhouse. In the Land of the Midnight Sun, it was the start of the longest and lightest day of the year and Pike, general manager of United Keno Hill Mines Ltd., had a clear, high-in-the-sky view of the idled rig, owned by the territory's largest transportation firm, White Pass and Yukon Route. His gaze zeroed in on the load. The flatbed brimmed with hundreds of rock-filled sacks, smothered with a canvas tarp. The driver was nowhere to be seen—must have taken a break and walked the short jag to the Elsa Coffee Shop for a cup and a smoke.

As the wall clock ticked, Pike's initial curiosity turned to alarm. Something was up and it wasn't going down well. No UKHM transports were scheduled for that afternoon. If they had been, company trucks, not WP&YR, would do the hauling. Besides, the company packed its ore in containers, not sacks anymore, and there must have been more than two hundred sacks on that rig. Who had hired it? What was it carrying? And given that UKHM laid claim to near every square inch of soggy muskeg and stony slope in the Mayo mining district, where the hell did the rocks on that truck come from? He'd have to find the driver. Likely he was gabbing with the guys but whatever, he'd been in there now for more than twenty minutes.

Apart from its six operating mine sites, UKHM had about six hundred mineral claims, most of them dating back to the 1920s and '30s. With little competition, company policy was to accumulate as many claims as possible, either through buying existing claims or, as some people put it, by waiting for the old-timers to die and then jumping on their claims.

A slight man on the minus side of medium with dark, shiny hair greased back in the fashion of the day, Albert Edward Pike was a powerful, pugnacious and widely disliked man. Arrogant, autocratic and cruelly dismissive, he was nicknamed "Little Hitler" by miners and other men, many of whom had emigrated from war-ravaged Europe. Employees stiffened and spoke only when spoken to when around Pike, then in his mid-fifties. They'd learned the hard way to keep their opinions and suggestions to themselves. The less said the better. Pike ran a tight ship. But it was under his watch that the vessel hit a squall.

"Pike made life hell for anybody who worked there," recalled former UKHM chief geologist Al Archer, who worked in Elsa from 1957 to '61 and then again from 1962 to '65. And for most workers, there was precious little they could do about it. They simply had to take what Pike dished out. As Archer put it, "People were trapped—they had no place to go."

Elsa sits smack in the middle of the Yukon Territory—in other words, beyond away. It was a significant locale at the time, however, as Elsa was the site of one of the most productive silver mining companies in the world. In its heyday in the 1950s and '60s, UKHM was the second richest silver mine in Canada and the third richest in the world, spitting out up to 6 million ounces of silver per year—about a third of the nation's total output.

Pike not only ran the mine, he ran the town of about six hundred people. A mining engineer who graduated from UBC in 1933 and toiled in several BC mines before going north, he became the UKHM mine manager in 1954 and was promoted to general manager in 1957. Through a chain of events that started with his sighting of that White Pass truck, Pike would leave the north the same year as Dad.

"The mine is the town's only reason for being," wrote author Jack Hope in his 1976 book *Yukon*. "There are no other businesses or sources of employment… There is no elected town government; all that happens here is subject to the approval, or disapproval, of the mine manager."

On that portentous summer day, Pike assessed the situation outside, turned to his production manager Bruce Lang and pointed out the window.

"Recognize that haul?" he asked.

"No," said Lang. "I have no idea what it is or what it's doing."

"Well, you're going to know about everything very soon. Get over to the coffee shop, drill that driver and find out who hired him, what's in his load and where it came from."

But by the time Lang had covered the distance between the main office and the coffee shop, the White Pass driver was back in his truck and rumbling through town, hanging a curtain of dust behind him. The driver had 32 miles to go on a gravel road to hit Mayo, where truckers stopped for lunch at the Chateau Mayo Hotel before the exhausting haul to Whitehorse. Tidal waves of fine grit and windshield-cracking pebbles were hazards of summer transport. Drivers always turned their headlights on and many preferred to travel in winter when, ironically, visibility was better and ice and snow made the roads smoother.

As Lang entered the long log building that housed not only the coffee shop but the Elsa library, the barbershop and a beer parlour, cigarette smoke and high-level chatter filled the air. The volume dipped as soon as he entered. Addressing four fellows hunched at the counter, Lang said, "Hey, anyone know what that White Pass driver was doing here?"

"Looks like he took a wrong turn," said one guy Lang recognized as an underground worker. "He came in to get directions to Mayo. Must not be from around here."

Lang wasn't the most popular member of the supervisory team and the workers hesitated to divulge anything that might get a buddy in trouble.

"What was he hauling? Who'd it belong to?" Lang said.

"Never said, only that it came from some claims far side of Faro Gulch, past Keno."

"Whose claims?" asked Lang.

"Didn't say," volunteered a second man.

When Lang returned to the main office, Pike was standing by the phone.

As Lang relayed his meagre intelligence, Pike started dialling.

"Pike here. I've got a job for you," he said into the receiver. "No, no… will you just shut up and listen? There's a White Pass semi loaded with ore sacks coming into town. When the driver stops for lunch grab me some samples. Five or six, minimum. I want them here on my desk first thing in the morning."

Later that afternoon, outside a Mayo café, a posse of men swarmed over the back of the White Pass truck, helping themselves to several chunks of rock. The next morning Pike scrutinized the samples, turning them over again and again in his hands. Perplexed and increasingly apprehensive, he called his geologist, Al Archer, and the next day drove up to Calumet to see him.

"Know what this is?" Pike said, thrusting a fine-grained, silver-grey chunk of raw ore into Archer's right hand.

Without any hesitation, Archer replied, "Do I? I know exactly what it is. And I know exactly where it comes from—the Bonanza Stope in the Elsa mine."

By that point, the WP&YR truck had chewed up the more than 250 miles between Mayo and Whitehorse, along with two other heavy-laden semis that had failed to come to Pike's attention. In Whitehorse, their loads of sacked ore were packed onto two White Pass and Yukon railcars and carried over 110 miles and one international border through a mountain pass to Skagway, Alaska. There, once transferred to the 4,000-ton ss *Clifford J. Rogers*—the world's first container ship—the ore sailed 1,645 miles down the British Columbian coast to Vancouver. At the West Indies wharf in North Vancouver, the sacks were once again pilfered and samples stolen—this time at the behest of a Vancouver-based consulting geologist named Aaro Aho—before traversing, again by rail, 722 miles to their final destination, the American Smelting and Refining Co. (ASARCO) in Helena, Montana.

Over the following month, Pike would be frantically preoccupied and would learn a great deal, all of a highly suspicious nature: three WP&YR trucks had picked up ore from a loading site on Duncan Creek Road, out of sight of Elsa; the drivers were directed to take Duncan Creek Road straight into Mayo, thereby bypassing Elsa completely, but one driver got turned around and stopped at the Elsa Coffee Shop for directions; the ore in question supposedly came from a group of claims called the Moon claims, a patch of scrub in the hinterland northeast of Keno; and, once smelted, the silver released from that ore would fetch more than $160,000, easily half a million dollars in today's currency.

Most disturbing and indeed infuriating to Pike, the ore shipment was registered to Alpine Gold and Silver Mines Ltd., a company he'd never heard of. When all this information and more was relayed to UKHM vice-president and managing director P. N. Pitcher in Toronto, alarm begat action. In early July, Canada's chief mining inspector, A.T. Jordon, visited Elsa. Shortly after, the head office of UKHM contacted the RCMP's General Investigation Service in Toronto.

The Mounties, in turn, called the United States Federal Bureau of Investigation, which ordered ASARCO to hold off smelting the two railcars of ore pending an investigation.

On August 6, Inspector J.L. Vachon of the RCMP's Whitehorse detachment announced an investigation into the odd ore shipment, which he believed was stolen from one of UKHM's premier operating mines.

The next day, an unidentified Whitehorse RCMP spokesman hinted that the theft was the work of "a skilled international ring."

On August 10, criminal charges were laid against the registered shipper of the ore, owner of the Moon claims and former chief assayer of UKHM—my father, Gerald H. Priest.

CHAPTER 2

Unexplainable

We aren't spliced according to the law.

THEY WERE A COUPLE IN CONTRAST—a maddening mismatch. Not exact opposites, but different to such a degree that friends wondered why it took them so long to see the inaptness. Perhaps it was love-lust. Or simply a blind need nested so deep it hid like a slow-growing cancer from their consciousness. At least that may explain the long-lasting attraction and part of the impending disaster.

He was 6 foot 1. She was 5 foot 2. He wanted to be older. She yearned to be younger, and lied about her birth year to everyone, including emigration officials. She outlived two husbands. He predeceased two wives. He was fair with a high forehead, fine, swept-back honey-brown hair and eyes big and blue as a northern sky. She was brown-eyed, gypsy-eyed, with dark arched eyebrows, light olive skin and a waterfall of blackness cascading over her shoulders. Where he avoided the sun, she worshipped it. Where he was indolent to the point of squalidness, she was enterprising and exact. Her best colour was scarlet, his dove grey. He shunned the modern world. She embraced it. Born in a city, he was happiest in the bush or a town the world forgot. Born in a rural Russian village, she was happiest in a metropolis offering a decent opera and a symphony. He was a devout atheist. She was born and raised a Mennonite, although the brand never took. She saved every letter, card and note he ever sent her (257 letters and 26 cards, plus 3 Canadian National telegrams). He tore up or burned almost every one of hers. Before they met, she had had a capital-L hell-raising, heartbreaking, action-packed, screen-scorching, passion-packed, thrilling, explosive, rollicking, rough and raw Life. In Technicolor. Until she entered, he'd lived a sepia-toned existence—narrow, dreary, punctuated by a strained home life, fleeting friendships, a lacklustre stab at university and tedious work in underwhelming jobs for two-bit mining companies in remote small-town BC. If not technically a virgin groom, he was so emotionally. At their October 13, 1951, wedding in a Fraser Valley Mennonite church, he knew only the bride—no family, no friends, no acquaintances. His best man was a Mennonite fellow she'd asked to stand up for him.

They were Gerald Henry Priest and Helen Friesen, Dad and Mom.

I was born August 29, 1953, at the Mayo Clinic, not to be confused with the famous medical practice and research centre in Rochester, Minnesota. Actually, it was the Mayo Hospital in Mayo Landing, Yukon Territory, but "Mayo Clinic" has a better ring. Today, the village—named after mining explorer and former circus acrobat Alfred S. Mayo—is simply called Mayo and has a population of about 230, mostly members of the Na-Cho Nyak Dun First Nation. The settlement is now a rag of its former self, its only claim to fame recording the hottest and the coldest temperatures in the territory: 97 degrees Fahrenheit and 80 below respectively. The two-storey wood-sided hospital where I arrived was torn down soon after and the replacement hospital was eventually downgraded to a nursing station. But at the time of my birth, Mayo was hopping. The centre of administrative, economic and social activity for the district,

Mayo had more than eight hundred permanent residents and was the transportation hub connecting UKHM workers and their families with the "outside," and bringing powerful political, financial and industrial leaders to the rainbow's end.

Back in the day, Canadian Pacific Airlines operated bi-weekly DC-3 flights from Mayo to Whitehorse, where you could connect with CP flights to Vancouver and Edmonton, as well as to Seattle and Fairbanks, Alaska, via Pan American Airlines. All this at a time when there were fewer than ten thousand people in the Yukon Territory, an expanse larger than the state of California, and bigger than Belgium, Denmark, the Netherlands and Germany combined. Today there are about thirty-five thousand residents, far fewer than at the time of the Klondike Gold Rush. The territory's small population and vast wilderness appeal to summertime tourists, frontier types and a few low-density fans. Three-quarters live in Whitehorse, the territory's capital and only city. The Yukon of the 1950s and '60s was a very different place. Our family—Mom, Dad, Omi, Vona and I—were five of nine thousand people. In Elsa and its sister settlement up the hill, Calumet, we were five of six hundred.

Dad was born August 27, 1927, in Edmonton, the middle son of three boys of poor, decent and undemonstrative—in a WASPish kind of way—parents. His relationship with his elder brother Bill was tainted with jealousy from an early age, when Dad concluded Bill was his parents' favoured son. His younger brother Ronnie was a quiet, gentle soul who always lived a somewhat shadowed life. The family never recovered from the Depression but proudly bore their scars and dents, forever identifying with the underdog. Owning their own home remained a pipe dream their entire lives. Gerry's mother, Alice May Russell, was born in Minnesota, and family rumour had it that her father Bertram disowned her when at eighteen years old she left home to marry the man she loved. Gerry's father—born in England—was a printer, and like his father before him refused to upgrade his skills. As newspapers advanced from hot metal to cold type, the family drifted from one small BC town to another, fleeing technological innovation. Occupational nomads, they rented modest dwellings in Nelson, Powell River, Prince Rupert, Revelstoke, Kitimat, Williams Lake, Kimberley, Maple Ridge and Slocan City, to name some of their short-lived hometowns. From Edmonton, where Gerry attended elementary school, the family moved to Nelson to join his paternal grandfather, who also worked as a printer. Apparently, my great-grandfather came from a long line of sailors but hated life at sea so vehemently that he quit the navy and settled in the mountains. His grandfather, our grandfather insisted, sailed against the Spanish Armada with Lord Nelson.

Gerry finished high school in Nelson and enrolled at the University of Alberta to study chemistry. He didn't last a year, and signed up for a short course in assaying techniques. Unlike my mother, who couldn't stop talking about her past, he rarely shared his memories of early life. All I know I gleaned from his letters, a few documents, brief conversations with his aunt, and my memory. Chances are, before he met Helen, he never ventured outside western Canada, though he claimed otherwise. I heard vaguely of one early girlfriend in Nelson, named Nancy, who died young in a car crash.

Dad grew into a quiet, clever, well-read and well-spoken young man. He could exude the aura of a refined gentleman, the kind who dined at the Ritz and presided over high-level business meetings. Or carry the role of a maverick leading a pack train of horses through a winding, high-peaked pass. But most of all, when his guard was down, he squirmed in his own skin. He was a fretter and a finger-kneader. Only his full, well-formed lips betrayed a sensitive and petulant temperament that was so out of step with his time. By nature, he disdained parties, crowds and gatherings of more than three or four people and was most himself when seated at a kitchen table with a dog at his feet, a cup of coffee or a freshly rolled cigarette in hand and one agreeable companion across the divide. Preferably female.

We learned early and often that he had a snarky streak bordering on cruelty. Was that a gleam in his eye? Or a glint? A smile? Or a smirk? When I was two or three, he could trigger my tears by scowling in my direction. As my chin began to quiver and my lips crumbled, Mom would say, "Stop it Gerry!" and he'd throw his head back and guffaw, then lean over and kiss me. Most often, however, he was witty, affectionate and spectacularly original. An enthusiastic playmate, he would give us "the works," which entailed tickling us till we screamed for mercy, giving us rides on his feet and on his back, and taunting us to come and get him. We charged straight on, scrambling all over his towering body, one scaling the heights to his shoulders and the other hiking up his legs while grabbing his outstretched arms. We'd bend down and put our hands through our legs and he'd flip us ass over teakettle from behind. Come winter, he'd throw us full force into bottomless snowbanks over and over until he was gasping for breath.

We were six and seven when the town got phone service. There was no one to call but—surreptitiously—Mom would dial 27 (his office) and hand the heavy black receiver over to us. "Hell-ooo," a male voice cooed. "This is the Big Bad Wolf. I am so looking forward to eating… pork tonight." We quivered with excitement and just the right amount of fear. He loved to play practical jokes. Once he dared Mom to swallow a teaspoonful of Tabasco. She did, and after the choking and coughing subsided she spat in his face. But she wasn't finished yet: she squatted down, crossed her arms and kicked her legs straight out, executing a furious rendition of the "hopak," the Ukrainian Cossack dance, before she collapsed in a fit of breathless giggles.

Vona was fidgeting and fiddling with a wiggly tooth. Dad swung her up on the bright yellow Arborite kitchen counter, "just to take a look."

"No, no. Promise you won't pull it!" She squirmed and pulled her head away.

"I won't pull it. I promise," he said calmly, looking her straight in the eyes. "Now, open up and let me see."

Slowly she leaned a bit forward and opened her mouth wide.

"Ah, there's the culprit," he said. "And a wicked brute he is. Now I've got a little string here and I'm going to lasso that bad fellow."

"No, no! Promise you won't pull it. Promise!"

"I won't pull it! Okay?"

Carefully manipulating the string, he gently tied it round her tooth, all the while listening to her muffled pleas.

"Now," he said. "I want you to look out the window at the stars in the sky and count to three."

"Wha? Why? You won't puhl? Righ?!"

"I won't pull it. Just look at the stars and count to three."

Vona slowly turned her eyes toward the window and mumbled, "Onth. Thwo. Thee."

Yank.

Gerry's intellectual air was accentuated by large, thin wire-rimmed glasses set on his finely formed nose, and below a smooth, broad forehead that at twenty-six years of age already showed signs of expansion. By thirty, his receding hairline was firmly established, giving him an even greater appearance of braininess. But it was the age of John Wayne, and he boasted a macho side too. A broad tattoo spread out on the upper side of his right forearm. A long-horned steer with droopy eyes—*Texas*, it said in the wavy banner below. I would sit on his lap and stroke the outline of the creature beneath the filigree of his fair arm hair. He could make the steer move by twitching his arm muscles.

"Have you been to Texas, Daddy?"
"Yes, dear," he said placidly. "Before I met your mother, I travelled around Texas, Colorado and Wyoming and even Mexico, where I picked up a bit of Spanish. But it was too hot and dry for me so I bid 'hasta la vista' to all my senoritas!"

We heard and knew far more about the western American states and even Mexico than any part of Canada, despite the fact that the farthest east he'd travelled had been Alberta and the farthest south Seattle.

Trained at a basic level in chemistry and employed as an assayer—someone who determines the mineral content of ore—Gerry's real passion was to be a mountain man. With a horse to ride, a pack horse to haul the gear, a taciturn companion and a tree-lined trail. During four summers (1958 through 1961) he lived his dream, negotiating passes, canyons, creeks and rivers through the Rocky Mountains—once from Sundre, Alberta, to Revelstoke, BC, and another time from Sundre to Nelson, BC—on horseback. It was the Kodak era, when ordinary men and women developed a skill and passion for photography. Self-taught, Gerry evolved into a better-than-most amateur photographer, snapping, developing, printing and enlarging his own large-format black and whites. For colour, he preferred slides and 8 mm home movies. Other than mountains and horses, he focused his lens on his wife and young daughters.

Music in the form of lone-note folk melodies, work songs, sea shanties, classic cowboy songs and old ballads was a constant. He whistled, yodelled, played the guitar and piano by ear—chording grandly with his left hand, trickling arpeggios with his right—and sang, his tender tenor caressing the high notes. We cherished his serenades, especially when he attached a head contraption to his mouth organ, as he called it, that allowed him to pick and strum the guitar and suck and blow on the harmonica all at the same time! Why hasn't he been discovered by Hollywood yet, we wondered. His favourites ranged from "Whoopee Ti-Yi-Yo" to "Green Grow the Lilacs" to "Beautiful Brown Eyes" and, in a family of four females, "I Got No Use for the Women."

I got no use for the women.
A true one will never be found.
They'll stick with a man when he's winning,
And laugh in his face when he's down.

Mom was born November 24, 1924, in what was at the time southern Russia and is now the Ukraine, although that may change any day now. Named Lolya, or Helen, she was the second child and only daughter of Maria Reger and Abraham Friesen. She had an older brother Peter, and a younger brother Alexander who died of diphtheria at eighteen months. Her parentage was from a long-established, large colony of Russian Mennonites, an Anabaptist sect that, in the late 1700s, traded Prussia for southern Russia when Catherine the Great offered them expansive tracts of black gold in exchange for religious freedom and exemption from military service. Helen, however, never considered herself a true Mennonite. God knows she tried, and revered Jesus as *the* wise one, but she was never baptized—and full-immersion adult baptism is a must-do in the Mennonite Brethren faith. After years of quoting slips of scripture and memorized Bible stories, she sadly concluded that when it came to the meaning of life, "Nobody knows." Over the years, she increasingly turned to classical literature for explanations of human nature, particularly Dostoevsky, Hardy and Tolstoy.

When her family moved away from their large extended clan in the Ukraine to Ebental, a small village in the foothills of the Caucasus

Mountains, Helen mixed with more Russians than Mennonites and her agnosticism deepened. As a young girl, she aimed to one day defend Mother Russia as a fighter pilot. But German was her mother tongue and heritage. And in 1930, when her mother learned that her parents, sisters and brothers had been loaded in cattle cars and shipped to Siberia, two children dying along the way, the Soviet regime became their enemy. For Mennonites and other victims of Stalin's holocaust, the Caucasus region was no safer than the Ukraine. Three years later, her father collapsed and died at the age of thirty-five after learning he was to be brought before the NKVD, the Soviet secret police and forerunner to the KGB.

Within two years, her mother married another Mennonite—Heinrich Werle, a university-trained agronomist responsible for ensuring the late August harvest of the area's wheat crop. The state, aiming to be progressive at all times, forbade the use of horses and insisted farmers use combines. However, there was not a combine in sight, only a darkening sky that threatened rain. Werle ordered farmers to hitch up the horses and bring in the harvest. Once the crop was secured, he was banished to a northeastern hard labour camp.

In 1940, Helen and her mother moved to a larger town, Stepnoye, where Helen attended high school and her mother found employment as a store clerk. Previously, she'd worked as a milkmaid. Helen's brother Peter, now seventeen, stayed in Ebental to care for the family's small house and few animals. The following year he too was arrested and summarily sent to the Gulag, where as far as his mother and sister knew, he'd disappeared and probably died. (As fate would have it, Helen would be briefly reunited with her brother again—fifty-six years later.) In 1941 the Nazis marched into the Caucasus, their commandants riding in long, low black Mercedes. Maria welcomed them as liberators—they had a common language and a common hatred. When the Russian army launched its massive counteroffensives in the winter of 1943–44, Helen and Maria retreated by foot, horse and cart, and cattle car along with the Germans. The only belongings they took were a few clothes, a handful of family pictures and a precious home-cured ham, useful for bribing train conductors.

Like other war survivors, Helen would later keep the best stories to herself. But certain dramas she divulged. At seventeen, her first sweetheart, a Russian partisan, a resistance member, knocked on her bedroom window one night, swept her up on his horse and galloped into the woods where his comrades were hiding. He introduced Helen to his commandant and then returned her home before her mother noticed her absence. And when Helen and her mother first arrived in German-occupied Poland, nineteen-year-old Helen was forced to attend the Bund Deutscher Mädel (Hitler Youth school for girls). After two days of lessons on how to be a good German wife, mother and homemaker, she and a girlfriend scaled a wall and fled.

Making their way to Germany, Helen and her mother were greeted by bombs and falling brick shattering heaven and earth. Terror spread like a plague as Helen and thousands of other civilians dove into basements, ducked under beds, bellied beneath railcars and fled from the fury of Allied forces. But the struggling Reich was desperate for skilled workers and Helen secured a respected job as a Russian–German translator for Kommission 28, a division of the German Reich evaluating applications from "Volksdeustch"—refugees who claimed German ancestry and were fleeing Eastern Europe. Helen worked long hours but at the end of some weeks, she danced till her bare feet bled. During that year, her mother was in a sanitarium recovering from tuberculosis.

At the war's end, Helen and her mother crowded into a small room shared with two other families in a former barrack in the American Zone—the most desirable section of Allied-occupied Germany. But with identification papers nailing them as Russian citizens, they were slated for repatriation to the land of their birth. In the American Jeep motoring east, Helen wept and in faltering

English told the Yankees what the Russian army would do: rape them and then, if they lived, heave their ravaged bodies onto a Siberia-bound train. The soldier turned the truck around. When a chest x-ray was required for emigration to Canada, Helen disguised herself as her mother and went through the examination twice so that her mother's Swiss-cheese lungs would not be revealed. In the fall of 1948, Helen and her mother boarded the ss *Cynthia*, landing in Quebec City ten days later. From there they chugged across the country to Matsqui, BC, where Abraham and Helene Rempel, the Mennonite family who sponsored them, gave them a home, a community and work in the fields, primarily picking berries and hops. They worked to pay back their boat and train fares, which the Rempels had paid—$500 for both.

Although Helen's identity papers stated she was twenty-two, she was twenty-four and felt great pressure to marry. Marriage during the war was unthinkable, though, despite proposals from the United Nations: a Russian, a Pole, an Italian, three Germans and an American. She knew what war did to husbands, brothers, fathers and sons. Once in Canada, however, amidst a Fraser Valley enclave of Mennonites, she soon had a marriage offer from a young man who planned to work overseas as a missionary. He was kind, fair-haired and not far from handsome. She declined, not least because she felt her travelling days were done. It was complicated. Mennonites were honest, industrious and generous, but, in her view, simple-minded. They were her people, but she was not wholly of them. Her world was not a temporary testing ground where God and the Devil battled for each soul. Where only piety, prayer, charity, righteous living, Bible study and full-immersion baptism brought peace of mind, and where only death brought eternal happiness. While Helen had no doubt God guided her through the war and ushered her safely to a new land, her world was an exhilarating mystery, full of ambiguity and equal parts fear, sorrow, joy and pleasure. She'd tasted the richness of a cosmopolitan life and wanted more. After crossing two continents and the Atlantic Ocean, she felt reborn—and not in any religious sense. What better way to cement her new self to her new nation than to marry a real Canadian?

Later, in the Yukon, Helen was an exotic, if somewhat peculiar, beauty—a cardinal in a town of sparrows. A flat outdoor surface was rare in Elsa. No sidewalks, no streets, only roads covered with snow, ice, mud, dry dirt or gravel. Yet Helen dressed in taffeta gowns, billowing skirts, velvet jackets and tight side-zippered slacks, all of which she sewed herself after seeing them worn on the silver screen by the likes of Lana Turner, Rita Hayworth and Elizabeth Taylor. Once home from the movies, she would quickly sketch a dress or other article of clothing and trace precisely sized outlines on newsprint or scrap paper. With help from her nimble-fingered mother, she'd create a chic wardrobe, and had no qualms about showing it off in a jerkwater mining town. The dresses fitted her petite figure like a hug, and with a full skirt flaring from her cinched waist down, she rivalled any southern glamour queen.

As the mother of two girls born 360 days apart, she designed and dressed her children in matching ensembles; everything from fluffy butterfly dresses to plaid cowboy shirts to traditional Ukrainian dancing costumes with shamrock green skirts, puff-sleeved blouses and hand-embroidered aprons. She always wore pumps with two-inch heels and never owned a pair of jeans. Gentle and trusting by nature, when you met her, she would smile shyly, lock your eyes with hers and extend her delicate, manicured hand for a firm, warm touch. If she'd met you more than once, she'd greet you with an embrace. She never coloured her nails but filed them into almonds and painted them a shiny clear finish. She was the spirit of vitality and spontaneity, as long as you didn't look too closely. Tragedy called, and for decades she answered with a disarming mix of grace, instinctive practicality and childlike charm.

CHAPTER 3

The Brunette Flower

What of the wonder of my Heart,
That plays so faithfully its part?

HOW DID THIS DISPARATE TWOSOME, who began at opposing ends of the Northern Hemisphere, ultimately meet, bond and, for a long while, have a really good time? After paying back their ship passage, which took two years of Fraser Valley farm work, Helen and her mother Maria confidently moved to Vancouver, where they planned to settle permanently. They shared a house with a Mennonite family at 451 East Forty-seventh Avenue in South Vancouver, a growing and tight-knit enclave of urban Mennonites, anchored by three large Mennonite churches. Maria found employment as a "dayworker," or cleaning lady, and Helen as a receptionist at a dry cleaner's. As someone who had come to life on city energy in Prague, Vienna, Strasburg, Berlin, Frankfurt and other European cities and then laboured two years on a farm, Helen revelled in what little Vancouver had to offer: shops, shows, fashion and free concerts in Stanley Park. And she began to make a few friends, in particular a newlywed woman named Gisella whose husband, Egon Busse, and his mother had been on the same transatlantic ship Helen and her mother were on. Gisella told Helen that Egon had found well-paid work somewhere far up north but that she missed him terribly.

On January 10, 1951, Helen received a mysterious letter. The return address bore no name, only: Torbrit Silver Mines Limited, Alice Arm, BC. Alice Arm—now one of the most inaccessible ghost towns in the province—was then a remote mining community in a thickly forested fiord called Observatory Inlet, an arm of lengthy Portland Inlet, 85 miles northeast of Prince Rupert on the BC coast, near the Alaskan border. The town, built for the families of mine employees, was 17 miles from the mine, and located deep in the traditional territory of the Nisga'a.

The one-page handwritten letter was in German and its signature—fluid and bold, with the first letter of each part dwarfing the rest—was *Gerald H. Priest*. The signature was obviously penned by a different hand. Mr. Priest had heard "good things" about Helen through Egon, his assistant, and asked if she would be interested in exchanging letters as a way to improve her English. She was intrigued and on January 13, 1951, wrote back. Monday was mail day. On Tuesday, he responded.

Weekly and then twice and thrice a week, Helen's and Gerry's missives flew north to south and south to north like migrating birds. Often typed on Torbrit Silver Mines stationery, Gerald's letters told of 50-foot snowbanks, blizzards, bears, ravens and mountain goats, of families of geese and grouse. Most often, though, the pages bore the burdens of his heart, which lured her into the labyrinth of his mind. In impeccable English, he poured out selected fragments of his history, his aspirations and his beliefs. Often, they echoed her desires and dislikes. She loved going to shows and movies. He did too and would take her to one next time he was in town. She loved music. He listened to opera and the classics whenever he had a chance. She loved to dance. He would like to learn how. She couldn't swallow the litany of Old Testament "thou shalt-nots," but believed in God and the teachings of Jesus. He preferred the United Church and once walked 17 miles to attend a service, and 17 miles back.

Helen corresponded in tentative English at first, but it didn't take long to improve. The new language, which she had started studying in Germany, came easily, and she was soon writing two to three pages, enchanted to be corresponding with a pensive, sensitive and philosophical soul, someone grounded in goodness but searching for deeper meaning—as was she. By mid-February, Gerry was sharing his innermost musings and broodings:

Feb. 16/51
One thing about these places, a person has a great deal of time to do nothing but think, and that would be good if a person always came up with the right answers. But they don't. After awhile up here, a person begins to consider himself as separate from the rest of the world, as if he were standing still and the whole world were moving around and never quite touching his own sphere. That isn't right though and occasionally, I have to give myself a good mental shake and come back to earth.

In March, after learning that Helen had lost her job and was looking for another, he offered to lend her money. And confessed that he too was a true believer.

March 4, 1951
I so hope I don't offend you… it's just that I earn a lot of money here and I get very little satisfaction out of it, it just goes to the bank every week and I don't feel as if it's doing any good… I get the feeling sometimes that time is going by and I'm not getting anywhere, not in a material sense, but spiritually. It seems everywhere a person looks these days, why there's only unhappiness. I really don't know and sometimes I wonder if

people haven't lost the simple art of living honestly and simply.
I guess a person just has to figure out what makes a decent and
God-fearing life and try to live by it.

God flits in and out of his letters. But his deity is far removed from
the austere patriarch of her upbringing.

March 10, 1951
It's too bad that often we're blinded by work and worry so that
we can't see all the wonderful things God has given us… I look
around me here and see such a number of hard, bitter, twisted
people, I think "what an awful shame"… Whenever I feel bad, I
think of that Psalm, "I shall lift up mine eyes unto the hills from
whence cometh my help." Probably that's misquoted, because I
don't read the Bible enough to fix any of it in my mind… too
many religious people think that to believe in God one has to go
around with a long face, singing Hallelujahs right and left, and
denying themselves any kind of pleasure. I can't see that at all.

And by this time, his sign-off changes from "all my best wishes" to
"all my love." By April, German expressions of endearment creep into
their letters. He calls her Schatz (Treasure). She calls him Liebchen
(Sweetheart). As a pale, spring sun softens the heavy snows blan-
keting the dark woods, and hummingbirds and robins reappear, his
mood lightens. Slightly. He teases, writing that their correspondence would flow easier if she were Spanish, given that he is fluent in
the language, and throws in a few Spanish phrases. "You teach me
German and I'll teach you English. But there are things I'd like to
say that wouldn't take any language at all." In April, he suggests they
exchange pictures. She agrees, knowing like all women that looks
are her greatest asset. Despite the flirtations, though, his pen, more
often than not, records sentiments of alienation and eerie isolation.

April 7, 1951

It's about 8 in the evening here, Loyla, not dark yet but just that soft gray that comes to the mountains at dusk. Out my window, long streamers of mist float down the valley and along the sides of the mountains. Sometimes I think they look like lost souls just drifting by and not going anywhere… I like to sit here and look down the valley and watch it grow darker and darker. It makes me feel sad and lonesome and so far from everything. But still I do it so I guess I enjoy it.

They both have pictures taken at professional photo studios—his in Prince Rupert—the custom of the day. In early May, Helen's picture arrives in Alice Arm and that settles it. They must meet. A date is set for mid-June. He will show her the Vancouver sights: Stanley Park, Grouse Mountain, a harbour cruise. He puts her picture in a thin, gold-rimmed oval frame and places it on his table, which doubles as his writing desk. Her dark eyes follow him to every point in the room. He tells her he will rent a car and have two weeks in Vancouver as he has given notice at the mine and accepted a position at the Prince Rupert pulp mill. But that too would be only temporary, he writes, given that he and his father plan to start up their own newspaper in some as yet undetermined BC small town. He'll never go back to Alice Arm.

May 3,1951

Lately, I'm afraid, I've been thinking less and less about my work and more and more about you… I'll try not to be shy, so that we can talk about lots of things. I'll tell you how pretty I think you are and what dark and lovely hair you have. About how long it's going to seem from now until we meet, about the nights I've lain awake and thought of you, oh yes Loyla, I'm so sure I can find a great deal to say to you.

As their first date draws nearer, Gerry becomes more restless, more miserable and dissatisfied with where and who he is, telling Helen that many men lead "wasted lives" and that "for more years than I like to think of, the world has been a dark and lonesome place for me." Nature, however, soothes his soul and comforts his heart. He concurs with Victorian-era poet Bliss Carman: "The greatest joy in nature is the absence of man." One night he wakes at midnight to hear a large flock of wild geese overhead, returning north for the spring. What wonderful birds they are, flying across the moon in arrowhead formation. And when they mate, he writes, "it's for their whole lives."

On June 15, Gerry rents a mint green Cadillac convertible and drives to Stanley Park, where they rendezvous at the third bench on the main walkway. He wears a doeskin brown suit, a white shirt and a cornflower blue tie. She stands when he approaches, dressed in a rose red, waist-hugging, full-skirted frock. His knees buckle. She's the most terrifying creature he's ever met.

Helen continues to work during the days but for two weeks they spend every other waking moment together. They take in movies, go for long drives and ride up the Grouse Mountain chairlift. Mostly they walk, talk and sip the intimacies of courtship. Where had she learned to kiss like that? Soft, slightly open lips with a firm backup. A girlfriend took her to the graveyard one night and taught her how, she confesses. Their union will be passionate, playful, spiritual and intense. She is infinitely better than he deserves, and he wishes only that she love him half as much as he loves her. An incessant kidder, a tease and a joker, he continually seeks declarations of her devotion. He also meets her mother, a short, plump, pink-cheeked and green-eyed woman, who blushes and smiles but doesn't say much.

Toward the end of the second week, Gerald goes to O.B. Allan Jewellers on Granville Street and buys a 14-karat gold diamond engagement ring with a speck-sized single-cuts bracketed by two minuscule single-cuts. That evening, on a hidden pathway on Little

Mountain, also known as Queen Elizabeth Park, he proposes. She accepts with one condition. My mother, she says, is part of the deal. He replies, "I'll take seven mother-in-laws if I can have you."

Lovesick and nearly broke, Gerry returns to Prince Rupert and takes a position as an analytical chemist for Skeena Cellulose, a pulp and paper plant. His starting salary is $350 a month, rising to $400 after one year. Known as Canada's wettest, darkest city for its record levels of precipitation, the town is rough and weather-beaten and housing options are grim. He lives in a small, scruffy two-bedroom wood-sided house at 528 Seventh Avenue West—with his parents. His plan is to move them into a furnished apartment and then move Helen and her mother into the house after the wedding. But within a month, his taste for the new job sours and he begins looking for work elsewhere. Jobs up north are plentiful and pay well, he tells Helen, and they would only stay a year or two. Would she be willing to move north? She is aghast. Even farther north? But where would that be? "Wherever, that would be so hard, especially now that Mama has made friends at her church." "Yes, of course," he writes. "I understand. We will not go north. That's for sure."

In August, Helen flies to Prince Rupert to meet his parents. Poor and proud of it, they greet this foreign-looking, foreign-sounding young woman politely and coolly. After a dinner of corned beef hash and boiled beans, the men retreat to the living room to listen to records on the phonograph, while Helen helps his mother Alice, a mouse of a woman with cobalt blue eyes, do the dishes. In the kitchen, Alice wears a net over her short tightly permed hair. A low coal fire smoulders in the small airtight heater attached to the stove.

"So, Helen, Gerry tells me you are German," Alice says, wiping a large oval platter.

"No, no, not German, Mrs. Priest. I come from Russia." Helen turns back to the sink and plunges her hands in the warm, soapy water.

"Really? But German is your language, your culture. Can you cook meals men like Gerry like to eat? A roast beef with gravy and Yorkshire pudding?"

"What is Yorkshire pudding?" Helen asks. "I have never, but I will try. Please show me the recipe."

Outside, the rain has let up. Steel grey clouds hang over the hills circling the town like a forever fog. The dark trees creep slowly down, trying with time's help to someday push the town into the sea.

"Can you bake a pie? Men like a good pie."

"I have never but I would like to try."

The next day Helen spends the afternoon in the kitchen and produces a grand dinner. Her Yorkshire puddings are light and fluffy, the beef not overdone. The apple pie is perfect. Gerry and his father praise her skills. That evening Alice washes and Helen dries.

"Can you knit and mend, Helen?"

"Knit? No, but I can sew and embroider and crochet."

"No, you will need to knit."

"Please give me instructions and I will try."

After the dishes are done, Alice gives Helen a ball of wool, a simple pattern and knitting needles. She catches on quickly, knitting and purling several rows.

The following day, Alice leads her into their bedroom. She goes to a dark wooden dresser and opens the top drawer, rummaging and then pulling out a pair of brand new black lace panties and two lace-trimmed black garter belts.

"Take these. You will need them to keep your husband happy."

On her final day, when the men are out, her future mother-in-law flings her final salvo: "Helen, listen to me. Don't marry my son. If you do I can promise you one thing—he will break your heart."

Helen wants him more than ever, just to prove the old hag wrong.

On October 13, 1951, Gerry and Helen wed. The ceremony takes place at Matsqui Mennonite Brethren Church, not far from where the Rempel family had welcomed Mom and Omi to Canada, and the reception follows at the Rempel family home. Helen borrows a wedding dress from their daughter Helene, who married the year before and is now Helene Klassen.

Helen knew every guest and participant, even the best man, who was a Mennonite fellow Gerry had never met. In fact, other than his bride and her mother, the groom knew no one. His parents were invited, but begged off due to the travel expense and a visit from a distant relative. His two brothers didn't attend. And neither did his two uncles, two aunts or a single friend. Indeed, his marriage was the first church wedding he'd ever experienced.

Ten days later, Mr. and Mrs. Gerald Priest arrive in Elsa, a small, rugged mining community, in the Yukon Territory.

CHAPTER 4

Elsa—The Silver King

Thank God! there is always a Land of Beyond

WE THOUGHT WE KNEW COLD but this was something cruel, sharp and cutting like a knife. The cold cracked our thermometer, and for the better part of a week the town shut down: no school, no mine, no coffee shop or cookhouse. Everyone sheltered indoors. For us children, this weather-enforced internment was the most excitement we'd had since Mr. Harper's dog got eaten by a wolverine. When we scraped Jack Frost's fingerprints off our single-paned windows we saw grey—the air thick and murky, silent and primed to kill. Too cold for human, beast, bird or even snow. Dad said it was 70 below and we weren't so much as to poke our noses outside without wrapping *two* woollen scarves over our faces, thick enough to choke us. Then he filled a tin bucket with water, opened the door a wedge, and as a razor sliced into the room, Vona and I held our breaths and hid behind his legs. He flung the bucket skyward, and as the water droplets reached their apex and descended, they transformed into pellets of ice. Pointing at the glint on the ground, he said, "That is how your blood will look if you inhale one exposed lungful of outdoor air."

Although we liked school and missed playing outside with our friends, we weren't miffed. School was good. The town was good. Home was best. We lived in a one-storey, three-bedroom, red cedar squared-log home known as a Panabode in a hiccup of a town at the top of the world. The map on our classroom wall proved it: pink Australia sat down at the bottom and we—pink too, like all the Commonwealth countries—were perched at the top left corner of Canada. If you went farther left you hit blue Alaska. And if you went a bit higher you'd slip over the North Pole and slide down the other side to Russia—where we knew life was worse than terrible. Somewhere on the far right of Russia, close to Alaska, Mom's brother and Omi's three surviving sisters and four brothers had disappeared. Dead or alive, we didn't know. We did know they experienced cold as extreme as ours. But that's where the parallels ended.

We weren't innocents. Along with spoonfuls of cod liver oil, we swallowed tales of Communist atrocities, near-death escapes from the evil NKVD and anti-starvation tips. Turnips could keep you going a remarkably long time. If you had some. But what happened when you didn't? One night our grandmother divulged a story about Stalin-inspired starvation in the Ukraine that had gone on for so long that after eating all the dogs, all the cats, all the mice, all the birds, all the leaves off the trees, all the grasses in the fields and all the roots under the ground, people began eating each other. Hansel and Gretel was a welcome change.

By the time we started school, we knew bad things could strike anyone at any time. Anyone "outside," that is. Because we lived "up north," in the land of smiles and safety, we were far removed from the threat of forced labour camps, diabolical dictators and atomic annihilation. Here we were well sheltered, well fed and well loved. We led a privileged life in one of the richest silver towns in the world. A town most people have never heard of, but one that in its heyday generated more wealth per capita than most cities in Canada.

Elsa sat on the south slope of the McQuesten River Valley, 300 miles north of Whitehorse, a broad buckbrush, alder, aspen, willow and black spruce terrain spread out like a thick tweed on a high mountain plateau. Named after the sister of a lucky prospector, Elsa began in 1924 as a particularly promising mining claim among hundreds of claims in the silver-lead-zinc-rich Keno–Mayo mining district. By the 1960s it was the second largest silver producer in Canada, and at one point was the third largest in the world.

Most people today, if they think of the Yukon at all, associate it with the 1896 Klondike Gold Rush that put the territory on the map. A remote version of the Wild West, the Klondike has been milked like a menopausal cow for more than a century: Dawson City Disneyfied; the silhouette of straggly men scaling the Chilkoot Trail appropriated as an icon for an SUV and the word "Yukon" stolen for another; a squatting goldpanner etched on the territorial license plate; and summer recitations of Robert Service's Victorian-era ballads in Dawson for up to 60,000 tourists a year—that's 2 tourists for every man, woman and child living full-time in the Yukon today. In his poem "The Spell of the Yukon," Service attempted to capture the allure of a land forged like no other, although the "spell" works on certain misfits, misanthropes and malcontents only. (Yukoners today call those folks "the colourful 5 percent," although in truth it's closer to 95 percent.) Known as the Bard of the Yukon, Service wrote: "there's some as would trade it/For no land on earth—and I'm one." Well, not exactly. Service spent only twelve of his eighty-four years there. Before his stint in the Yukon, he worked as a banker on Government Street in Victoria in a grand stone building now housing the Bard & Banker Pub. Later he frequented warmer, more cultivated climes in Paris, California and the French Riviera. He could afford it. His *Songs of a Sourdough* and other books of "Gunga Din" style verse (moulded after Rudyard Kipling) and his novel *The Trail of Ninety-Eight* sold like cheap wine. People couldn't get enough of his cleverly rhymed octets and narratives of melodrama, pathos and rugged individualism, though the literati viewed his poetry as mere doggerel.

In truth, the Klondike was a flash in the pan, a frenzied three-year boom and bust that cost hundreds of lives and enriched only a fraction of the 100,000 desperados who set out for the north, drawn by tales of gold just waiting to be plucked, practically underfoot. But after a spasm of placer mining—the exposing and flushing of precious metals in sand and gravel streambeds—the easy-to-get gold was gone. The wealthiest spent their fortunes in a flurry of excess and died penniless. By 1899 the vast majority of gold seekers had fled to juicier sluice boxes in Alaska and BC. Once the largest city in western North America north of San Francisco, Dawson had dwindled by 1903 from 40,000 to fewer than 5,000. By 1912, it had shrunk to 2,000 people and was inching toward ghost town status. If not for the federal government's decision, in 1959, to make it a National Historic Site and pump millions of dollars into restoration, it may well have become a ghost town. In fact, for almost two decades—the 1920s and '30s—the entire territory, an area the size of Texas, took on a haunted quality as the population sank to around 4,000.

But as the gold rush lost its lustre, placer mining underwent a metamorphosis. By 1906, the Yukon saw its first industrial placer mine operations. These highly capitalized ventures used dredges to move massive amounts of earth, and cannons to shoot highly pressurized jets of water, which dislodged rock and sediments to root up the gold. Such indefatigable gold seekers had the financial backing to persist, and they soon scattered east and north to the Stewart and McQuesten Rivers and deeper into central Yukon to Duncan Creek and its tributaries. There they did indeed find placer gold but not in the amounts hoped for. Instead they encountered a high mountain plateau, lit gentian and rust in the fall, and rimmed with snow-topped peaks, gently flowing streams and slopes of quartzite masked by distinct layers of glacial deposits. This was a far different landscape than the wide, delta-like Dawson country lying at the confluence of two large rivers. Here, prospectors eyed hills where fortune of a different flavour ran through the bedrock in undulating veins. The best could recognize rock protrusions that hinted at another precious metal—silver.

Early prospectors named two prominent heights of land Keno Hill and Galena Hill. Anywhere else in the world, people would call these summits mountains. Keno Hill rises to 6,480 feet and beside it the broad tabletop of Galena Hill reaches an elevation of 4,389 feet. Back then, pre–global warming, permafrost permeated as far as 262 feet down on the north slopes of these hills. The word "keno" refers to an old-time gambling game and so befits any mining venture. Galena is a shiny silver-coloured mineral containing mostly lead and sulphur, and is distributed abundantly in the earth's crust. Only in a few places, however, does it also possess high concentrations of a silver mineral called tetrahedrite, and in only a fraction of those cases is there enough tetrahedrite to be valuable. The early prospectors in the Keno–Galena Hill region spied just such rock in exposed surfaces, a find that led to the discovery of buried, silver-rich veins that would usher in a whole new era in Yukon mining history. For most of the twentieth century, these two mountains relinquished much of their prehistoric payload, allowing generations to thrive in one of the most remote, extreme and majestic places on earth.

Where most people see rock, rubble and dirt, prospectors and geologists see float, overburden, outcrops and other signposts pointing to promises of another Eldorado. Geology is a hands-in-the-dirt science, and this particular geology necessitated guts, time, brawn and dogged determination—and the financial means—to tough it out. In the early days, hardrock mining was a wretched enterprise. Apart from the endemic silicosis and lead-arsenic poisoning, men were routinely mangled, blasted, crushed, concussed, suffocated and frozen. Alcohol and lots of it may have been the only way to put up with that existence, even if it hastened the inevitable. Men concocted brews from any carbohydrate available, including flour, molasses, rice, raisins and dog food.

Excavating, crushing and transporting millions of tons of boulders and rock demanded heavy equipment, mills and concentrators, and all the grinding apparatus needed to process massive amounts of ore. Even though the precious metal in question was silver, not gold, those involved deemed their sacrifices worthwhile. And it was silver, not gold, that carried the Yukon into the modern mining era. But not just any kind of silver. In order to compete with less isolated silver mines in places like Coeur d'Alene, Idaho, and Cobalt, Ontario, Yukon mines needed ore rich enough to make up for the far greater transportation costs. Silver from the Elsa–Keno area was of an extremely high grade, routinely assaying over 200 ounces per ton.

Close to a hundred years ago, silver discoveries on Keno Hill proved so promising that New York tycoons the Guggenheims—who also had their fingers in the Klondike goldfields—bought claims and working mines there. By 1918, the mountain was a patchwork quilt of more than five hundred claims. In 1923, there were a thousand. The area was gripped by a full-scale silver stampede. Throughout the 1920s, Keno City and the surrounding creeks and hills were crawling with thousands of people. Today, mining on a much smaller scale has resumed in the area, but with Keno's year-round population at ten or so, the town teeters on the brink.

In 1921, a Montana-born man was sent by Alaskan gold mining interests to explore the area. He was so taken with its silver potential he built the foundation for decades of long-term investment, exploration and prosperity in the Keno–Galena Hill area. Livingston Wernecke was a mining engineer and geologist with surplus skill, dedication and enterprising spirit, enough to form the Treadwell Yukon Mining Company. His Wernecke Camp, a settlement on the mid-northwest slope of Keno Hill, included bunkhouses, a machine shop, a mill, a mess hall, teachers, medical facilities, a recreation hall with a pool table and bowling alley, and family homes. It was more than a camp, it was a community, and the overture to what Elsa would become: an industrial worksite where women and children were not only welcomed but also considered necessary for employee contentment and company success.

For Wernecke—an exacting, educated and shy man—almost no mark of civilization was missing from his town, seen in contrast to nearby Keno City, which descended into all-night drinking, fighting, gambling and whoring. The Keno scene attracted some miners for a time but it also cost the lives of both men and women. In the 1920s and '30s, a stable of eight women with names like Vimy, Vancouver Lil, Jew Jess and Silver Fox worked the saloons and brothels of Keno City. Most worked for organized vice rings based in Vancouver and at least one of them, Silver Fox, was murdered.

Wernecke had a piano and a dairy cow hauled up to his mid-mountain abode. In her 2009 profile of Wernecke, Whitehorse author Jane Gaffin writes that the Wernecke Camp was located "in a pleasant grove of scattered spruce, overlooking a panorama of colourful sunsets. Lightning streaked over the McQuesten River Valley and caribou wandered among the log cabins and frame buildings occupied by the staff and their families. The setting was akin to having heaven served on a platter." No doubt the occasional reindeer roast also graced the plate.

But like all divine repasts, this one didn't last. The Depression, plummeting silver prices and the eventual depletion of most of the accessible, high-grade ore on Keno Hill forced Wernecke to shut the mill in 1935. The town was abandoned only eight years after its birth.

When I was about four or five, my Dad took Vona and me on an overnight outing to Wernecke Camp. It was a rare adventure, given that we were daughters and not the sons Dad so desperately wanted and did not get. After her first child, a girl, doctors ordered Mom not to have more as the pregnancy revealed trouble from a childhood encounter with a serious disease. She disobeyed, however, and I arrived, another great disappointment. To some.

While most buildings in Wernecke had been dismantled or left to time and weather's whims, as is the Yukon way, some homes were eerily intact. We peered in the windows of fully furnished rooms, some with the kitchen table set with tablecloth, silver (of course) cutlery and china, all covered with a fine layer of dust. I imagined that little green men from Mars, as we called aliens in those days, had come down and snatched up all the people, forbidding them to take any belongings. The doors had no locks but we were not allowed to enter or touch a thing. "Someday," Dad said, "the people may return."

By the mid-1920s, attention shifted 12 miles west to Galena Hill where a Swede named Charlie Brefalt discovered promising silver veins. One discovery he named Elsa, after his sister. A second, straddling two claims, came to be called Hector–Calumet. Legend has it that Brefalt was out grouse hunting when he accidently stumbled on a rusty vein of ore among the bushes that would later assay at a startling 3,000 ounces of silver per ton. More likely, however, his find was due to nothing more than the usual toil and tenacity of area prospectors. Years later, a vein in the Elsa mine would contain silver concentrations more than double that. Buildings were soon erected at the base of Galena Hill near the Elsa adit—the horizontal entrance to the mine—and in 1935, Wernecke moved his mill to Elsa, where it crushed 150 tons of ore a day. Two years later, he constructed a 14,200-foot aerial tramline from the Hector–Calumet mine near the top of Galena Hill to the Elsa mill below. His company bought options on the Galena Hill claims, and as silver prices rose, so did Treadwell Yukon's prospects. His spectacular rise to success ended abruptly, however, in 1941, when he died in a small plane crash off of BC's coast.

Wernecke's sudden death, coupled with the war, temporarily silenced Elsa and the whole region. The war dealt two strong blows to Treadwell Yukon: a labour shortage and the US government's decision to stop buying foreign silver, an ill-advised move given that the Americans would soon need all the silver they could get. After the war, in 1946, two Toronto-based mining companies—Conwest Exploration Ltd. and Frobisher Exploration Ltd.—joined forces to buy what remained of the Treadwell Yukon holdings. The new consortium called themselves United Keno Hill Mines Ltd., first because they now held rights to more than thirty-five different mine sites scattered over the area, and second because Keno Hill was the first to be explored. Nonetheless, UKHM chose Elsa as its main townsite and northern headquarters, and over the company's lifespan, most of the silver taken from the area came from Galena Hill, not Keno Hill.

Apart from a four-month hiatus when the mill burned down in 1949, UKHM would unearth silver, zinc and lead continuously for the next forty-two years. Silver accounted for 80 percent of the ore's value. A mini-empire, UKHM owned sawmills, lumberyards, a transportation system, part of a coal mine and even a greenhouse. It operated ferries, maintained roads and helped operate the docks in Skagway, Alaska. That's because UKHM chose to ship its ore to a smelter thousands of miles south in Montana, USA. In 1962, Canadian mining giant Falconbridge Nickel Mines Ltd. took control of the company and initiated an aggressive and successful exploration program. As with all natural resources, and especially in the north, much of that prosperity flowed south to shareholders in cities such as Toronto, Montreal and New York. Regardless, UKHM powered much of the Yukon economy for four decades, and brought more wealth to the Yukon than the Klondike.

Elsa was that engine's heart.

CHAPTER 5

My Elsa

Oh how good it is to be
Foot-loose and heart-free!

I LEFT ELSA BUT IT NEVER LEFT ME. It is here inside, a hard, gleaming gem of good things. The mustard-yellow woods amidst a black-green forest sliding into a crimson valley rimmed by violet, snow-splashed crags, all crowned by a turquoise sky. The many nights we motored home along the Mayo road, rocking in the back seat, sleepy but sensing the cold and beast-filled void just a window away, until, as we climbed a hill, rounded a corner, a cluster of lights drew us home like a lifeline at sea. Springtime, climbing Crocus Hill: a birch grove carpeted with cupped blooms of lavender and white. Picking wild blueberries and cranberries at the top of Keno Hill… the air crisp, fresh and sweeter than any fruit. Sometimes, on Sundays when the roads were clear, we'd go for a drive just to see if the other side of town was still there. A shower on a blue-sky summer's day with sun shining through the rain meant either a fox's wedding or a monkey's birthday. Winter and 40 below, Vona and I racing through supper, stuffing our bodies into tubes of wool and then running out to play with Alan Mitchell, Darryl Andison,

David Mills and Dale Ekens. We'd toboggan down an icy hill in the blackness until someone got a wooden projectile in the gut. Or we'd jump off the pipebox into snow pillows so deep our boots got stuck and we yelled to be rescued. Some nights we played nicky nicky nine doors until Mr. Wall threatened to whip us good if we knocked on his door one more time.

All my Christmases were white, as were my Halloweens and Easters. Winters—six months of sub-zero cold and snow, and for half that time all-day darkness—were the best. On Christmas Eve we gathered at the community hall where Santa called us by name and presented us with the perfect present. Living so close to the North Pole meant Elsa was Santa's first stop. Crystal daggers hung from roof edges, growing so pointed and heavy that grown-ups knocked them down with shovels and picks before the ice pierced some kid's skull. We'd spread out on the snow, five-pointed angels, under stars so big and bright we reached to pick them like apples from a tree. On cloud-covered nights snowflakes drifted into our open mouths like frozen bits of sugar lace. Hours spent studying the phosphorescent light streams shimmering above—neon green, purple and pink ribbons swimming in a jet-black sea. Nothing separated the outside from my insides. And when I closed my eyes and pulled the covers up at night, the cosmos came along.

One night we wandered past the mill, past the mine, past the coffee shop to the first bunkhouse, where the single miners lived and where my sister and I were forbidden to go. Plunked on a rise of land, the bunkhouse was a hulking shoebox of a building with two floors of small six-paned windows and dim hallways with communal showers in the centre of each level. It was home to about 140 single men. I'd never been inside but everyone knew it as a tough and grungy place with pockmarked walls and splintered doors. Two men shoe-horned into a single room with opposing narrow iron cots and space for one trunk of belongings each. Housekeeping services consisted of a mop and a bucket but no soap. Miners were expected to clean up their own messes. Or not. An open door released a stink of tobacco, beer, urine, and sweat.

On this night, we heard accented voices spit out words I didn't understand—and didn't want to. "We're not supposed to be here," I whispered to Vona. "Don't be a baby," she shot back as she and the others moved deeper into the blackness behind the bunkhouse's back steps. The voices were harsher now and hateful. Two dark-haired hulks emerged, swaying and clutching each other's shoulders. Something glinted and wavered in the air. They shuffled, shoving each other down the stairs, tugging at each other's shirts, a fog of breaths suspended before their faces. Lurching toward us, one shouted, "Hey, who there? Scram, you little rats!" Without so much as a snow-squeak, we lit out running till our lungs ached, heading straight for our houses. The next day the town buzzed with the news that there'd been a stabbing at the bunkhouse. One man had been seriously wounded.

From 1953 to 1963, Elsa was home. They don't make towns like that anymore. Along with Calumet, its sister settlement four miles up Galena Hill, Elsa was a company town in an era when companies, particularly in the north, strove to keep employees and their families, if not happy, then content enough to stay put. In my day, Elsa was a remarkably accomplished, self-contained and well-endowed community of about four hundred people. Wages were generally higher than those "outside." As chief assayer for UKHM, with four to five workers under his command, Dad made from $600 to $700 a month, which was a good wage when the company charged only $30 a month for housing, heat and electricity, and subsidized the cost of groceries, beer and, for a time, even cigarettes. Water and steam heat generated at central heating plants at the mill travelled to homes and buildings along a pipebox—a long, raised, flat-topped wooden box containing insulated pipes that snaked through town.

Sewage travelled the pipebox in reverse. For kids, the pipebox was our house-to-house highway—we ran on top of it all the time, jumping off at will.

Housewives ordered essentials such as Squirrel peanut butter, Pacific powdered milk and Libby's canned Bing cherries from the cookhouse, where Chinese men baked bread and cooked meals for the miners. In the mid-fifties, "fresh" (previously frozen) prime rib roast sold for 75 cents a pound, bread for 25 cents and butter for 75 cents a pound. Specialty items were pricier: a package of Velveeta cheese slices was $8.19, and Jell-O chocolate pudding mix was $4.12. Almost every imaginable fruit and vegetable came in a can, including oranges, peaches, pears, spinach, peas and beets. Mom so longed for fresh food that one winter she cut out magazine pictures of pineapples, tomatoes, cucumbers and watermelons and glued them to the front of the kitchen cupboards. One week later she ripped them down, saying they only made her sense of deprivation worse. In the early sixties, a real grocery store appeared where customers could pick whatever goods they wished off the shelves. A sign on the building, which sold everything from hats to ham to Hershey bars, read: "The Elsa Market is owned and operated by UKHM Ltd. to supply a service to company employees, their dependants and residents of Elsa. All unauthorized persons are required to do their shopping elsewhere."

Such preferential and paternalistic treatment lasted well past the 1960s. Joe and Louise Volf ran the Elsa Market from 1966 to 1989, when the UKHM mine—and the town—shut down for good. "The company liked us to take special orders for German sausage or exotic cheeses from Denmark to please employees as much as we could," Joe says. "We were not allowed to make a profit. In fact we were told not to make money and I was scolded once for charging too much."

Not all requests, however, were granted. When Joe asked the company to stock underarm deodorant, the response was "No—let them smell." The Volfs, then retired and living in Mayo, look back on their Elsa days with fondness. "It was one of the nicest companies in the country," Joe says. "They took care of people. And we had a nice place to raise our three children. "

My best friend growing up in Elsa, Darryl Andison, spent more years in the town than he cares to admit. After high school graduation in Mayo, Darryl worked for UKHM, above ground, until the mine closed eighteen years later. His work, on the bull gang, the green chain and as a carpenter's apprentice, was a tempting trap: United Steelworkers Union wages, room and board for $2.60 a day, including good food and lots of it, and "beer that was $1.50 a glass in Elsa and $4.25 in Whitehorse."

Many company employees, including my dad, received a month's paid holiday a year and an annual paid trip outside to either Vancouver or Edmonton. For Mom, Vona and me that meant regular summer outings to Vancouver, where we stayed with my grandmother in her Mennonite friends' homes, while Dad traversed the Rockies on horseback or canoed a Yukon river or two.

An entity called the United Keno Hill Mines Recreation Club donated hundreds of dollars every year to a huge range of sport, social and hobby clubs. The money came from UKHM commissaries such as the beer parlour, coffee shop and pool tables, the objective being to do "the most good for the most people of the community." It was corporate socialism of a sort, and it worked. The company even handed out engraved silver and copper medals to eight- and nine-year-olds on Children's Sports Day.

Children's Races
30 yd. Girls 7-8 ys.1. A. Priest 2. L. Bennett 3. M. Grundmanis.

Wheel Barrow Race
Girls: 1. V. Priest, A. Priest; 2. M. Grundmanis, S. Conway. 3. L. Bennett, G. Swizinski.

Egg and Spoon Race
1.A. Coyle 2. A. Priest 3. M. Grundmanis

The Tramline, August 31, 1962

Things to do in Elsa? There were a few: curling, choir, bridge, badminton, bingo, ski club, rod and gun club, ladies' and men's baseball, square dancing, Brownies and Cubs, handicrafts, library, English lessons, first aid classes, film club, a branch of the Canadian Legion, a women's social group called the Silver Queens and a camera club that my dad initiated, presided over and eventually became the sole member of. A weekly mimeographed newsletter—called *The Tramline* after the tower and cable system carrying ore from Calumet to Elsa—and astutely edited by indefatigable long-time Elsa resident Virginia Grundmanis, reported everything from dances, major-run movie showings, club meetings, church services, dentist visits, cooking tips, community concerts and bazaars, who was visiting whom, who went on vacation and where, who was back from vacation and whether they had a tan, who had an operation, new arrivals and permanent departures, to items lost, found or for sale, the weekly temperatures, precipitation and mining accidents. *The Tramline* always finished with a flair such as "Most husbands know how to manage a wife but their wives won't let them." In the early days Dad, who viewed himself as a bit of a wordsmith, was a frequent *Tramline* contributor. Writers were not named but the following has G.H. Priest all over it:

> *"SABRINA" Set against the luxurious background of the fabled '400', Sabrina is a Cinderella story of a chauffeur's daughter, Audrey Hepburn, who, after a trip to France, is transformed from a gangly legged adolescent to a drenchingly beautiful young woman. William Holden and Humphrey Bogart, the scions of the family who employ her father, become enraptured by her*

and what happens is as romantic and frothy as the first rose of
summer with a bug on it and twice as sweet.

The Tramline, September 13, 1956

The almost imperceptible creep of time combined with the material simplicity and communality of Elsa life created a universe apart. Before 1960, Elsa and Calumet residents didn't have long-wave radio or TV stations or telephones. Short-wave radio was another matter, and Radio Moscow came in loud and clear. Don White, who later moved to Port Hope, Ontario, spent part of his boyhood in Elsa. "We got the results of the 1954 Grey Cup from our buddies in the USSR. Don't think they were cheering for the Als that year."

Major transportation hurdles isolated the community even more. All vehicles heading south, including transport trucks, had to cross three rivers—the Yukon, Pelly and Stewart—by ice bridge in winter and by motor ferry in summer. Ferrying the long, heavy trucks across a full, rushing river was often a harrowing exploit, and breakup and freeze-up periods—when the rivers were neither wholly liquid nor solid—meant no one went anywhere by road for one or two months. Even taking on the 32-mile gravel road to Mayo in the winter was a challenge. Most people, Dad included, put their cars up on blocks for the winter and hunkered down for months of quiet domesticity, relieved by weekly movie nights, concerts, drop-in visitors and impromptu all-night parties. Custom dictated that one couple went next door for drinks and then the foursome continued to the next house and so on until unsuspecting souls would be rudely roused in the wee hours by a mob of twenty or more inebriated but friendly folk.

There was no hospital, but we did have a clinic of sorts and a resident doctor. More often than not, somebody's wife was a nurse. Dr. Kirk also treated pets, including our dog Caesar when he came home yelping with a snout full of porcupine quills. Babies were born either 32 miles down the dirt road in Mayo (as I was) or "outside" in Whitehorse, Edmonton or Vancouver (as was Vona). As for dental care, the company brought in Dr. B.H. Wischert twice a year to drill, fill and pull. Sometimes his dental office was set up in the post office, sometimes the school and one summer he plopped his black and yellow chair of pain outside in a clearing just above the school steps.

COMMISSARY ANNOUNCES REDUCTIONS
Effective Saturday, January 7th, 1956, cigarettes purchased by the carton will be less 25 cents the regular price, that is Canadian cigarettes will be $3.25 instead of $3.50 and American cigarettes will be $3.75 instead of $4.00.

The Tramline, January 5, 1956

In my day, Elsa was a patchwork of white, tar-paper frame structures trimmed in either dark green or bright red, and highly varnished Panabode log buildings. Homes, mining offices, churches, sheds and other places could be of either style, but if your home was a Panabode, your dad had a better job than dads in other kinds of homes. Houses sat along one side of three roads carved out of the bush, punctuated on the south end by towering, snow-covered Mount Lookout, officially known as Mount Haldane and once home to a healthy population of grizzlies. On the north end of town, the main road split, to the right climbing the hill to Calumet and to the left meandering to Keno City, about six miles away. If you took the road south, you'd arrive in Mayo. A company-sponsored bus made regular and frequent trips between Calumet and Elsa in an effort to keep residents connected. For years, Vona and I took that bus to Calumet every week for piano lessons with Mrs. Lopp, a German immigrant like many others in town.

Elsa's attributes included a Catholic church, a cookhouse where single miners and staff ate, a coffee shop/beer parlour/barber shop/library, bunkhouses, the mine shaft (a cold black breathing maw), the railcar track, compressor houses, machine shops, electrical shops, the sprawling crusher and mill (deafening roars and dust fumes), Dad's assay office (smelly four-room wood-frame hut accessible via a long flight of stairs), the Elsa Market, the Royal Bank of Canada (perhaps the smallest branch in the country), a few white wood-frame homes, the log-cabin Anglican church, the rectory and a large, square white tar-paper shed we called the Three-Door Garage. Somewhere along the strip was an RCMP station with two full-time Mounties. Then, perched on a short slope, came the Walls' white and red-trim abode, fronting the road leading to our house, the last in a row of three copper-coloured Panabodes. From our big single-paned living room window we gazed out over the McQuesten River Valley, where wolves hunted and howled. Beyond lay a vast blanket of northern boreal forest that petered out at the alpine treeline.

We walked to our three-room school, on the road below, by following a short path through the bush. A ways beyond the school, through more bush and across a road, was a collection of flimsy homes known as Flat Creek, where several miner families lived. Below Flat Creek huddled a hidden handful of wood-heated shacks housing three or four Indian families. For some reason, that area was known as Millerville. The houses lining the highest road were large two-storey mansions with basements and breathtaking views and even, in summer, green lawns. One was a guesthouse for government officials and UKHM executives visiting from Toronto. That road was also where the general manager, assistant manager, mine manager, general superintendent, doctor and other boss-men and their families lived. During my time, the chief geologist and engineers lived in Calumet, where the geology department had its own log building.

Joe Stevens underwent minor surgery last week when Dr. Clark removed a growth from his lip. Although Joe was never noticeably handicapped by this formation, the doctor thought it best that it be removed. No time was lost by Joe, as he appeared at work the morning after the operation as spry and energetic as ever.

The Tramline, July 26, 1956

A big booster of the Elsa–Keno area was the late geologist Aaro Aho. His 2006 book *Hills of Silver: The Yukon's Mighty Keno Hill Mine* is the definitive history of the Keno–Elsa district up until the mid-1970s. A member of the Yukon Prospectors Hall of Fame, Aho spent thirty years scouring the territory, many of them in the Keno–Galena Hill area. He dubs his chapter on UKHM's prime time—the fifties—"The Halcyon Years."

"During the early 1950s camp spirit at United Keno was excellent," Aho wrote. "In those days… the district was still relatively isolated and people felt that they had to co-operate in order to survive. Housing was spacious, comfortable and cheap… Doors were never locked, even when one was leaving for a month's holidays, yet there were no recorded thefts." Well, okay, there was one.

On the home front, Vona and I were fuss-free playmates and did nearly everything together; we would dance, sing, play piano duets and trade secrets using our code language, Pig Latin. The latest games, books and records from far away magically arrived in the mail. My parents belonged to both the Columbia Record Club and the Book-of-the-Month Club, and Dad frequently came home bearing plain brown paper packages.

My Elsa was full of daily marvels, laughter and loving kindness, but I know that for others it held the opposite. Mining towns could be rough, lonely and brutal. For some single miners, it was as soul-destroying as a prison sentence. "The typical underground worker," writes Jack Hope, "rises at seven, eats in the mess hall, takes a company bus to his shaft at eight, works till four in the damp, unlit tunnels, showers in the 'dry,' busses back to town, eats an early dinner, and spends the long evenings reading, talking or, most commonly, drinking in the company beer parlour... The drabness and danger of days underground is at least matched by the monotony and frustration of social life aboveground."

Digging and blasting under the earth can also be bad for your health.

FATAL ACCIDENT IN ELSA MINE: People of this mining community were shocked to learn of the tragic death Tuesday evening of popular Heinz Alff, Elsa miner, in the first fatal accident on UKHM properties since January, 1953. Deceased was operating a mucking machine when he was killed instantly by a fall of loose ore in the 521 drift in the Elsa mine. Employed at UKHM since 1952, he is survived by his wife Gerda of Elsa and by his parents in Germany.

The Tramline, April 26, 1956

Married or single, people socialized laterally in hierarchical layers as firm and impervious as sedimentary rock. The top crust consisted of mine managers, geologists, engineers, the doctor and the clergy. Then came skilled staff such as electricians, carpenters and millwrights. As UKHM's chief assayer, Dad was staff. Next came the miners, first those who lived in houses and had families. Many lived in Flat Creek, Elsa's very own wrong side of the tracks. The single, recent-immigrant miners from countries such as Germany, Italy, Czechoslovakia and Hungry were housed in bunkhouses. Near the bottom of the social strata were the few Chinese men who baked bread and cooked meals for the miners. Their real homes (and families) were in Vancouver or China and they alternated one-month shifts with a replacement group of men. Last and least were the Indians, as they were known. In school, we studied the brave Iroquois, the river-canoeing Algonquin and the noble Plains Indians who built teepees, killed buffalo and rode painted ponies across the prairie—just like the "red skins" on the movie screen. But our Indians were as good as invisible. I do not recall any local Indian students in our school, or ever being taught about the local Natives—an Athabascan people called Na-Cho Nyak Dun, based in Mayo. Our adopted aunt and uncle—Mayo-based big game guides Louie and Dolores Brown—revered their Indian wranglers, especially one named Lonny Johnny, but I never spoke to him and, for the most part, in my world, Indians existed in books, movies and deep in the bush. Except for once a year, at Halloween, when we returned from trick-or-treating in knee-high snow, pillowcases full of frozen candy. Mom allowed us to choose one treat each. The rest, she said, would be given to the Indian children.

An Indian petitioned a judge of an Arizona court to give him a shorter name.
'What is your name now?' asked the judge.
'Chief Screeching Train Whistle,' said the Indian.
'And to what do you wish to shorten it?' asked the judge.
The Indian folded his hands majestically and grunted, 'Toots'.

The Tramline, November 23, 1956

Along with the racist, classist and colonialist attitudes of the fifties came free-for-all sexism. Working single women didn't work for long. They married, left town or did both. Still, if my mother was any indication, most women didn't mind the trappings of domesticity: homemaking, handicrafts, child-raising and husband-taming.

Elsa men were tough, taciturn and a little wild, or so they liked to imagine. But a happy wife made for a happy life. The women weren't submissive housewives, but productive and spirited team players who proudly navigated the mud streets in high heels and muskrat coats and enjoyed distilling town gossip, playing bridge and hearts, giving friends haircuts and Toni permanent waves, babysitting each other's children and drinking cup after cup of percolated coffee.

When it came to emotional and spiritual survival, few men made it without a woman. As retired mining engineer and former UKHM employee Bob Cathro wrote, "Successful family life was impossible without a very strong spouse." Given the era and a culture that took every opportunity it could to publically denigrate women so as to better elevate men, inner strength was the only way a woman could maintain self-respect, let alone sanity. Anti-women diatribes permeated books, magazines, music, movies, advertising, newspapers and radio so deeply they were rendered invisible by their ubiquity. On February 18, 1965, *The Whitehorse Star* ran a cartoon of two men watching a dogsled team. The lead "dog" is a large, block-headed woman with a fridge for a body. With great effort, she strains forward as four dogs run behind her. The musher, the man on the sled, cracks his whip. Under the cartoon the text reads: "Tried that with my wife Effie one time—durned if she didn't bite me."

In May 1961, the American men's magazine *Argosy* ran an article by Dick Adler titled "Steak for Men Only." My mom saved it not only for the terrific sauce recipe but also for Adler's prose: "Women and steaks are not compatible. By their very nature, females are timid, trusting, unadventurous and generally ill-equipped for the exacting task of engineering a slab of sirloin to the peak of perfection." In our family, Mom did 80 percent of the cooking. Omi, who lived with us for the first eight years of my life, did the other 20 percent. And Dad, who never so much as fried an egg, thought nothing of saying, "I make the living—you make the living worthwhile."

From table manners to bedroom techniques, every family generates and nurtures its own curious habits. Children, of course, think their family defines normal and all others are weird. One of our quirks was the persistence of German endearments despite my dad's claim that our home was his Anglo-Saxon fortress. We were too much of a hugging, kissing, touching family to be truly English anyway, and when my paternal grandparents visited we sat on our hands. But what we called each other in private was embarrassingly juvenile. To this day my sister and I refer to our parents (both dead) as Mammy and Pappy (pronounced "puppy"). And almost till the day they parted, they called each other Liebchen (Sweetheart), and were always holding hands, kissing hello or goodbye or goodnight, or touching each other affectionately. Omi was short and plump in a delicious, doughy way, and her wide, deep lap was highly coveted and routinely fought over. Second place was Dad's lap, which wasn't so cushiony but comfy nonetheless.

As babies and toddlers, my sister and I heard and spoke more German than English. Dad left the house and German ruled. We reverted effortlessly to English when he returned. Unlike Mammy, Omi never took an English lesson in her life and for a few years spoke haltingly and said little in Dad's presence. Vona and I were called Kleine (Little One) and Schätzlein (Little Treasure) and Süße (Sweetie). Then one day, when we were approaching school age, Dad laid down the law: no more German in *his* house. Besides being the tongue of "the godless Hun," it was guttural and ugly, and if his girls heard and spoke more of it, they'd have trouble learning proper English. Furthermore, Dad said, the quickest way for Omi to learn better English was to force her to speak it.

My sister's name, Vona, is a strange one. Mom told me she pulled the name out of the air but the truth is more interesting. Vona was supposed to be a boy, just as I was later. As her pregnancy ripened, Mom tired easily, and quickly became short of breath and dizzy.

Doctors detected a pathological heart murmur and suspected that sometime in her childhood she'd endured a bout of rheumatic fever, a disease that can permanently scar the valves of the heart. In early August 1952, at eight months along, Mom was sent "outside" to Vancouver's St. Paul's Hospital, put in a private room and restricted to bed rest. Doctors told her that, unfortunately, serious scarring of her heart valves meant her first child must be her last.

By strange coincidence, my Dad's elder brother Bill was at St. Paul's Hospital at the same time, undergoing surgery for a brain tumour that, within a year, would take his life. Meanwhile, my Dad remained in Elsa. In the fifties, it was not unusual for expectant fathers to be absent from the culminating event. Whether it was customary for a man to avoid visiting his terminally ill brother was another matter.

Aug. 29. 1952
Dearest Lambchen,
I was sad to hear that there'll be only one baby, Liebchen. If that's so, I hope for a boy because I want a son, oh very much! Maybe we could adopt one? But no, that wouldn't be nice either... Well, if it's a boy, how about the name Carl? I like that one. I'll make a deal with you: if it's a girl, you name it what you like and if it's a boy, we take Carl. Good enough? If you like Svetlana, that's good enough for me.

It was a girl, born September 3, 1952. Searching for a name, a name that would perhaps go a small way to assuage her husband's great disappointment, she recalled a Spanish love ballad he often sang, called "Juanita."

Nita! Jua......a....nita! Ask thy soul if we should part!
Nita! Jua......a....nita! Lean thou on my heart.

Only four years out of Germany, Mom chose the name Juana—close to Juanita, but not so foreign sounding. In old German, the "v" is sometimes pronounced softly as a "w," as heard in "Juana." For her middle name, Mom chose Gerina, a feminized form of Gerald.

Within four months of her return to Elsa with her new babe and her mother, Mom was again pregnant. Four months later, she received a letter from Dad, who was visiting his parents in Nelson.

April 6, 1953
I was around Alan and his little boy, who is sure ugly compared to Vona. As a matter of fact, I haven't seen any baby as nice as Vona anywhere. And soon a little boy? Ja? Everyone else has a boy so I just feel we are going to be lucky and come fall we'll have a little Paulchen!!

I arrived on August 29, 1953, in Mayo Landing Hospital, induced one month early to ease the strain of a full-term baby on Mom's heart. Dad was canoeing down the Stewart River at the time. The story goes that a friend greeted him at the Mayo dock with: "I'm sorry Gerry—it's another girl." My name isn't straightforward, either. Alicia is the name Mom gave me and it brands my birth certificate, but for all my Elsa years and about six years after, I was called Alice, my Dad's mother's name. Maria, my middle name, is Mom's mother's name. Occasionally, when we were alone, Mom called me Alicia, but otherwise I bore Granny's first and last names. Sometime within my first year Mom became pregnant for the third time. Doctors declared that the child, if brought to term, could kill her. Mom was flown to Edmonton where she had a therapeutic abortion and her tubes tied, a calamity neither she nor Dad ever mentioned. Over the next forty years, Mom would undergo six heart operations, four of them open-heart. Her first doctors predicted she'd be lucky to see the age of fifty.

Of the close to three hundred letters, cards and telegrams Dad wrote Mom, 99.9 percent of them declare his love and devotion to an operatic degree: "I love you more than life itself." "You are my whole reason for being." The exception was a wicked snippet concerning money, which of course he controlled completely and intended to keep it that way. In the fall of 1956, as Mom was convalescing in Vancouver from her second heart operation, Dad encouraged her to choose some new and necessary household fixings from the nation's largest department store. With delight she sat propped up in bed and selected a full couch, a chair, a faux-marble coffee table and two matching end tables from the more than six-hundred-page Eaton's fall catalogue; then she filled out the purchase form and phoned in the order COD—cash on delivery to Elsa! Dad was livid, writing her with accusations of selecting furniture "far more expensive than anything we had ever considered." He wired Eaton's and cancelled the order, and transferred all money in their joint account into his account. Any cheques she wrote would bounce. Then he set out the new rules. There was no more "our" money, only "his" money. He would allot her forty dollars a month for "house money" and "outside of that, you'll have nothing to do with money." Her new marching orders arrived on the day of their fifth anniversary.

You've been married to me for five years, have seldom been given any money of your own and have had to make do in the way of furniture. You've had very little money to spend on fixing up the house and not a great deal even for your children's clothes. That you've done so well, I have been proud. But we'll remember this— you've never been mistress in your own home. You've never been responsible for the running of this home, not even in the larger sense, the governing factor in the upbringing of our children. Your mother has been that simply because she's a stronger character than you. Natural enough under the circumstances.

You've not been well. I know that and sometimes feel I've let that influence me to a far greater degree than I should have. I'm not going to waste time crying of the disappointments I've had in marriage. You've had some too, I'm sure.

As officious, false and insulting as those words were, Mom simply turned the other cheek. She came home, new furniture arrived and for the greater part of time and from where we stood, we were an affectionate and fun-filled five: Pappy, Mammy, Omi, Vona and me. Vona was contrary, courageous and too clever by half. I was compliant, cautious and too credulous for words. Vona was happy playing with her plastic horses or drawing horses or reading about horses, or outside scrapping with someone, girl or boy, it didn't matter. I was happy playing inside with my Noah's ark set or my View-Master, or outside building rivers in the free-flowing spring melt or tearing through the bush with Caesar. We both were most content with our heads between pages. Dad teasingly dubbed us Thing One and Thing Two, after the two simian creatures in Dr. Seuss's *The Cat in the Hat*.

Mom was radiant, playful and infinitely inventive. Didn't have any shortening or butter for a pie crust? No problem. Cooking oil would do. And when I needed an Easter bonnet for the Easter parade (indoors of course), she turned a round bread basket upside down and wove purple and yellow hair ribbons through its wicker, then glued a downy toy duckling and fluffy white bunny on top. I won first prize. On rare occasions she would allow me to see her naked in the bath. But only after she was fully immersed and had placed her washcloth in a diamond shape strategically over her nether regions. As steam filled the warmed room and I stared at her mini-mermaid body, she said, "You know darling, Pappy is the only man I let see me like this."

Omi was our rock. When Dad and Mom went on camping trips or Mom went outside for any reason, she was our mother more than our grandmother. As a girl, she had fallen from riches to rags, having begun life in a wealthy, land-owning family who lost everything, including themselves, to revolution and anarchy. With her birth family and her only son imprisoned somewhere in the Gulag, she suffered lifelong survivor guilt, relieved only by her Mennonite faith. Despite her piety, she had no truck with the Anglican or Catholic churches in town. For many years in the Yukon, her only link to those she left behind was a heavy, cream-coloured plastic short-wave radio. She would spend winter evenings turning its dial in search of Russian- and German-language stations. Most often, though, she tuned it to Radio Free Europe, the US anti-Communist campaign dedicated to converting Russia into the Christian nation it once was. A twist of fate had terminated her long journey out of Russia, across Europe and across the Atlantic in northwestern Canada, just across the Bering Sea from her banished relatives.

We adored Omi. She loved us like a Siberian tiger. She told us true-life adventures, sewed us fancy outfits for everyday use and embroidered our household linens with cherries, ferns, flowers and long-tailed birds. For months the outside world was dark, grey and barren but inside, our pillowcases, tablecloths, tea towels and clothes burst with colours and shapes from a Ukrainian harvest. Omi was a skilled Mennonite cook who rarely measured ingredients; her kitchen mainstays were milk, cream, eggs and butter. Chocolate, however, was anathema: it had once been a key element in a concoction she'd mixed and ingested to successfully treat her tuberculosis during her first year in Canada. Take raw whole eggs (shells included), immerse in freshly squeezed lemon juice and let dissolve in fridge overnight. Then add melted pork fat and, to make the whole thing palatable, several ounces of melted chocolate. One year's bed rest near an open window, plus three tablespoons a day of her medicinal brew, and Omi was cured. It was near the end of this convalescence at the Rempels' farm that Omi, as she described it, "confessed her sins and received Jesus into her heart." When we asked what those sins could possibly be, she answered, "In the terror times, I did what I did to stay alive." Before her sudden conversion, she'd been a Mennonite but only nominally. In Canada she was fully baptized and born again.

Thanks to Omi, we knew our Bible, and recited grace before meals and prayers before bed. For me, God was a given: the winter sky, the autumn hills and the coming of spring were proof enough. For a while. As we grew older, Dad's relentless rationalism began to niggle at our beliefs. And as Omi's English improved, she couldn't resist swallowing the bait of Dad's scriptural scoffing. One evening, the discussion turned to the Genesis parable about the evil city of Sodom. Naturally, the Bible we read was a sanitized children's "story book." The original version of Sodom and Gomorrah is a brutal and sexually disturbing tale unfit for little ears. That evening the subject was Lot's wife and God's punishment for disobeying His order not to look back at the city of Sodom. She looked back and was instantly turned into a pillar of salt. We were horrified and gasped at the swift and brutal judgment of what we believed was a loving and benevolent God. Our faces were a mix of confusion and fear. Dad looked at us and then stood up and raised his arms heavenward.

"God, here I am," he called in jest. "Turn me to stone. I dare you! If you can do it, do it now. I am yours! Turn me to stone!"

He stood up and jumped on his chair, hands almost scraping the ceiling.

"Gerry," Omi wailed. "Please stop. Stop. I beg you. You must not tempt God! It is a sin."

"Ha-ha-ha-ha! How about a pillar of salt, God?! Come now, all-powerful One. Right now—a pillar of salt! Can you do it?"

Believer, unbeliever or agnostic, tempting fate, some say, is a fool's game. But at that moment, Dad had it all: a home rich with music, books and pets, and where he didn't have to boil a kettle or wash a sock; a well-paying job; a beautiful and affectionate wife; and two daughters who revered him as only little girls can. Or perhaps he saw things differently: four female dependants, an ailing wife who couldn't give him the son he deserved, a religiously fanatical mother-in-law, a tedious dead-end job for a company of fools and two daughters who revered him as only little girls can?

CHAPTER 6

The Nighttime
Is the Right Time

A man's a mug to slog away
And stint himself of ease,
When bureaucrats take half his pay
To glut their treasuries.

I N THE EARLY HOURS OF JULY 30, 1961, Frank Obella was alone
at the United Keno Hill Mines Elsa operation. As a compressor
operator, he'd just returned from a short stroll into the dark, damp
400-foot portal, an adit (horizontal passage) into Galena Hill about
400 feet below the original surface outcrop of ore. This subterranean
tunnel, the mine's main entrance, was situated next to the mine office,
change room and mill, and near other major UKHM operations. After
his routine inspection of the air pipe, Obella noted something odd on
his return to the compressor house. Inexplicably, a sudden drag of air
exited the system. The pressure plummeted by nearly half, from 110
pounds per square inch to 60. This sudden drop could mean only one
of two things: either the line had broken somewhere, or someone in
the mine had opened a valve to release a blast of air.

Air-pressure drops would be routine during a work shift when the mine was crawling with a crew of labouring men. But this was sometime between two a.m. and six a.m.—the four "dead" hours between the day and night shifts. Right now, with the cafeteria and beer parlour closed, all the miners were sleeping, showering, drinking or doing God knows what back in their closet-sized rooms at the bunkhouse.

Air compressors are vital to underground mining. They blow away dust particles or smoke, regulate temperatures and power machinery used to drill, push or lift rock. But in the Elsa shaft, compressors served an even more critical function. As a result of a thick cap of permafrost marked by cracks that leaked out oxygen-rich air from beneath, the Elsa mine had notoriously "bad" air. Compressors channelled fresh air into underground areas and forced out the bad air that could be dangerously low in oxygen, so low it could kill. That's exactly what had happened in the previous decade when two miners climbed several lifts to retrieve a mucking machine. As the pair rose higher within the mine, the air became thinner and thinner. One miner collapsed and fell back down to the floor, where he revived, but the miner who continued higher died of asphyxiation. UKHM geologist Al Archer had a surefire solution to the problem: a lit cigarette. Like the proverbial canary in the coalmine, when Archer's cigarette began to sputter, he knew it was time to either get the hell out or get a drag of fresh air from the compressor.

Naturally Frank Obella was perplexed about the sudden change in pressure. Who could be in the mine when both crews were off shift? And why? Ambling back into the shaft a second time to ensure he wasn't going loco, he spotted a man in the distance fading deeper into the darkness. With 200 feet separating them, Obella couldn't make out who the individual was, but noted his hard hat and his lack of a light. By now, Obella had reached the same air valve the retreating man had used.

"I turned the valve off and the man in the mine turned around and saw me," Obella said. "He looked at me for a second or two and then kept walking into the mine. He turned and looked at me once more and then turned left by the elevators."

Rather than pursue the man, Obella returned to the powerhouse where he phoned and woke mine captain Fred Southam. Outside, a northern dawn washed the sleeping town in a flat light, pale as skim milk.

Southam showed up about twenty minutes later, along with surface superintendent Jack Hogan, production superintendent Bruce Lang and staffer George Reynolds.

The group strode 500 feet into the adit—as far as the downward sloping shaft—and out again. They hung around for about an hour and then, after remarking that anyone in there would be impossible to find, left. As far as Southam and the rest of the crew were concerned, Obella had cried wolf. Someone asked if he'd been drinking before or during his shift. (Within a month, after only nine months with UKHM, Obella quit and returned home to Italy.)

Two weeks later, however, another compressor man, Joseph Keller, had a similar experience. Seated in the doorway of the compressor house, once again in the dead hours of the night, he saw two men cross in front of the lights from the doorway going toward the 400-foot portal. He recognized one as twenty-nine-year-old UKHM miner Anthony Bobcik and the other as thirty-five-year-old night mine captain Martin Swizinski.

Bobcik visited our home often over the space of a year or two, which I thought normal at the time but now seems strange. Unspoken town etiquette discouraged management, staff and miners from socializing with each other. In fact, Bobcik was the only underground worker Dad, who was staff, befriended to that degree. Like many others, we knew him by his nickname, "Poncho." He was built like a giant, tall and wide with dark greased-back hair, a ruddy complexion and a belly. Most often, he smelled of sweat and salami. Jolly, with an easy, runaway laugh, Poncho would scoop us up one at a time, twirl us around, but then abruptly release us. He promptly became awkward when Mom appeared, and avoided her eyes.

In *Cashing In,* Jane Gaffin notes Bobcik's commanding size— 6 feet tall and 220 pounds—and reveals details of his character and background. "He was a nonchalant, clever extrovert with an above-average intelligence," Gaffin writes. "He was fond of music, especially opera, but seldom socialized." Bobcik's father had been a wealthy farmer in Czechoslovakia until 1949, when he switched to running a trucking company. But the Soviet-dominated government expropriated both the family farm and the business.

Between 1951, when he emigrated to Canada, and 1957, when he moved to Elsa, Bobcik worked as a shoe-cutter in an Ontario factory and later as a trucker and logger in the Duncan area on Vancouver Island. As a new immigrant in a new land, he accepted hard work at grunt jobs as his destiny. Like other recent eastern European arrivals, he instinctively feared authority figures, and was suspicious of anyone with power.

Shortly after seeing the two men, Joseph Keller noticed the same sudden drag on the compressor that Obella had. Someone in the mine was using the air-powered machinery. Unlike Obella, however, Keller kept what he saw to himself. The bosses had ridiculed Obella over the alleged sighting earlier that month, which had amounted to nothing, and Keller was in no mood to give his superiors a reason to bad-mouth him. Instead, he returned to his station and hung out to see who would eventually emerge. But just as before, no one did.

The failure of the two men to walk out the main entrance of the mine was not magic, mystery or an employee's alcohol-fuelled fantasy. Up the hill and around the corner from Elsa, just off the Calumet road, was a second entrance, the seldom-used 200-foot portal. It was hidden from the main road and the town itself, and could be partially seen by the occupants of only one house—that of Butch and Virginia Grundmanis and their four young children, who were all asleep during the dead hours, as Butch worked day shift in the mill.

Soon after the development of the Elsa mine in the 1930s, ore near the distant 200-foot portal had been blasted away and removed. Now this portal was kept open primarily as an escape route in the event of fire, explosion, cave-in or other disaster. All the equipment needed to move piles of heavy rock in that section of the mine remained in place. Rail lines extended from inside the mine to the entrance. Rusting ore cars squatted idly. And the mine's compressor system stretched along its dim passageways. The 200-foot portal's entrance fronted a deserted spur of a road where anyone could come and go, virtually undetected. Just a jag up the hill, the road forked with the main path leading to Calumet and the smaller track, known as Williams Creek Road or Ballpark Road, leading to yet another byway called Duncan Creek Road. On the south side of Galena Hill, and out of sight of Elsa and Calumet, this gravel corridor provided an alternative route to Keno City and Mayo.

Between July and November of that year, UKHM Ltd. was in the last phase of excavating the richest vein of silver ore in its history and indeed one of the richest silver veins on the planet. Discovered in 1957 at the 525-foot level and called the "15-foot vein," this ossified river produced the highest silver assays UKHM ever obtained, up to a phenomenal 7,500 ounces per ton. At the time, the average grade of UKHM ore was a decent 40 ounces silver per ton. The five-month span in 1961 was the final stage of a three-year period during which this small, short vein was completely mined out. And some geological goblin had saved the best for last. At about 165 feet below surface, the vein blossomed into a silver rose of splendid mineralization. Miners call these buried treasures "bonanza" oreshoots, or stopes. The Spanish word *bonanza*, meaning fair weather, had been used for centuries to describe an especially rich metal lode. This one measured about 165 feet long, 100 feet deep and 7 to 10 feet thick. At its heart sat a 2,500-ton nut averaging 1,500 ounces of silver per ton. All told, what came to be called the Bonanza Stope produced 4.5 million ounces of silver.

Numbers like those are enough to quicken the heart of any prospector, miner, geologist or shareholder, perhaps even an assayer. Indeed, as Bob Cathro later wrote, UKHM's Bonanza Stope was so rich it had "the dubious honour of being one of the few sulphide oreshoots in Canada that was worth stealing." Pilfering nuggets of visible gold is relatively common in the mining industry, Cathro points out, but "the theft of a complex sulphide ore is practically unheard of because it requires smelting to recover the valuable metals." Also because, unlike nuggets, massive quantities of rock-bound ore demand a ton of heavy lifting. Fortunately or not, depending on your view, the Bonanza Stope occurred at the 200-foot level, about 400 feet from the entrance.

Archer, then UKHM's chief geologist, was intimately familiar with the Stope's fine-grained ore, which had a distinct silver-grey colour, as opposed to the more standard black-grey hue of Keno Hill ore. Back in 1957, Archer had discovered the 15-foot vein that eventually led to the Bonanza Stope. He knew its worth better than anyone, as well as its tempting allure. Archer jokingly said as much to Martin Swizinski during one conversation when the stope was being mined.

"I knew Martin quite well," Archer recalled nearly fifty years later, when he met me for lunch at Vancouver's Yew Restaurant, in the Four Seasons Hotel. A slight, frail, somewhat stooped man, Archer's voice matched his physique. His mind, however, didn't. Past eighty, Archer is one of the few principals in this story still alive. After lunch, he ushered me outside the restaurant to one of the hotel lobby's expansive couches.

"Martin and I often talked about how easy it would be to steal ore from that stope," Archer said. "A fellow could fill his lunch box with high-grade ore, say 20 pounds every day, and by the end of three years he'd have hundreds of thousands of dollars. The stuff was already broken up and lying around. Nobody would miss 70 tons of that ore. That was nothing!" The Bonanza Stope's total yield, Archer added, was somewhere between 75,000 and 100,000 tons of exceedingly valuable rock.

Like several other former UKHM staff members, Archer suspects Swizinski was Bobcik's partner during the odd events of the summer of 1961, mainly because, to do what he did, Bobcik needed help from someone in a supervisory position. Other arrows point to Swizinski's possible involvement. Most obviously, he was identified by Keller on that one occasion as being in the mine with Bobcik during off hours. And every two weeks, he was the senior man on night shift. In that position, Swizinski oversaw underground miners who worked the night shift five days a week. Crews worked one shift for two weeks, before switching over to the other.

Making off with mega quantities of raw ore from the Bonanza Stope was an undeniably fabulous feat, no matter when or how it was done. But it would have been impossible during the day shift, Archer says, "because a lot of authorized people wandered through the mine at will during the day—geologists, samplers, senior mine supervisors, safety inspectors, etcetera. None of these, other than the shift boss on duty, came during the night shift."

With senior mine employees absent during evening hours and all other employees out during the four dead hours, nighttime was the right time to fill a lot more than a lunch bucket with high-grade ore. Especially when the treasure was positively begging to be taken. Both day and night shifts followed a standard routine. Each crew began by collecting the "muck" left behind by the previous shift. Muck is broken rock blasted from a rock roof or wall and scattered on the floor. Each two-man crew of miners gathered about 20 tons of muck per shift. Crews next erected wooden posts and beams in a process known as timbering to support the roof, fortify walls and prevent cave-ins. Holes were then drilled into the rock and loaded with explosives. Just before shift end, the explosives were detonated, creating yet more muck for the incoming gang—four hours later.

The only exception to this regime occurred in the Bonanza Stope, where it was common practice to leave ore on the ground for longer periods of time. That's because UKHM, like many other mining companies, used small amounts of the Bonanza ore as a sweetener to enrich the lower-grade ore produced from other UKHM mines. This mixing ensured a higher return when the mined ore was later smelted. In most cases, such a move made sense. But not with the Bonanza Stope. Archer, who was more familiar with the Bonanza's geological idiosyncrasies than anyone, knew that a good portion of the silver-rich vein ran close to the surface and as a result had oxidized into a clay mineral. To extract optimum value from such rock required bagging, processing and smelting it separately from less valuable ore. By mixing the rich, oxidized ore with less rich ore, UKHM lost money, as much as 25 percent of the ore's value. But when Archer gave Pike his expert opinion on this matter, the chief said, "Go back up there to your hole and don't bother me again."

And that wasn't the only instance in which Pike's autocratic decisions cost the company. A federal government tax incentive gave mining companies a three-year tax-free period for anything that was considered a "new mine." And the Bonanza Stope was exactly that. By mixing the tax-free ore with taxable ore—and keeping sloppy books—UKHM ended up paying far more tax then they needed to. Not a lot further down the road, Pike would have to answer for his mistakes.

But there was more. Pike's practice of using only small amounts of Bonanza ore meant large volumes lay around for longer than usual, likely for weeks at a time. Other miners eyed the enticing silver-laden hoard. One, who had served jail time for a previous ore theft, talked up the idea of making off with the muck and disguising its origins by saying it came from elsewhere. Rock laundering, in other words. But that was just talk—talk that burned Bobcik's ears back at the bunkhouse.

As night-shift boss, Swizinski knew when the mine was clear of workers and safe to enter on the sly. Bobcik rendezvoused with his partner by entering the mine through the 200-foot portal. He quickly reached the Bonanza Stope via a crosscut, which ended at a ventilation door. These doors were placed in inactive sections of the mine and kept closed to avoid loss of compressed air. Beyond the door, Bobcik continued into a new crosscut and encountered a tugger—a winch powered by the compressor and used to push, pull or lift rock. From there it was only 40 feet or so down a gradual incline to the Bonanza Stope, where freshly blasted treasure awaited.

The task was physically gruelling and mentally methodical. First, Bobcik and his co-worker shovelled, hand-sorted and loaded chunks of ore into five or six burlap sacks—backbreaking work. Using the tugger and a slusher, they pulled the 100-pound bags up to the 200-foot level. A giant mechanized shovel, the slusher worked best when moving rock downhill, taking advantage of gravity, and was normally used to direct ore down to the 400-foot portal. But the slusher also moved rock uphill. By running the slusher in reverse, the thieves shifted roughly half a ton of ore, in a matter of seconds, up to the rail tracks leading out the 200-foot portal. From there, they loaded the sacks into railcars, pushed the cars about 400 feet into a dark, inactive recess of the mine, pulled the sacks out from the cars and hid them. On most nights, they performed this operation three or four times—lifting, pushing, hauling and hiding more than a ton of ore each visit.

A month after the mysterious nighttime sightings, two off-duty miners were heading home from an early morning hunting venture when they came upon Bobcik and another man in the midst of moving ten heavy burlap sacks. The encounter took place on a lonely part of Duncan Creek Road. The second man immediately dashed off into the bush while Bobcik coolly got into his truck and drove away.

The Law of the North dictates that season and weather determine people's outdoor plans. Getting the ore out of the Bonanza Stope had been a relatively risk-free if exhausting accomplishment. Adding to the challenge was the fact that Bobcik and his partner had to work their own shifts either before or after their nighttime exploits. But now what? Although they'd managed to stash a tiny portion of their massive haul in an out-of-the-way spot in the bush, could they safely relocate the rest? Left languishing in a hidden nook in the mine, the sacks might as well be packed with cardboard. During the light-enhanced nights of July and August, the duo had no chance to move the ore without risk of being caught, as the scare with the hunters had proved. And winter months, which began in October, when back roads became impassable and fresh snowfall exposed tire tracks, were precarious too. After much thought, Bobcik and his partner chose to leave the bulk of their sacked booty in the mine drift, near the entrance of the abandoned 200-foot portal.

Hours and hours of hard labour lay ahead. The bags, numbering around 660, still had to be dragged out of their shady niche; placed on railcars and pushed to the road; then lifted into a pickup truck—at best a two-ton, four-by-four; and cached somewhere safe, somewhere hidden, somewhere no one would go. They'd hit on the right time to scoop the ore from the stope; now, during the winter of 1961, they'd have to find the right place outside the mine. Any spot they picked had to be relatively near the mine as the ore had to be re-bagged in new sacks that didn't bear UKHM's brand, and they certainly didn't want to be seen before that happened. But once that was done there was an even more challenging aspect. Somehow, they'd have to find a way to pass themselves off as the legitimate owners of the ore.

CHAPTER 7

Buying the Moon

There's a race of men who don't fit in,
A race that won't stay still,
So they break the hearts of kith and kin,
And roam the world at will.

A BLUE-PURPLE HAZE ENGULFED the poorly ventilated room along with smells of sulphur and smouldering metal, and although this hellish state was normal and indeed expected, workers took it as a smoke signal to get out. There was nothing to do but amble to the Elsa Coffee Shop for an extended cigarette and coffee break, and wait for the noxious cloud to dissipate. Such was the art of assaying in the 1960s, and such was the workday of Dad, UKHM's chief assayer.

Assaying is to hardrock mining as laboratory testing is to medicine. Both analyze tiny portions of larger samples to obtain critical information that would otherwise remain invisible. In both cases, the results can be disastrous: a patient's lab results may signal imminent death, and an ore assay may scuttle a prospector's dreams. But while medical tests often bring good news—confirmation of a pregnancy or a patient's receptivity to treatment—it is rare for an ore assay to point to an Eldorado.

Once someone finds a good mineral deposit and a mine begins operations, assays are done continuously to calculate the content of the ore so that management knows the exact value of what is pulled from the earth each day and will later leave the mine property for processing elsewhere.

During the thirteen years that Dad was UKHM's chief assayer, he and his crew worked out of a four-room, wood-frame white tar-paper building in the middle of the camp, next door to the mill where the ore was crushed, and a two-minute saunter from the multipurpose Panabode building housing the Elsa Coffee Shop, the barber shop, the beer parlour and the library.

Dad found his chosen vocation mind-numbingly mundane but that didn't stop him from being good at it. He was known for his precise and exacting assays. But as talented a technician as he was, he found time for other, more personal pursuits. "A man's home is his castle," he liked to boast, but his office was his true citadel. And in a musty shed behind the office, my Dad set up a suspended wooden barrel strung between ropes and when he had a few free moments, would straddle and hone his equestrian skills. He frequently brought Caesar to work too—especially in the summer, when our shepherd chased and killed rats and mice.

George Duerksen, who worked twice for my Dad, once in 1952 and again in 1957, recalls a boss who was easy to work for, if a tad on the anti-social side. "I admired your Dad and enjoyed working for him. But he was shy—wouldn't look my wife Margaret in the face," Duerksen told me, adding that Dad once cautioned him about marrying beautiful women: "You have to be careful marrying a racehorse. It's not like keeping an ordinary horse—you have to keep your eye on 'em, have to be protective." Duerksen also recalls a man who had it made by mining world standards. "His job was as soft as they get."

But not all of Dad's colleagues found him so pleasant. Bill Richter, who worked day shifts in the office for three years, described his boss as "moody, quiet and almost conceited," adding, "His favourite subject was suicide. He was rather morbid and enjoyed talking to anybody about this."

By 1961, Dad had served ten years at UKHM. To mark his decade of service, the company presented him with a gold-plated Omega Seamaster watch engraved with his initials, G.H.P., and theirs, UKHM—an indication of how well the company was doing. I wear it now, my one inheritance from my father other than a pill-sized vial of gold dust. But after a decade's indebtedness to The Man, did Dad eye his memento as a milestone or a millstone? As a child, I wanted for nothing. Still, money, or the lack of it, was a sensitive although infrequent late-night conversation topic between Mom and Dad. As a new bride, Mom had been promised "only one or two years" up north, "until we get some savings under our belts." But as one year melted into the next and family savings added up to skimpy to nonexistent, she longed to live and raise her girls in the city. Omi couldn't tolerate the isolation and extreme weather anymore, and told us with shiny eyes that after much prayer, she had decided to move back to Vancouver before the first snowfall. Besides, my mom would say, the Elsa school only went to grade seven, and Vona and I would soon have to leave for a larger centre. Many families sent their teenagers to the high school in Whitehorse, where they boarded with other families.

In August 1961, a vacancy opened in the assay office where my dad supervised four employees. The job went to Anthony Bobcik. Poncho was quite literally moving up in the mining world, although he was taking a pay cut to do so. Freed from the hard underground labour of shoring up freshly blasted tunnels with heavy timbers, drilling rock walls and shovelling heavy loads of ore, Poncho would now spend his days above ground working as a bucker. As such he would crush up small baseball-sized chunks of rock delivered from the mine, which was the first step in the "dry" assaying process. "Wet" assays dealt only with crushed powder samples from the mill.

By then, the bulk of the ore Poncho and his partner had stolen from the Bonanza Stope was tucked away in its temporary hiding place, not far from the 200-foot portal. The spot was well chosen, near a rock pile where an old tunnel and ceiling had caved in, blocking the passage. No one venturing into the mine's back entrance was likely to follow a tunnel known to dead-end. A stand of rough-hewn timbers was also stored nearby, providing a further shield for the ore stuffed into hundreds of old UKHM-stamped burlap sacks.

Poncho's new job didn't require any special skills. An ad in *The Tramline* noted that a high school education would suffice, and that "previous chemical experience" was an asset but not a prerequisite. He and another man performed dry assays, while Dad and an assistant did wet assays and a fifth employee (typically a woman) parlayed her household skills into cleaning the beakers, bottles, trays and other assay equipment. Poncho's task was straightforward muscle work. In the furnace room, he pulverized rock chunks into particles as fine as talcum powder using a hinged, tapered metal crusher. The other worker maintained the furnace at temperatures approaching 1,700 degrees Fahrenheit. The rock powder was then placed in a clay pot along with a flux—a mixture of charcoal powder, cream of tartar, lime and other dry ingredients—and the whole mélange was cooked in the furnace. Metals such as silver, lead and zinc fused together, while rock minerals became cinder-like fragments known as scoria, from the Greek word for rust.

But the process wasn't finished yet. Poncho then chipped away a small piece of the cooled, hardened and fused ore and placed it in a shallow porous cup called a cupel. Cooked again, any remaining lead and zinc in that sample fused to the cupel's surface, leaving behind a bead of pure silver. Flat on the bottom and rounded on the top, the bead resembled a pewter-coloured Smartie. Dad often brought handfuls of silver beads home to show us what he produced, and they would end up strewn about the house, on dressers, tables and windowsills. Back in the assay office, each bead was weighed and that figure, when compared to the weight of the original sample, determined the silver content of the larger volumes of ore.

Wet assays also gleaned information about the content of raw rock, but in another way. Fine rock particles were mixed in beakers with various liquid chemicals and heated to trigger chemical reactions that revealed lead or zinc. It was this fiery alchemy that regularly produced billows of blue stinky fumes, driving the staff to the Elsa Coffee Shop.

A few years after Duerksen's departure and a few months after Poncho's arrival, there was a noticeable increase in the number of impressively large silver beads produced in the assay office. This marked the beginning of months of assays revealing off-the-chart silver concentrations—during which time the Bonanza Stope was mined.

Almost from the moment he began working as an assistant assayer, Poncho enjoyed a special status. He was, as fellow assay office worker John Bourdeaux recalled, Dad's "bosom pal" and would spend "considerable time up in the wet lab talking with Gerry. He did so little work that it became annoying to me and I started to keep my own record of his times."

In an office where the workload was already lighter than in other places, Poncho set a new slacker standard. But complaining did his workmates no good. It was the complainants Dad found fault with, not Poncho. And as Dad and Poncho conferred more frequently and for longer periods—on occasion their coffee and cigarette breaks stretched to two hours—the rest of the assay crew learned to keep their mouths shut.

As a stellar Yukon fall yielded to a dark and increasingly frigid winter, Dad and Poncho concocted what they saw as a surefire solution to their predicament. Obviously, the ore inside the 200-foot drift couldn't stay there. Moving it was the easy part. Harder by far was sneaking all that rock out of town from under the noses of UKHM bosses without raising a whisper of suspicion. And then hauling the load thousands of miles by truck, rail, ship and then rail again across the international border to the smelter in Montana, the same facility UKHM used. Yet getting it there would be for naught if they couldn't convince the smelter that the large high-grade ore shipment was legit. The shipment would need some credible paperwork verifying its source and ownership.

Who better to point them to a potential source of riches than the mine's own chief geologist? Dad approached Archer, asking if he knew of any claims in the Keno area where quartzite rock occurred. There was not much to choose from, given UKHM's practice of snapping up any excuse for a claim as soon as it became available, but Archer pointed him to the Moon claims.

Archer made his suggestion after consulting an old geological report. While the report indicated there might be something of value on the Moon site, it was clearly not a property UKHM was interested in.

The Moon claims had sparked interest from prospectors and miners since 1921 when a treasure tramp named Bjonnes staked them and named them Doris, perhaps in memory of a lost love. The Norwegian either found nothing or what he did find was long gone by the time the claims were re-staked thirty years later by a prospector named St. Louis. Almost a decade after that, prospector John Strebchuk staked the property again and christened them the Moon. His choice of moniker mirrored the Moon site's location—in the outer limits of nowhere, far past Keno, beyond the old Wernecke townsite, near the bottom of Faro Gulch. The claims were most easily reached during winter when ice and snow solidified the McQuesten Valley's bogs and creeks. But getting to the Moon in the summer meant trudging 8 miles northwest from Keno City on a tattered old mining road skirting the edge of a ridge and then clambering down a gully.

Archer's opinion that the Moon claims might hold promise was exactly what Dad and Poncho wanted to hear. Around the same time, as if destiny was in on the heist, Poncho, Dad and the third man were suddenly forced to move the bulk of the stolen ore in a hurry. Mine superintendent Bill Case notified the two shift bosses that the tunnel near where the stolen ore was cached would soon be re-timbered in preparation for new mining activities.

It was about this time, March 1962, that Dad began going out late at night. Well, late for an eight-year-old. One mid-week night we'd eaten supper, helped dry the dishes, practised our piano and done our homework when he hurriedly kissed us goodnight and put on his heavy coat, boots, leather hat with woollen flaps and thick gloves.

Normally, this was Mom and Dad's time to listen to records or read a book to each other or take Caesar for a starlit stroll. Many nights we drifted off to the sounds of Patti Page's "The Tennessee Waltz," Harry Belafonte's "Scarlet Ribbons" or the Norman Luboff Choir's haunting western ballad "The Colorado Trail." But no songs would be heard this particular night.

"Where are you going, Pappy?"

"I'm going to see a man about a dog," Dad said with a small smile as he went out the door. We had a dog. Why was he talking about another? Caesar was all the dog we needed. As Dad was fond of saying, "Give your heart to a woman and you'll get it back. Give your heart to a dog and he'll take it with him to his grave."

The next night and the next he went out to see a man about a dog again. When we turned to Mom for an explanation, she said: "Your father is helping an old prospector named Charlie North, and it's very good of him to do so. Now, you each choose a favourite story and I'll read two tonight."

As his evening outings continued over the course of that strange week, I noticed how tired Dad was. Sometimes he nodded off right after supper, sitting in a chair. Sometimes he came home for lunch and slept for an hour. And on Saturday, he cut his workday short, returned to the house and crawled into bed for a long nap.

Over the space of five cold nights, Dad helped that mysterious prospector move six hundred or so burlap sacks of ore, first by railcar to the mine entrance, then into Poncho's Dodge Ram Power Wagon and finally off the truck again, before the bags were dragged and tucked securely into their new temporary home. The location was a short drive down Williams Creek Road, not far past the ballpark, to a hiding spot near Duncan Creek Road. A narrow moss-covered ditch ran back from the road and was completely concealed by bush and tangled willow scrub. The chance of anyone poking around there was next to nil, the area having long ago been rejected for any mineral potential, and the road nearby rarely used in any season. Once they had all of the ore at the new site, and with the winter moon as their witness, the three men cut open the bags and dumped the ore onto a growing pile, which was quickly covered by snow.

Having laid down the rock, it was time to lay down a paper trail. Not a simple mission. Perhaps at this point, perhaps at another, the third man came down with a bad case of the heebie-jeebies. He'd been a key player in the theft but for whatever reason he now wanted out. For a price, of course. Dad and Poncho, on the other hand, were gearing up to execute what they saw as the perfect theft. Back at the assay office, they fine-tuned the details of the final and most audacious stage of the plan.

Meanwhile, at home, another more threatening drama was playing out. Mom was spending long periods in bed. When she attempted the slightest physical activity, such as walking up a gentle incline, she gasped for air. Once, while hanging laundry on the outdoor clothesline, she fainted. She tried to downplay our worry but I saw the fear on Dad's face and prayed for God to heal her soon.

My prayers were answered but not by any celestial powers. In late April 1962, Mom flew "outside" for her second heart operation at

Vancouver General Hospital, under the care of cardiac surgeon Ross Robertson. Dr. Robertson knew her well, as he had performed her first operation. This second one was basically a repeat of the first: a "closed commissurotomy," a blind procedure done prior to the invention of the heart-lung machine. The surgeon cut open her left lower chest, spread her ribs and made a tiny incision in an artery adjoining the left chamber of the heart. Inserting his index finger deep into the incision, the surgeon felt for the mitral valve and freed it of any built-up scar tissue. Her four subsequent heart surgeries would be open procedures, which was a great improvement, as surgeons could see what they were doing and where they were doing it.

During Mom's absence, Omi, who had moved into a Vancouver basement suite the previous fall, flew north to look after us. It was a cold May and snow still smothered the ground, but inside the house spring miracles burst forth: Mitzi, our tabby, crawled into a loose pocket under the couch and had her first and only litter of four kittens. We named them, checked their progress daily and wrote Mom about all the news each week. On more than one night I woke from a nightmare in which Mom had died, and at that point I wasn't totally sold on the idea of heaven. But she came through the operation and was recuperating, first in hospital for two weeks and then another two weeks with Vancouver friends Angus and Carol MacDonald. Angus was a consulting geologist and had worked extensively in the Keno area, including for UKHM.

My sister and I took turns sleeping with Omi. Omi's greatest fear now was that her daughter would succumb during an operation, ending her maternal relationship with her "girls." Co-habiting with Dad in a world without her daughter would be impossible. She understood correctly that he could never live with her. Dad was slovenly to the point of squalour, and she was the quintessential Germanic woman. It made for a vexing household arrangement. Born into wealth, Omi was raised by Russian nannies and sent to the finest all-girls school. Yet every Saturday she knelt down and washed and waxed our kitchen's checkerboard linoleum floor before baking several loaves of bread. Every Tuesday she did the laundry, including my dad's underwear (which he used to brag only felt comfy after five days' wear), using a state-of-the-art wringer washer. She hung the laundry outside where it froze stiff as cardboard in colder weather. She ironed the sheets before they went on the beds she changed, and embroidered the pillowcases we slept on. She even washed and polished the leaves of our giant, trailing philodendron houseplant.

At around 8:30 p.m., after telling us our Bible story and bathing us in kisses, Omi would turn out the light, and then pray in the darkness while we floated to sleep, rocked by her soft-voiced German. When Mom didn't die but recovered quite nicely, Omi showed her gratitude to God by fasting one day a week for the rest of her life. On Thursdays, till the day she died, she only drank water. However, Omi yearned for her independence, her like-minded companions and the warmer, sunnier climes in Vancouver. She loved us more than her own children, she often told us, but needed to be with her soul-sustaining Mennonite community, which was thriving in "Little Deutschland," a neighbourhood in southeast Vancouver centred on Fraser Street and Forty-first Avenue.

As Omi filled her Yukon days attending to our home, her son-in-law and us girls, Dad wrote Mom of his promising business venture.

May 2, 1962
About the other thing Liebchen—don't worry or let it keep you in suspense at all. Things are going just fine, and if it's successful— just dandy!! If it isn't, we've got the most valuable things of all, each other and the children. Ja?

At the end of that month, on UKHM letterhead embossed with the words "Elsa, Yukon Territory," he wrote: "I still have lots to do with my business here and imagine that most of my Sundays and spare time will be taken up with it."

Summer arrived, Mom returned home, all the kittens had new owners and Dad was indeed busy. In June, he and Poncho inked a private deal—the first of a growing pile of papers signed or initialled by the two—regarding the soon-to-be-purchased Moon claims. They agreed to split the cash value of the ore shipment equally, but with a small percentage of the total going to the third man. Once the initial "mining" was completed, Poncho would gain full ownership of the claim and be free to explore it as he wished. Three days after they signed the deal, Dad bought the Moon claims from John Strebchuk for $1,000. Then he wrote the Yukon Territory's mining inspector, stating that he intended to mine the Moon "on a very small scale." If a claim holder did not do a minimal amount of work on his claims, they reverted to the territorial government and became free for someone else to stake. Dad told us about his claims, but we thought little of it—even then, we knew that the Yukon grows prospectors like the Prairies grow gophers.

Shortly after, another letter, penned again in the UKHM assay office, was mailed to the American Smelting and Refining Co. in Helena, Montana.

Dear Sirs,
I should like to enquire about the possibility of marketing a small shipment of hand picked high-grade silver ore… If I could manage an average of, say, 2,000 oz of silver and 25% lead, what could I expect to receive after deductions for transportation, smelting, etc.? How would it be advisable to ship providing you would accept it?
Sincerely,
Gerald H. Priest.

Over the following fall and early winter, there was a lull in the activity and as far as Vona and I were concerned, life was blissfully normal. In October, Poncho quit the assay office and moved to Keno City and we rarely saw him. But as 1963 got underway, Dad initiated a flurry of correspondence, along with numerous phone calls, and also purchased some extraordinary goods. He bought a Ski-Doo for the princely sum of $988.49. Such an exotic contraption had never been seen in Elsa and would be the first such machine operated in the region. When it arrived, Vona was beside herself with excitement. Me, not so much. It sounded like an angry mosquito and chewed up the snow like the war tanks I'd seen in the movies. I didn't see the point of all that noise and stink but Vona jumped at every opportunity Dad offered for Ski-Doo rides, up and down hills and along snow-packed roads.

In March, Dad bought a pair of Ojibway snowshoes, snowshoe harnesses and a towing toboggan. The next week, he phoned the Northwest Sack Co. in Vancouver and ordered seven hundred heavy twill sacks at thirty cents apiece, along with seven hundred specialty sack ties. By late March, all the goods had arrived, and it was time for Dad to take his holiday.

"Pappy is gone taking his ski doo for his Easter Holidays. He has gone to his claim. Tomorrow he will come home," Vona wrote in an April 1963 letter to our adopted aunt and uncle, Dolores and Louie Brown. "Our ski doo is yellow, round, and [has] a curved windshield. There is one ski. A large one in the middle and two rubber tracks on the side. The seat can come off and you can put hammers and things like it [inside]. The toboggan is six feet long, made of plywood. About 2 and half feet wide. I can drive the ski-doo all by myself. I know how to stop and start it."

While on holiday, Dad let a few select people know of his good fortune. He'd discovered "float," a surface deposit of silver-rich ore, on his claim, he told one man. "He was going to mine this float and haul it out," said mill worker Joe Sekulich (not his real name). "Poncho was trying to build a road to the claims the summer before but had wrecked his Cat. So Gerry was going to use his snowmobile and toboggan to haul the stuff out. He expected to make seventy or eighty thousand dollars, but first he'd have to break it up in little chunks and put it in sacks so he could haul it to the road where the White Pass trucks could pick it up."

Offering his help, Sekulich built Dad a special sacking stand so that he could more easily load the ore during his wintertime forays. Days later, Sekulich bumped into Dad in Elsa during the Easter break. "He had a beard and was dressed for the outdoors. I asked him how it was going, and he said fine."

Johnny Yandreski (not his real name), who drove his pickup truck daily between Elsa, where he worked, and Keno City, where he lived, also helped Dad during the early spring of 1963. "He asked me if I would take some stuff for him from Elsa to the junction of the Wernecke and Klondike Keno Roads. Since I drove that way all the time I said yes. A couple of days later, I stopped by his house and he had about five bags of grub and tools and a sleeping bag. When we got to the Wernecke–Klondike junction his motor toboggan was parked right there."

Yandreski would shuttle Dad back and forth a few more times. However, Dad was tight-lipped about what he was doing on those cold days and nights, and Yandreski knew it was bad form to pry a prospector. Still, he was puzzled: there weren't any snowmobile tracks along the roads. If Dad was using his fancy machine to haul ore, he wasn't taking the most obvious route.

Poncho, meanwhile, was busy on other fronts. At the end of April, after returning to Elsa from a trip, he wrote Toronto lawyer Richard Irwin Martin asking him to incorporate a new mining company. Martin had experience with mining companies in Ontario.

Since I have left, Priest has been taking out ore from the claims, hauling it with a snow toboggan. The ore is such as I have never seen at United Keno. I want you to come up here to the Yukon and prepare an agreement. I want you to incorporate a new company called Faro Silver and Gold Mines.

Shortly after, a new company was registered with an official address on Church Street in downtown Toronto, not far from the financial heart of the nation, including the well-heeled owners of UKHM. But it wasn't called Faro Silver and Gold. The company's name was Alpine Gold and Silver.

A few weeks after that, on a Friday, Vona and I came home from school and received stomach-churning news: in four days we would be leaving Elsa forever. Mom, Vona and I flew to Vancouver on June 4, leaving Dad and Caesar behind to join us later. Dad said he would find a good home for Mitzi. Much later we learned he took her out back and shot her. His last day at the assay office was the following Saturday. Then, he got down to business—the first grunt work Dad had done since the frenzy to pull the cached ore out of the mine more than a year before. Poncho, Dad and Ed Sivak, a miner they'd hired, shovelled, sacked and tied up the ore into 671 bundles and hid them deep in the gully off Duncan Creek Road.

On June 21, the first of three White Pass and Yukon Route trucks arrived at the Duncan Creek site and more than two hundred stuffed sacks were heaved onto its flatbed. The following day two more WP&YR trucks were loaded, and soon headed for Whitehorse.

By then, another family had laid claim to our house, the only home I'd known. Such was the demand for desirable Panabodes in Elsa that they were spoken for immediately after an outgoing family announced their departure. But Dad had no feelings for the house or community where he'd spent the past dozen years. His last letter to

Mom before leaving Elsa and the Yukon for good (or so he thought) was a typical amalgam of fact and fiction.

Elsa, Y.T. June 18, 1963
My dearest:
Please forgive my writing—I'm writing from my tent, and it's kind of cramped. My hands are awful stiff and sore too, from handling ore.

I got your letter and I'm glad to hear that everything is fine there. Things couldn't be better here, everything is just dandy and in only a few more days, (next Sunday or Monday) I'll be in that truck with Caesar and heading south. I'll send you postcards as I go down the highway.

I've only been back to Elsa once since I cleaned up the house (yes, I swept the floor—and, oh yes! Dorothy Chisholm got our house) the camp already looks strange and not at all like the place where we lived so long. I'm living out in the bush here—last night a bear came while Caesar and I were down at the creek. He ate up my sausage and cookies and butter, and was just making off into the bush with my garbage pail under his arm. He dropped it and ran away fast when the brave Caesar went charging after the villain, roaring like Puff, anyway, the bear got away and I had a big mess to clean up.

We do lots of running around in trucks, and that suits Caesar fine. He was very lonesome and sad the first few days after you left and didn't eat much. But he is fine now, and loves the bush.

Well, my dear this is Tuesday—on Friday & Saturday we load the big trucks and then that's where the Yukon and I shake hands. Tell the children I think of them (many thanks for the Fathers day card!!) and of course I'm missing you and loving you so very much.

Bye for now, darling—I love you,
Gerry.

CHAPTER 8

Smeltdown

A man once aimed that my life be shamed,
and wrought me a deathly wrong;
I vowed one day I would well repay,
but the heft of his hate was strong.

I N VANCOUVER, WE WENT FROM NEEDING NOTHING to needing Christian charity to get by. I felt hidden, almost beneath the earth, invisible in our beige-wallpapered, white-particleboard-ceilinged sub-basement near the graveyard. Suddenly, our homemade one-of-a-kind outfits were billboards of shame. We had a few plastic animals while the other kids had store-bought clothes, strap-on roller skates, bicycles and televisions. Our bicycles were still in Elsa, and belonged to other kids by now. The highlight of the week was Friday afternoons when we were allowed to watch half an hour of *Fun-o-Rama*—next door.

Omi's Mennonite friend Mrs. Krause owned the 1920s wooden clapboard house, and lived upstairs. Back then, even a war widow with a little chutzpah and a low-paying job could buy real estate in Vancouver. Besides being industrious, thrifty and honest, Mennonites knew God had made the earth and He wasn't making another. And with no Lucifer around to usurp private property, home ownership became the eleventh commandment. Until our sudden arrival, the basement suite had been Omi's rented home, but while we lived there, waiting for our promises to become reality, she moved in with a nearby friend and continued to work as a cleaning lady. Four days a week, she caught the early morning bus to the homes of various "ladies" who lived far to the west or north, across the Lions Gate Bridge. Her employers adored her and often gave her gifts and excess groceries. On weekends Omi walked over pulling a rectangular upright cart packed with homemade zwieback (two yeast rolls baked on top of each other), cheese, ham, eggs and apples, and sometimes a creamy, crumbly chunk of halva.

Only our place wasn't home. It was four neat rooms, smelling of hairspray and fried onions, full of prissy, stiff furniture, crocheted doilies and, on the walls, framed Bible quotations such as "Delight thyself also in the Lord: and He shall give thee the desires of thine heart." None of our belongings—our maple beds, the hand-carved wooden moose lamp with the log cabin and forest in the shade, our upright piano, our sapphire blue painting of a glaring tiger in the jungle, our fifteen-volume *Compton's Pictured Encyclopedia* set, our cherished books and records—were here.

Caesar was missing too and we ached for his quiet, princely presence. Pierre wasn't a real dog, although he eventually wormed his way into my heart. Caesar was temporarily with our paternal grandparents in Revelstoke, and would join us once we had our own house. Letters quickly arrived from the grade three, grade four and grade five classes back in Elsa. All three classes shared one room in our old school and their missives indicated how close-knit our community was. "Dear Girls," read the grade four letter. "We bet you are having more fun than a barrel of monkeys. We suppose Vona has her horse and Alice has lots of animals and you feel like floating sky high." I didn't write back.

We asked Mom when we would have our own house. "Soon," she said, and then added the chilling phrase: "Don't worry." Around this time Mom took up a lifelong habit of nestling her right hand under her left breast, against her heart.

For the most part, Dad had vanished, appearing sporadically with little mention of where he'd been or was going. When he was home, he sat at the kitchen table slurping coffee spiked with half a can of Pacific evaporated milk and two sugars, circling his fingers with his thumb and blowing smoke castles in the air after each deep draw on his hand-rolled cigarette. Niggling and tickling us, he elicited our squeals and hoots as usual, but his troubled face troubled us. Vona devised a plan to smooth his brow: *Smile at him. Be kind to him. Laugh with him when something is funny. Be friends with him and play with him if he wants to.*

He was our father and could do no wrong. To Vona, he was the Pied Piper of her heart. He now called her Pal and they shared a passion for all things outdoorsy and western. If possible, she would have become a boy, but being a tomboy would have to do. By this time, Vona clearly was "Pappy's girl" and I was "Mammy's girl." Jealousy, which had woven its way into the family fabric from my earliest beginnings, was now firmly entrenched. Still, we continued to do many things together quite pleasantly. One family pastime was writing separate nonsense poems about a chosen topic and then reading them out loud. For whatever reason I kept a few. This time the subject was outer space.

Mom wrote:

> *Up so high into the skies,*
> *Go astronauts today,*
> *And ride around the world those guys,*
> *To think! What next they'll play!*

Vona wrote:

Beyond the eerie planet Mars,
We travelled on past distant stars,
When what appeared but a meteor falling,
Then a Martian saying, "Avon calling"

I wrote:

Space. Where everything is free and black,
And empty, you quack,
I'll marry a star
And we'll go far, to all the universes;
We'll steal the ladies' purses
Ah space you go on forever,
So clever!

And Dad wrote:

Oh space, I salute thee!
And root-a-toot thee.
While Russkies and Yankees
Merrily scoot through thee.
But one bit of you causes me tears,
And that is the part of you
Between Vona's ears!

More often than not, domestic frivolity was the exception to the rule. Dad was frequently gone. And when we asked Mom or Dad what was happening, their responses were vague or dismissive. One of his favourite retorts was simply "Little pigs have big ears." Then one day we got a long distance call from Montana of all places. When Mom got off the phone, she said Dad was in America, where ore from his claims would be processed at a giant smelter, and soon he would come home a rich man.

A few days after Pennsylvania Railroad boxcars #87796 and #23346 slid into the American Smelting and Refining Co. (ASARCO) rail yard in Helena, Montana, the FBI stepped in. So far, the facts were few and straightforward: one, two boxcars containing 671 sacks of silver-rich ore were registered to Alpine Gold and Silver Ltd., a Canadian company; and two, a corporate Canadian silver producer in the distant Yukon Territory, United Keno Hill Mines Ltd., disputed that claim, alleging the ore was stolen from one of their richest mines. UKHM had a long and lucrative relationship with ASARCO. But Alpine Gold and Silver was a newcomer and a nobody.

Over the previous month, UKHM officials had moved quickly, efficiently and, almost certainly, illegally. Al Pike started the shenanigans when he ordered someone to pilfer samples from one of the ore-laden trucks the day they were picked up from the Duncan Creek Road loading site. Several days later, consulting geologist Aaro Aho dipped into the sacks while they sat at the West Indies dock in North Vancouver. By then, Pike had already reported the suspected ore theft to the mine's parent company, Falconbridge, in Toronto. Falconbridge alerted the RCMP, who called the FBI, who issued a stop order on the smelting. Without that order the ore would have been smelted soon after arrival, thereby obliterating the evidence.

But Pike didn't step back and let the Canadian and American legal authorities handle matters from there. On instruction from UKHM's vice-president, P. N. Pitcher, Pike rushed down to Helena, where he met smelter superintendent Ernest Hase. Aided by another smelter employee, the men scooped ore samples from eleven different sacks in the boxcars. No impartial witnesses were present. But after decades of dealing with UKHM, ASARCO officials assumed Pike was right, and actually facilitated his rummaging through and helping himself to what was the property of Alpine Gold and Silver Ltd. That Pike had no search warrant and no charges had been laid didn't bother a soul.

After identifying what appeared to be concentrates (a powdery substance produced from crushed ore that has been separated from useless rock), Pike hurried back to the hotel and phoned Pitcher.

"Looks to me like there's mill concentrates in those sacks… Yeah, from our mill. The ore? Hah! No way it came from the Moon. It's ours," Pike said.

"Hold tight, Al," Pitcher cautioned. "The cops are on it. They've brought an FBI guy up to speed and they're handling things down there. An agent is on his way to see you now."

Shortly after the call, FBI special agent Bruce Lanthorn showed up and for the next hour the two men talked, then headed back to the smelter. Tall, dark-haired and Marlboro-man rugged, Lanthorn looked like he knew more about rodeos than hardrock mining, ore and smelting. But after twenty-three years with the Federal Bureau of Investigation, he knew a thing or three about crime.

Standing in front of the boxcars with Hase, Lanthorn turned to Pike.

"How much do you reckon those rocks are worth?"

"Well, if the initial assays are correct, that ore averages 1,650 ounces of silver per ton. It's very high-grade material. I'd say the silver alone is worth more than $150,000," Pike said. "And there's lead and zinc in there too."

"That's a fair chunk of change," Lanthorn replied. "Lock these doors and seal them. If there's any doubt about who owns what, we don't want anyone tampering with the evidence."

Chances are Lanthorn knew full well about the three different meddling incidents. With the boxcars sealed, he hoped that was the end of it. Now he awaited the arrival of Alpine's "authorized representative," who was expected at the smelter soon. Two days later, Lanthorn returned to meet the man from Alpine, Gerald Henry Priest.

If Dad was shaken when greeted by an FBI agent at the smelter's executive offices, he didn't show it. For the past five days he'd been holed up at East Helena's Harvey Hotel, only making one trip to the smelter to see the loaded boxcars and note that "grab samples" had been taken to determine the rough grade of the ore, a normal procedure. Ostensibly, he was returning to witness the crushing of his ore. But no doubt he'd been forewarned that UKHM had, in his words, "set the hounds of hell" against him. It was ten in the morning when Lanthorn produced his badge, told him the FBI was investigating the possible illegal transport of stolen goods across state lines, and warned him that anything he said could be used against him in a court of law. Dad countered with courtesy and confidence and answered Lanthorn's questions without so much as a hiccup. In fact, he volunteered details about the ore and its origins, even drawing a map of the Moon claims and the location on Duncan Creek Road where the ore had been picked up just a month earlier. The impression he gave was of a man with nothing to hide.

"By far, the vast majority of the shipment is made up of highgrade silver ore that I mined from my Moon group claims," Dad said. "The rocks consist of tetrahedrite, galena, sphalerite and antimony."

"You're talking Greek to me," Lanthorn said.

"Excuse me, sir. I should know better. Those are basically different minerals appearing in the ore and contain copper, lead, sulphur and zinc along with silver."

"Thank you. Now, when exactly did you acquire the Moon claims?"

"On July 10 of last year, sir. There are four claims in the Moon group, registered in the Mayo Mining District of the Yukon Territory. I don't suppose you've had a chance to visit the Canadian north?"

"I'll ask the questions here, Mr. Priest," Lanthorn said, turning the conversation back in the desired direction. "How and when did you mine this ore?"

"Last summer I collected about one and a half tons of float from the surface of the claims. Then earlier this year, in February, March and April, I mined a larger deposit, leaving a hole in the mountainside about 25 feet long, 10 feet wide and about 5 feet deep. You can go up there and see it for yourself."

"Float? What's that?"

"Sorry, sir. Fifteen years in the mining world has made me forget my manners. Allow me to explain. Geologists refer to ore that sits on the surface as 'float.' Usually that ore was deposited there eons ago by glaciers or gravity or melting ice. On my claim, I believe, an enormous boulder rolled down the mountainside a very long time ago and ended up on the Moon. The Moon's ore was exactly that—float covered by about two feet of dirt, moss, rocks, boulders and snow. Once I determined the float was there, I had to remove the surface debris, then use a hand drill, a sledgehammer, and a pick and shovel to break up the rock and hand-mine it."

"Sounds like a hell of a lot of rough work. Did you have any help?"

"No sir, I worked alone and I've got the calluses to prove it!"

Dad spread open his wide, long-fingered hands with their reddened palms and thrust them before Lanthorn.

"I see, Mr. Priest. Anybody see you do this?"

"Prospectors are a secretive bunch, and with good reason," Dad continued with a chuckle. "You see, the whole Keno area is shot through with veins of silver, lead and zinc. Sometimes even gold. And prospectors circle those hills like ravens over a dead muskrat. Mostly to no avail though because United Keno snatches the good claims and jumps on new ones the minute they become available. Promising claims are hard to come by. I happened to get lucky and buy a good one. A very good one, as it turns out. But to answer your question—except for telling a few people, I kept my mouth shut. I did my utmost to avoid being seen in case I had a chance to buy more claims in that area."

"Uh-huh," said Lanthorn. "How did you transport 70 tons of rock from the Moon claims to the pickup spot? Must be more than walkin' distance between those two and through some pretty tough country."

"Oh it was the hardest labouring work I'd ever done, let me tell you. And I did most of it in the winter. Because by late spring and summer the McQuesten becomes a swamp. I had to bag the ore, and then use my motor toboggan and tow toboggan to haul the bags up a series of switchbacks out of the valley to Hanson Lake Road, where my truck was. I could haul up to 1,000 pounds a trip. On some days I made five round trips, other days seven or eight."

"Go on."

"Well, after loading the truck bed, I drove south out of Keno City about four miles to the Duncan Creek cache site—here," Dad said, stabbing an X on his hand-drawn sketch. "The cache was hidden from the road by a large clump of willows."

"And all this time you were employed by United Keno Hill Mines?"

"Yes, sir. Chief assayer for more than twelve years. Resigned just last month. I worked on my claims during weekends and on my month-long holiday in April."

For Lanthorn, who had never travelled to the Yukon, Dad's story seemed plausible. Why wouldn't it? Isn't that what prospectors did—find buried treasure? In the course of the conversation, Dad mentioned a fellow named Anthony Bobcik. Dad said he'd told Bobcik about the claims, Bobcik did some bulldozer work on them and had helped Dad re-bag the ore at the Duncan Creek pickup site.

"Would you consider Anthony Bobcik a friend?"

"A friend? No sir. I pick my friends as carefully as I pick my women. Bobcik was my employee at the assay office until last year and later offered to help out on my claims. He didn't work for free—we have an arrangement. Bobcik is... a business acquaintance."

But there was still something to reveal. Those bags carried more than crude ore, and Dad had every reason to believe Lanthorn knew as much. Because Al Pike possessed samples from one of the White Pass and Yukon Route trucks, and had snatched more samples at the smelter, information on the exact nature of the bags was flowing between UKHM, the RCMP and FBI offices like spring runoff. In the Yukon, the rumour mill spun and speculation among miners, prospectors, truck drivers, bartenders and housewives was rife. Dad told Lanthorn that 10 percent of his motherlode contained ore concentrates and ore precipitates but that as UKHM's chief assayer, he had every right to possess this material.

Concentrates are tiny granules of either zinc or silver-laden ore. Precipitates, or as Dad called them "rejects," involved inflicting yet another chemical process on lead concentrates to arrive at leftover leftovers, what then assistant mine engineer Bob Cathro called "the last squeak of the pig." The end result of this alchemy was fine, dark particles, very high in silver content and often melted and formed into small silver beads.

"I took twenty-seven sacks of precipitates and concentrates from the basement of the assay office and dumped them over the ore," Dad said. "As chief assayer, I acquired this material over many years and it was rightfully mine."

"How so?"

"Well, up until about three years ago, when some underworked official at the company rewrote the rules, there was an unwritten agreement between mining companies and assayers that any leftover material from the assaying process belongs to the assayer. That's the way it's always been, and the way it remains at most mining companies."

Dad had a point, even though it was a thin one. While there was never a policy stating assayers could help themselves to the highly valuable end product of their work, a custom existed whereby some assayers did exactly that. At UKHM, that practice was encouraged by a slipshod security system.

George Esterer was the assayer at the MacKeno Mine in Keno City until the late 1950s. Earlier, he worked with Dad in Elsa and the two became good friends. As he said to me years later, "The silver beads left over from the assaying process were the assayer's to keep. I've never seen that in writing, but that was the way it was."

"How much are those precipitates and concentrates worth?" Lanthorn asked.

"Oh, not much. Maybe $300 a ton. They were just rotting in the basement and would be rotting there still if I hadn't taken them."

Lanthorn wrote a summary of their conversation and Dad generously added a page of his own. Then, with Lanthorn and the smelter's chief accountant D. G. De Grooyer as witnesses, Dad signed the document with a flourish.

For the time being, Lanthorn's inquiry was largely over. But for Corporal George Strathdee and Constable Lauren McKiel of the RCMP's G Division, the work had barely begun. Over the next eighteen months the two overworked Mounties would spearhead one of the most complex criminal investigations in Canadian history. The task would drain the federal and Yukon governments of more time and money than any Yukon investigation to date.

George Strathdee wanted to leave the Yukon from the moment he arrived. Transferred from Ottawa to the remote community of Teslin, southeast of Whitehorse, he and his wife Verna were raising a young family. By June 1963, the date of the transfer, Verna was pregnant with their third child. If the move from the nation's capital to the out-and-beyond weren't enough, Strathdee's next assignment would strain his family life close to the breaking point.

Within weeks of his arrival, Strathdee and the rest of the Yukon's Mounties received devastating news. A Beaver aircraft piloted by Sergeant K.M. Laughland had been en route to Whitehorse from Mayo when it banked and crashed into a slope near Carmacks. All aboard were killed: Laughland, in his early thirties, three other policemen in their twenties and a fifty-six-year-old prisoner. The RCMP lost its entire investigative unit based in Mayo. Elsewhere in the Yukon, the corps was already struggling with staff shortages. The Whitehorse detachment was nine members short and smaller detachments were understaffed as well.

The plane crash had far-reaching consequences for policing in the Yukon. In the event of a major crime or investigation, the RCMP's senior brass had no choice but to cobble together a team from whoever was left.

Elsa had its own two Mounties, Mike Dwerimchuk and Terry Kushnivuk, but Dwerimchuk was on an extended leave when news of the possible ore theft surfaced. Constable Lauren McKiel, based in Whitehorse and recently transferred to the Yukon from Yellowknife, became the first Mountie assigned to the case.

According to McKiel, the Elsa Mounties had little trouble keeping a lid on the bunkhouse, where miners commonly referred to Dwerimchuk and Kushnivuk as "Meesta Mike and Meesta Terry." But the irreverence ended there. "They were big enough to burn diesel fuel," McKiel said. "You had to have a bad case of stupid to take on either of those fellows. When they walked into the bunkhouse because there was a row going on, everybody stood up beside their beds. If a fight was going on they'd say: 'It's over. If I have to come back, somebody's going to jail in Mayo.' Very seldom were they called back."

But defusing a drunken brawl was one thing. Investigating a potentially record-setting ore heist was another, especially when the theft involved one of the most powerful mining companies in the country, an international angle and a bully of a mine manager. McKiel understood the complexity of the situation almost immediately. His superiors took longer.

"I was on the case by myself because somebody opined that you could just go up there and clear it all up in a couple of weeks," McKiel recounted for me, on the phone from his home in Liverpool, Nova Scotia. "That's all there'd be to it. You arrest someone. Charge them. And everything would be fine. We didn't have any idea what we were up against."

After a week on the case, McKiel told the detachment's chief: "This is not a nut we're going to crack easily. This is going to be very complicated... we're going to need experts in mining geology who can tell us where this stuff came from and what it contains."

McKiel returned to Elsa with a promise that help would be on its way. Two weeks later Strathdee was put in charge. He had a reputation as an exceptionally "tenacious" investigator. "He'd chase you right off the edge of the earth," McKiel said. "But he was fair as fair can be. Didn't have a mean bone in his body. But I tell you, if he was on your ass, you'd better get off the road."

If someone had a scrap of information, no matter how flimsy, Strathdee would find a way to talk to him. One winter day—and Yukon winters begin in August—a prospector who lived in the bush said he had valuable information relating to the case. But the only one he'd talk to was George.

"George was slight, thin as your finger," McKiel said, "and I was 6 foot 4 and 220 pounds. We were Mutt and Jeff. And this guy wanted the skinny guy."

So off Strathdee went. When he arrived, the prospector ushered him into his cabin and offered his guest a mug of homemade hooch. "The guy never did have any information, but he wanted to talk," McKiel recalled. "In the meantime, George is sucking back all this green beer. Well, he gets a raging case of diarrhea and is up three-quarters of the night. And then he calls the office the next morning at 7:30 and says he'll be down at 8:00 and to keep the door open."

"I think I can just make it from the car to there," Strathdee told his partner.

Five minutes before eight a.m., McKiel ducked into the washroom while Kushnivuk watched by the window. "Here he comes!" Kushnivuk yelled. And with that, McKiel flushed the toilet twice in rapid succession. Then the two constables retreated to their desks.

Strathdee sprinted from the car to the bathroom, his pants half undone, and slammed the door. Seconds later, McKiel and Kushnivuk heard a scream and convulsed in laughter like a pair of schoolyard pranksters. Everyone knew that you didn't sit on a toilet right after it had been flushed because the water pumped through the raised pipebox in Elsa ran burning hot to prevent freezing.

Everyone, that is, who had spent enough time in the far north. Clearly, Strathdee had much to learn, as his now smarting bottom attested. He would not be lured into the same trap again. There would be other bumps along the road though, in the gruelling months of investigations ahead.

CHAPTER 9

Three Honourable Men

In the little Crimson Manual it's written plain and clear,
That who would wear the scarlet coat shall say goodbye to fear;
Shall be a guardian of the right, a sleuth-hound of the trail—
In the little Crimson Manual there's no such world as "fail"—

A SHEERING MIST FELL GENTLY OVER NEARBY Georgia Strait on the summer's day I met retired Mountie George Strathdee, almost fifty years after he detailed Dad. We met at a Fraser Valley golf course clubhouse. A tall, trim seventy-nine-year-old, Strathdee had fine brown hair parted neatly to the side and brown button eyes. He briefly perused the menu through thin-framed glasses, and then ordered a Reuben sandwich and glass of lager.

As we waited for our food, Strathdee said that no one, least of all he and Lauren McKiel, had any idea how tough, trying and time-consuming Dad's case would be. Most of the mine's employees, along with the region's wider community of tramps, prospectors, independent geologists, outfitters and woodsmen, hated UKHM. Al Pike was universally feared and/or disliked, and regarded by many as "an arrogant bastard," Strathdee said. McKiel described Pike as "the toughest mine manager I ever laid eyes on. It was his way or the highway."

But it wasn't just Pike—a big part of the problem was UKHM's whole approach to mining in the region. Strathdee told me about how one day, while in the UKHM main office, he saw a large patchwork map of the Keno Hill area showing all the staked claims and known ore veins running through them. "UKHM knew *exactly* where the rich veins went and would wait patiently until a prospector was ready to sell." The intent was to wait them out and buy up all the productive claims. "There were big problems with UKHM. They were not popular," Strathdee continued. "There was so much bad feeling about the company [that] we got very reluctant witnesses to testify against the two men."

As a result, when word spread that two men were suspected of stealing ore from the company, many people sided with Dad and Poncho. Still, it didn't take long for Strathdee to figure out that Dad's statement to FBI agent Bruce Lanthorn about mining the Moon claims didn't quite add up. The story had parallels to Poncho's tale told to McKiel during a lengthy interview early in the investigation. Poncho wasn't a suspect at that point, but rather a potential key witness who could offer insights both as a prospector and as someone who'd worked with Dad.

"I sat down with him in his cabin in Keno City and over the space of four and a half hours wrote a twenty-nine-page-long foolscap Q&A. He started talking and didn't stop," McKiel recounted. "Basically he told me your father found the ore on the Moon claims and they'd mined it and kept quiet. It was theirs, and they were waiting for their cheque."

This was the first McKiel had heard about a link between the two men and the Moon claims. But that admission didn't raise any suspicions. Not yet. Like Lanthorn, who'd regarded Dad's account as plausible, McKiel initially viewed Bobcik's story as "straightforward and logical." Less than a month later, however, the two Mounties changed their minds.

"Priest's story of transporting (as well as mining) the ore from the Moon Claims by motor toboggan during February, March and April, 1963 is ridiculous," Strathdee wrote in an official police summary in late August of 1963. "The distance from the Moon Claims to the Duncan Creek Loading Site is approximately 18 miles through extremely rough terrain. After looking over the area, I formed the opinion that the shipment had come from Galena Hill and not from Keno Hill, on the far side of which the Moon Claims are located. The only mine on Galena Hill producing ore as rich as that believed to be in the shipment is the Elsa mine and it was conceivable that the shipment could have been high-graded through the 200-foot entrance to the mine, which is near the top of the hill and not used regularly as an entrance."

The Moon claims story may indeed have been "a pack of lies," as McKiel would come to call it, but proving so in court would tax the Mounties' investigative skills to the max.

Pike and other UKHM officials insisted that the entire shipment originated from the Elsa mine, but with their knowledge of the law the Mounties pursued two separate leads. Down one path they would establish that the ore came from the Elsa mine and demonstrate who stole it and how. Down the other they would prove that the ore could not possibly have come from the Moon. The Mounties vigorously pursued both avenues, burning through months of time, energy and money.

As the two detectives delved deeper, questions multiplied like mosquitoes in July. If the ore had come from the Elsa mine, how had Dad and Poncho stolen it so easily and without any witnesses? As chief assayer, Dad never ventured underground. And proposing that Poncho, a miner, had staged and executed the disappearance of 70 tons of rock by himself was beyond belief. They must have had inside help. But who? Could McKiel and Strathdee persuade anyone to testify against the suspected thieves? And if the silver ore originated from the Bonanza Stope, as Pike, Archer and others claimed, how could they prove it now that the Bonanza existed in memory only? Two years before, all that rich ore had been excavated, mixed with other ore and smelted, and the stope backfilled with tons of waste rock. There was not a single sample of Bonanza ore left to compare with the ore in the suspected shipment.

As Strathdee and McKiel interviewed miners and managers, they learned of the mysterious goings on at the Elsa mine two years earlier: shadowy figures identified by one worker as Bobcik and Swizinski inside the mine in the dead of night; drags on the mine's compressor system during off-shift hours; Bobcik and another man caught in the headlights of passing pickup trucks while struggling with heavy bags in the early dawn of a new day. But while all of this appeared incriminating, there was nothing concrete to link the shipment to those men—especially Dad, who was never seen near the mine, let alone in it. Any defence lawyer would make moose meat of a case trying to connect the two.

Even so, Strathdee and McKiel's suspicions intensified as they learned that not all the ore could have come from the Bonanza Stope, but that some must be from other areas in the Elsa mine; that other mine workers had toyed with the idea of stealing ore from the stope but had never played it through; and that the stolen ore had, in all likelihood, been squirrelled away in the maze of underground tunnels for months before being cached above ground.

The conclusion was inevitable. As former Elsa Mountie Jim Lambert told me, "You don't need to be Sherlock Holmes to figure out there had to be a third or even a fourth man... Because when those guys took the ore out of the mine, they had to know nobody would be there to see them. There had to be someone in an administrative position who knew the shifts."

Lambert served two years in Elsa, from November 1963 to 1965, and while he wasn't involved in the investigation, he was "very attuned" to the rumours swirling through town. Part of his job entailed interviewing recent immigrants, mostly miners, for their Canadian citizenship eligibility. "I was constantly talking to people… and I would ask them about current events, the capital of Manitoba, and it was a perfect time to slip in, 'Do you think anybody was with Priest and Bobcik?'"

One man's name kept popping up, Lambert said. The same man Strathdee and McKiel began to suspect: Martin Swizinski.

Originally from Alberta, Swizinski worked briefly for UKHM in the Elsa region in 1951. From the time of his return to UKHM's employ in 1955, he rose steadily in the mine hierarchy to become a shift boss and mine captain. By the time the investigation began, he was "very highly thought of" by his bosses, peers and work crews, and was granted time to shepherd Strathdee and others around the mine to collect ore samples that might be used as evidence against Dad and Poncho. On that level, at least, he was "cooperating" with the investigation.

But Strathdee and McKiel knew something Pike didn't. Documents obtained through searches of Poncho's cabin, Dad's office, the bank, the two men's vehicles and various businesses where one or both had made purchases included a three-ring binder with papers referring to a three-man operation. The three men's identities were noted by first initial only: G, for Gerald; P, for Poncho; and M—which the two Mounties believed was for Martin.

Frustratingly, few such pieces of paper existed. One contained a list itemizing vehicle fuel purchases by the gallon, fuel drum purchases, long distance phone calls, lumber and pipe purchases, and auto parts purchases. Beside each entry, one of the three initials appeared. For example, in April 1962, G, P and M purchased a tremendous amount of fuel within a short timeframe. McKiel and Strathdee believed this was the critical period when the bulk of the ore had been rushed from its hiding place inside the mine to the Duncan Creek site.

The other document was a more intriguing set of sixty-nine handwritten entries on three assay office worksheets. Written by Poncho, who struggled at times with math, the entries recorded not only the volume of ore moved, but also the assays for each sack of ore. Beside these entries were notes about whether or not M was to receive a cut, how many ounces of silver were estimated to be in each bag, and an entry of the ore type. One among many entries noted 273 sacks of ore, assaying at 4,000 ounces of silver per ton, with M owed a percentage of the sale.

When everything on the pages was added up, G and P were each to receive 44.1 percent of the proceeds and M was to receive 11.8 percent. With the lion's share of the spoils going to Dad and Poncho, M must have played a lesser role in the theft. Likely, at some point M wanted out.

Although the documents strongly indicated that three individuals were involved in the theft, nothing tangible linked Martin Swizinski—or any other "M" for that matter—to Gerald Priest and Anthony (Poncho) Bobcik, financially or otherwise.

In the absence of such evidence, the Mounties were stymied in their attempts to prove the theft was orchestrated from within the Elsa mine. Dad and Poncho were sticking to their story that the ore came from the Moon. And Swizinski wasn't talking. When the Mounties finally got around to questioning him, he repeatedly maintained that he knew nothing. Strathdee asked if he would consent to taking a polygraph test. Swizinski said yes. But there was a hitch. The Yukon RCMP did not have a polygraph machine and the equipment would have to come, along with an operator, from Alaska. A request was issued. As the day neared for the scheduled test, Swizinski told Strathdee he'd changed his mind and now refused to take it.

McKiel and Strathdee always believed Swizinski was the third man. So did Archer and Cathro. Mom was also on that list, telling us Dad had told her Swizinski helped out. But Swizinski was a popular fellow and "seemed to be on a first name basis with everyone he knew." No one would speak a word against him. The investigators reluctantly concluded that unless someone talked, they had no evidence that the heist had been a coordinated inside job, involving one of the mine's most trusted senior workers.

"The subject has been interviewed twice, the second time quite thoroughly," Strathdee wrote in one of many internal memos on the subject of Mr. M. "He remained calm and denied everything. Further interviews will not be attempted until more definitive evidence is available. We are, however, reasonably sure that he is the person represented as 'M.'" Strathdee hoped that further interviews with Dad and Poncho might elicit "sufficient information to positively connect him" with the heist.

His expectation was not unreasonable given that the two sleuths had amassed a great deal of evidence against Dad and Poncho. But neither suspect implicated Swizinski. And Swizinski never implicated them. Years later, Mom told my sister and me that Dad, Poncho and Martin had sworn a pact of silence in the event that one or more of them were ever caught. They thought of themselves as "three honourable men" and honourable men do not rat each other out. But there was another part to the vow—one more difficult to keep. If someone was caught and imprisoned, they had agreed, the others would help that man's family as best they could.

One peculiar thing workers at the assay office noticed in the months before Dad and Poncho left was that both men loved being at work. If Poncho worked nights, he'd show up at the office during the day, and vice versa. Dad, meanwhile, showed up at the office in the evenings, despite having a day job. And sometimes he went in on Sundays. "I often saw his car there at night, but I don't know what he was doing," one former worker told the RCMP. As more assay office workers were questioned, McKiel and Strathdee discovered that Poncho did more on the job than just crush rock. "He was accumulating precipitate," fire assayer John Bourdeaux told Strathdee. "It was being found all over the office." In fact, Bourdeaux found three large bags of the material in a drawer in the back office. Danny Skobeyko, a bucker in the assay office, also found small bags of precipitates in the office and knew of bags stored beneath the fire assay office. "We suspected Poncho and heard rumours that he was buying precipitate from the workers in the mill," Bourdeaux said.

After hours, employees often found Poncho in the furnace room, handling large crucibles that Bourdeaux and others believed he filled with precipitates to create solid pieces of silver. Bourdeaux also told Strathdee that Gerry once hauled another fire assayer over the coals for cooking a high-grade sample in the oven. When Poncho said "That's okay—it's mine," however, Gerry shut up. And now and again Gerry himself came down to the fire assay office and smelted small amounts of silver.

What Poncho and Dad were busy doing in the assay office in 1962 was, first, verifying the grade of "their" ore, and second, amassing precipitates from the mill that would be added to the shipment.

If Poncho was buying precipitate, someone in the mill was selling it. The police eventually zeroed in on mill worker Siegfried Haina. Through him they got their first big break in the investigation. After a three-hour interrogation by Strathdee, Haina confessed that he sold 600 to 700 pounds of precipitates to Poncho.

The arrangement had started innocently enough. Poncho had asked Haina whether he would like a chunk of solid silver and showed Haina a sample of his work from the assay office. Haina said he would and Poncho replied that he'd be happy to make him one but would need a small amount of precipitate matter from the mill.

"So I gave him a small sack full, maybe 6 or 7 pounds," Haina said.

The early afternoon sun shines on the deserted main street in Mayo during Gerry's preliminary hearing in 1963.

Elsa, as seen from Galena Hill looking west toward Mount Haldane, known by locals as Mount Lookout.

i

Omi, born Maria and third from left, was the eldest of thirteen in Russia, and the only member of her family to escape the Gulag.

Gerry as a boy flanked by younger brother Ron, left, and elder brother Bill, right.

elen and Gerry make merry by the Christmas tree.

Frontier family from left to right: Helen, Vona, Alicia and Gerry Priest.

Caesar was no sled dog but would tolerate anything for his girls.

tory time! Gerry Priest reads to Alicia, left, and Vona around 1956.

ust and high heels: Helen, centre, dressed up for a summer walk with icia, left, and Vona.

The Panabode house where Helen raised her girls was a perk for families of salaried employees. Most miners were single, hourly workers and lived in bunkhouses.

Helen in the fully stocked pantry. "I make the living—you make the living worthwhile," Gerry frequently said.

An excursion to Mayo Lake: in the physically and culturally isolated central Yukon, the outdoor getaway was a family staple.

With no TV, long-wave radio or phone service until 1960, kids like four-year-old Alicia made their own entertainment in and around Elsa.

That's right! A proud four-year-old Vona beams beside a chalkboard.

Sitting duck: while Omi perches on a stump, her granddaughters take aim with bows and arrows.

Alicia and Vona sit with Pierre and Caesar outside their Vancouver home on Main Street, around the time of their dad's conviction.

Mountain man: Gerry and his pack horses trek across the Rocky Mountains.

The town of Elsa, looking east, likely photographed for a United Keno Hill Mines annual report.

ROB STODARD

Gerry and George Esterer at the ghost town of Wernecke Camp. Men rarely
travelled without their rifles when foraying in the bush.

DOUGLAS MACKENZIE

Broken dreams: the decaying Wernecke Camp, where silver ore was
once plentiful.

Outside the Elsa Coffee Shop or Snack Bar, where alarm bells rang after a truck driver transporting hundreds of bags of ore stopped to ask for directions.

The United Keno Hill Mines assay office in Elsa, where plans for marketing 70 tons of stolen ore were first hatched.

or RCMP officers investigating the ore theft, operations in the Elsa mine
nd mill were among the darkest and dankest on earth.

isolated Elsa, highly anticipated events on the social calender
cluded choir, bridge, badminton, rod and gun club, square dancing,
irling and even cake-decorating classes.

Top left: Allan Fawley, seen here with diamonds from a Tanganyikan mine, was a globetrotting geologist and lead defence witness.

Top right: Known as the "Gladiator of the Courts," Angelo Branca was Gerry's lawyer before being named a BC Supreme Court judge.

Bottom: Judge John Parker presided over both of Gerry and Anthony Bobcik's trials. He later called Gerry "an odd bird."

:MP constable Lauren McKiel, left, and FBI agent Bruce Lanthorn outside
e Masonic Hall in Mayo during a break in the preliminary hearing.

b Cathro was a United Keno Hill Mines
sistant mine engineer who walked the Moon
ims and rejected them as a source of the
ver ore.

Vic Wylie, Crown prosecutor, faced an uphill
battle to convict Gerry after the jury in the first
trial could not reach a verdict on any of the
charges he faced.

Gerald, Helen and the girls, captured by famed Vancouver street photographer, Foncie Pulice, following a screening of *How the West Was Won*.

A few days later, Poncho gave Haina a piece of silver and asked him to bring him more precipitate. Only this time, he said, he'd pay for it.

"What did you say?" Strathdee asked.

"I said I can't go there," Haina replied. "And he [Poncho] said it's real easy, you can go there… He said he would pay me a dollar a pound and that he would kill me if I ever told anyone. I needed money to help my mother out because she was sick."

Before long, Haina was pinching precipitates out of the mill in loads of 40 to 80 pounds. Security was slack and it was a simple matter of walking out an unlocked back door and hiding it in the snow. Then he'd look around for Poncho and tell him he had more precipitates for pickup. Poncho paid Haina in cash, but Haina said the payments were always somewhat less than he was owed, and he was never paid for the last 80 to 100 pounds he delivered. Haina last spoke to Poncho two months before he sat down with Strathdee, right around the time the investigation was underway. The two men met at the Keno bar. "Don't say nothing about that precipitate," Poncho told Haina. "Nothing. You know what I told you before."

In total, Poncho bought 841 pounds of precipitate, the bulk from Haina, the rest from persons unknown. Notes in the three-ring binder showed that the costs for the precipitates were split evenly between G and P.

CHAPTER 10

The *Crème de la Crème*

It's easy to cry that you're beaten—and die;
It's easy to crawfish and crawl;
But to fight and to fight when hope's out of sight—
Why, that's the best game of them all!

RCMP CONSTABLE LAUREN MCKIEL flew from Whitehorse on a Canadian Pacific Airlines DC-6B dressed in a steel grey, narrow-lapelled business suit. Under his jacket and clipped to his belt, his short-nosed .38-calibre pistol gently nudged his right hip. It was August 6, 1963, and he was headed to Vancouver.

The groundwork was thoroughly prepared for Dad's quick and trouble-free arrest—or so McKiel thought. With a handful of search warrants to examine Dad's Royal Bank of Canada accounts, his vehicles, the moving company used to ship our belongings and the Vancouver basement suite where we now lived, McKiel thought he had all the angles covered. If things went according to plan, Gerald Priest would spend that night in a Vancouver jail and fly north the next morning for his first court appearance in Whitehorse.

But right from the start, surprises, mishaps and miscommunications arose that threw the Mountie's strategy off-kilter and heightened the urgency around Dad's arrest. For McKiel, it all added up to a missed opportunity—his chance to surprise Dad, sparing everyone concerned excess mental anguish, time and expense. Perhaps the biggest shock came during a refuelling stopover in Fort St. John. As McKiel re-boarded the plane, who should step into the cabin but Anthony Bobcik. Alarm bells rang. McKiel pressed Bobcik to talk, but a grunted half-greeting was all he got. His best hope now was to preempt any meeting between the two prime suspects before their arrest. Experience taught him that surprising a suspect with an arrest warrant could elicit a confession. But then, he didn't know Dad.

McKiel's reception in Vancouver did not bode well either. The member of the Vancouver Police Department who was supposed to pick him up was nowhere to be seen. After waiting thirty-five minutes, McKiel contacted the RCMP's airport detachment where the lone member on duty, Constable Duckworth, radioed the officer who was supposed to have fetched McKiel. The officer had been at the airport but waited at another terminal. Having given up and driven back to Vancouver, he was in no mood to make a second trip. Take a cab, McKiel was told.

Before doing so, though, McKiel was anxious to alert his superiors that Bobcik had been on the flight and would likely contact Dad. Making his way to the airport detachment's office, he asked Duckworth to call RCMP Sergeant J.O. Sehl at Vancouver's S Division. Frustrated and impatient, McKiel grabbed the phone, saying it was "imperative" that Dad be arrested immediately. But when he went on to outline his plans for the arrest, followed by a search of Dad's residence and vehicles, he was met with his third disappointment of the day.

A week earlier the Vancouver detachment had heard from the office of Angelo E. Branca, QC. The Vancouver lawyer knew an arrest warrant had been issued for one of his clients, a Mr. G.H. Priest.

"So when you have the warrant in hand," Branca's assistant had said, "give our office a call. Mr. Branca will arrange for Mr. Priest to be in our office. You can formally arrest him then."

"You know who Branca is, don't you?" Sergeant Sehl said.

"Yeah, I heard of him," McKiel said.

"He's one of the best. And you can be sure that if Priest hired him, Branca's already told him not to say a goddamned word to you or anyone else, and to trash or hide anything that might look bad. You'll get nothing out of Priest."

"What?" McKiel said. "Branca gets to say when, where and how we arrest him? That makes no sense. We may gain nothing by arresting him now. But maybe we will. Maybe he'll be spooked without Branca there. Maybe he'll talk."

"All I'm saying is Branca has rehearsed Priest. You're going to get no more out of him tonight than you would tomorrow. Besides, it's getting late and I don't have backup. Call a cab. Go to your hotel. Have a beer. We'll figure things out tomorrow."

McKiel knew when he was wasting good air. He called a taxi and headed downtown.

Angelo Branca was one of the top criminal defence lawyers in British Columbia, and arguably in Canada. Of Italian descent, he was dark-eyed, dark-haired and intense. Known for his intellectual clarity, his tenacity and his temper, traits shaped in part by years spent in the ring, Branca was Canada's 1934 amateur middleweight boxing champion. Oddly enough, he also had ties to the Yukon. After emigrating from Italy, his father Filipa Branca struck out for the Klondike and returned with $10,000 in his pocket (nearly $180,000 in today's dollars), one of the few to strike it rich in the Dawson goldfields.

Branca began his legal career in 1926, setting up shop in a second-floor office in the old Royal Bank building at the corner of Hastings and Main, not far from Vancouver's present-day police headquarters and provincial courts. During the Depression, he became known for his generous (and often pro bono) defense of poverty-stricken clients. He went on to defend both rich and poor with equal élan, and became known as the "Gladiator of the Courts." Of sixty-three murder suspects he defended, only four were convicted.

But Branca was also well known as a defence lawyer and prosecutor in notable cases involving the police. In 1935, he successfully fought for seventeen Vancouver police officers who had lost their jobs in a purge led by Vancouver mayor and reformist Gerry McGeer. All seventeen were reinstated. Twenty years later, he would successfully prosecute Vancouver police chief Walter Mulligan, who was operating an extensive payoff scheme involving a criminal gang. Constable McKiel was familiar with the Vancouver lawyer's formidable reputation, which only added to his agitation at the end of a long, frustrating day.

After a restless night, McKiel met RCMP constable Barry Wallace, who had been assigned to help him. The two consulted with Sehl and decided that since there'd been no arrest the previous evening, and since Bobcik had probably called Dad, the two Mounties would search bank and moving company records first. Arresting Dad and searching his car and our home could wait. Once arrested, he would be en route to Whitehorse within twenty-four hours.

The next day, Constable Wallace arranged for Dad to be in Branca's office by ten the following morning. At 9:50 a.m. on August 9, McKiel and Wallace entered Branca's office. Dad was there, sitting silently in a chair. Branca introduced himself, while Dad watched without saying a word. McKiel introduced himself and Wallace, then took out his RCMP badge and showed it to Branca and Dad.

"I am here to arrest Gerald Henry Priest," he said.

Without talking to Branca any further, McKiel turned to the gentleman seated behind him.

"Are you Gerald Priest?"

Flushed and flustered, Dad said, "Yes, I am."

"Can you prove that for me with some identification?"

Dad took out his wallet and showed McKiel his driver's license.

"Mr. Priest, you are under arrest."

As soon as the words left McKiel's mouth, Branca came out of his chair like someone fired out of a cannon. He started to rant and rave and peel a strip off Constable Wallace, calling him every name except a gentleman.

"You lying little shit! You said you wanted to interview my client—not arrest him! This is a fuckin' set-up. And by God," Branca continued, pointing at the two cops, "I will sue you and you before the next two weeks are out."

"I think, Mr. Branca, we can dispense with the theatrics," McKiel replied. "You just be quiet because I'm here to deal with Mr. Priest, not you."

Branca was stunned. He looked like he'd taken a hard left hook. Nobody spoke to Angelo Branca like that.

McKiel read Dad the charges: "One count of stealing ore concentrates worth more than fifty dollars and one count of stealing ore precipitates worth more than fifty dollars." There was no mention of the ore.

"Do you understand the charges, Mr. Priest?"

"I do."

McKiel handed him a copy of the warrant to read and warned him that anything he said could be used as evidence against him in court.

"Do you understand what that means?"

"I do."

"Do you have anything to say?"

Dad glanced at his lawyer. Branca rose slowly out of chair this time.

"He doesn't have a single goddamned thing to say."

"I asked Mr. Priest the question," McKiel said. "I didn't ask you."

"I don't have anything to say," Dad said.

"Fine. Then if you'll turn around, I will put these handcuffs on you and we'll be on our way."

Dad cooperated while Branca resumed berating Wallace.

"Nothing was said about a warrant for his arrest! Only warrants to search his house and car! You fellows came here under false pretences! You'll pay for this!"

On the way out to the police car, Dad turned to McKiel: "Guess you two fellows will be unemployed in a couple of weeks."

"I wouldn't bet on it," McKiel replied. "I don't know what you're paying him, but whatever it is, you got a pretty good song and dance back there for your nickel."

For our family, that day was like no other before or since. In the morning Dad had left dressed in a suit and tie, telling us he had a meeting downtown. A few hours later, red-faced and perspiring, he rushed into the house calling Mom's name. Two broad-shouldered men stood outside the back door—the only entrance to our suite. It was a warm August day and the sliding windows were half open in hopes of a cooling breeze. Vona and I watched as Dad and Mom hurriedly exchanged a few words, and then went into their bedroom where they chattered in agitated low voices and opened and closed dresser drawers. The two big men stayed put with their heads down and hands crossed.

"Children, go to your room and stay there," Dad said softly. From inside our room, we listened to shuffles, whispers and doors opening and closing for about five seconds before we sneaked out. Holding hands, we saw Mom and Dad clasped in an embrace as tight as a halter hitch. Mom had her back to us. Dad's face was folded inwards on her neck. His shoulders shook and out of his mouth came a mewling sound. Was Dad crying? In our minds, such an act was physically impossible, but our eyes weren't lying. Suddenly Dad pushed himself from her, grasped her shoulders and kissed her fiercely on the lips.

Then he turned and walked away with the two men. Mom ran to her room and threw herself face down on the bed. We clamoured to know what had just happened but knew enough to let her be for a moment or three. Vona had pretty much figured it out anyhow.

"Those were plainclothes policemen," she said. "And Pappy's been arrested!"

Mom heard us and called us into her room, where she hugged us and said the police had taken Dad back to the Yukon because there was trouble with his claim. But he would return soon and, most importantly, he had done nothing wrong. Nothing. Then she herded us to Little Mountain, as we called Queen Elizabeth Park, for a picnic of cheese sandwiches, pickles and apples. We stayed all afternoon. Later I learned that police officers searched our home and car while we were gone. The search yielded nothing. That night we all slept in one bed.

On the journey to Whitehorse the next day, on a stopover in Watson Lake, policeman and prisoner got off the plane last, after all the other passengers had disembarked. Flight rules forbade handcuffs on the plane but as soon as a prisoner's feet hit the ground, the cuffs went on. McKiel re-cuffed Dad and the two men walked back and forth on the tarmac behind the plane, out of view of the terminal. It was a cool August afternoon, under a blue, near-cloudless sky.

As they strolled south in the direction of the town, Dad turned to McKiel and asked, "Do you have a gun?"

"Yes I do."

"Is it loaded?"

"Yes it is."

"What would you do if I started to run away?"

"I'd shoot you," McKiel replied with a straight face.

"You would?" Dad replied, startled.

Shooting an unarmed, handcuffed prisoner was about the last thing McKiel would ever do. But Dad didn't know that. The two men kept strolling for a while, neither saying a word.

"Guess we better turn around and head back," McKiel said.

On the plane, the handcuffs came off and the rest of the long flight north continued without incident. In Whitehorse, a plainclothes detective met the two men and escorted them to the courthouse. Angelo Branca had arranged for a local lawyer to represent Dad. Bail was quickly granted, not contested by Crown counsel, and paid by Mayo MLA Raphael (Ray) McKamey.

Once the arraignment was completed, Dad and McKiel went to the Whitehorse RCMP detachment, where Dad was photographed, fingerprinted and released. "It was all very cordial," McKiel said later.

Cordiality, I'm certain, was the furthest thing from Dad's mind. Head held high, he strode to Whitehorse's Capital Hotel, downed a beer and rolled a smoke, then checked in and scrawled Mom a letter. He'd stay in the Yukon "until this is all settled" and try to find work. With lawyer's fees, moving expenses, storage expenses, car payments and hotel bills, not to mention money for our day-to-day existence, his bank account was dwindling.

"Believe nothing you read in the newspapers or hear on the radio—there has been so much falsity already," Dad wrote. "The investigation is grabbing at any silly thing it can. I know I must stand trial in the future but I am confident it will turn out just fine in the end."

Not long afterward, though, Dad's hope that McKiel and Wallace would be "sliced, diced and julienned" by Branca fizzled. And while Dad said Branca would "never drop me," within weeks the sixty-year-old legal legend was appointed to the Supreme Court of British Columbia. His days as a lawyer were over.

"The guy was truly brilliant," McKiel reminisced. "We respected his legal ability. He was a formidable lawyer. Your Dad picked the *crème de la crème*."

The stage was now set for one of the longest preliminary hearings in Yukon history, and over the next two years there would be not one, but two trials. It's hard not to be fatalistic about what's done and gone. And yet, forever etched in my mind is the question: Would Dad's fate—and ours—have been different had Angelo Branca stayed in the legal ring on his behalf?

CHAPTER 11

Up and Down—But Not Out!

Why join the restless, roving crew
Of trail and tent?
Why grimly take the roads of rue
To doom hell bent?

THREE WEEKS AFTER DAD'S ARREST, I started grade five and Vona grade six at our new school, Van Horne Elementary, located on Ontario Street, a couple of blocks west of Main Street. On the first day, my teacher, Miss Hildebrandt, told me to come to the front blackboard and write the name of the place I came from and the place I lived now. Proudly, I wrote "Elsa, Yukon Territory," which no one had ever heard of, but then misspelled Vancouver (omitted the "o") and everyone guffawed. After school, a boy asked me if my father was "the thief from the Yukon" he'd heard about in the news.

All in all, grade five was a year of firsts: the first time I routinely and repeatedly lied; the first time I failed anything (spelling and math); the first time I missed weeks of lessons due to chronic sore throats, swollen glands, fevers, stomach flu and the unfortunately named fungal skin infection ringworm; the first time food, even

Omi's borscht, tasted like glue; and the first time I fell asleep at night scratching mould off a cold, clammy bedroom wall.

We asked about our father every day, and about Caesar every other. And mom would do her best to calm us. Immediately after the arrest and during the plane ride to Whitehorse, Dad wrote Mom that he was engulfed in "a haze of pain and sorrow" and could not bear parting with her "that way" again. But once he was out on bail and circulating among sympathizers, Dad's dark clouds lifted and his spirits revived. His initial letters to Mom were full of buoyancy and bravado. Given widespread animosity toward UKHM throughout the Mayo–Elsa district, many people supported Dad, viewing the affair as a David and Goliath struggle. One of the most surprising people in Dad's corner was the man who paid Dad's bail, MLA Ray McKamey. A respected mineral exploration man from Mayo, McKamey had previously spoken out in the Yukon legislature about conditions at the Elsa mine, describing it as "a very dangerous mine to work in." Later, McKamey would win the federal Liberal nomination and run, unsuccessfully, against incumbent Conservative MP Erik Nielsen.

Although Dad had not found work—he would accept just about anything but hard labour—he was living rent-free in Whitehorse lawyer Henry Regehr's house and "working off" his meals at a local café. Regehr had expressed sympathy with Dad's case and was initially both Dad's and Poncho's lawyer. On the home front, Mom drew on our savings for bus fare and household essentials like toothpaste and soap, and Omi often filled our fridge.

"My lawyer is confident and so am I," Dad wrote at the time. "My head is high and will stay so. I came back from Mayo this morning and am cheered to find that all the people are on my side. Everything is fine here with me—remember that I'll always be the same person to you and the girls. So, chin up and as you told me once, we're down but we are sure not out!"

In another missive written in mid-September, he said, "We

will fight—99.9 per cent of the people are for me and people in Whitehorse from Elsa stop me and wish me luck… They [the police] still hope to break someone but that isn't going to happen."

When attorney Angelo Branca withdrew from Dad's case, however, he was devastated. While his new lawyer, John Molson, came recommended, he lacked Branca's impressive track record and pit-bull aggression.

Shortly after Dad's arrest, Poncho was arrested at his new home in Duncan on Vancouver Island and faced the same charges as Dad. No one stepped up to pay his bail though, so he languished for weeks in the Whitehorse Guardhouse. Then, on September 26, both men's charges increased to include "conspiracy to sell a substance containing a precious metal." This was legalese for trying to sell something that wasn't theirs. It was an odd charge, and as time rolled on it would prove to have its challenges for the Crown, UKHM and the accused.

Finally, the Mounties felt they had the evidence to charge Poncho and Dad not only with stealing precipitates and concentrates from UKHM, but 70 tons of silver ore. The trick would be proving it. All they needed was someone to squeal or an expert who could positively link the stolen ore with the Elsa mine. As they expanded their search, interrogating a range of miners, mine managers, mill workers, assay office employees, prospectors and geologists, the date for the preliminary hearing kept getting pushed back. It was originally slated for late September, then officials changed the date to sometime in October and finally inked it in for November 19.

By mid-October, Dad's letters bore a darker stamp, the late-night mutterings of a homeless, humiliated and frightened man.

Oh dearest, you are the only one who can ever know the depths
of my loneliness and longing—which seem to exceed anything
I have ever known or thought I could experience. You and the

children are my whole life, my whole reason for being or having lived. And my sorrow, shame and regret for having brought this situation onto us is unspeakable.

Those words were as close to an admission of guilt as he could muster. A confession, however, they were not. For in the same letter he wrote that no matter the evidence and witnesses mounted against him, "Fight I shall and go down if I must, bravely, with the knowledge that these difficult times have bound me to you with a strength that could never have come any other way. However this thing turns out, I must maintain a plea of not guilty. And that is as it shall be. That is better for you and the children—and for all our friends."

Nor could Dad divulge the deep disgrace he felt in the eyes of his father, who had always held him in high esteem and to whom he had sworn complete innocence. His parents wanted to attend the hearing and the trial, as did Mom, but with a dramatic touch Dad vetoed the idea, saying, "No one of my family must be there for I could not stand to see them suffer so."

By late October, Dad could bear his separation from us no longer, and came down by car with his friend Angus MacDonald, who worked as a geologist in Keno. Now that the preliminary hearing date was set, he had two weeks to spare before his legal battle began. He arrived on a Sunday. Mom had made a roast beast, as Dad called it, with Yorkshire pudding and gravy, and baked a lemon meringue pie. We were giddy beyond containment and for the first time since Dad left, I finished my plate and asked for more. After dinner, we bombarded Dad with questions: Had he been to Elsa? Who was living in our house? Who had he given Mitzi to? How was Caesar? And when would we all be together again in our own home? He answered every question to our satisfaction except the last.

In our hearts and eyes, he was the same Dad—bantering, mocking and roughhousing during the day, and mesmerizing us in the evenings with tales of adventure and horror. One of his favourites was "The Monkey's Paw," a Gothic story about a mummified monkey paw that grants its owner three wishes. A curse in disguise, the wishes have gruesome consequences and serve up a harsh lesson about desiring more than destiny grants. As he unravelled the yarn, he'd hide his long, thin hand inside his shirt sleeve and then, when we were least prepared, fix a beady eye on us while jutting out his now limp and contorted hand and dangling it in our faces.

One morning we woke to find him gone, back to the Yukon. That's when Mom told us what we intuitively knew: that Dad was accused of stealing ore, which he had not done, but he would have to stand trial. She didn't know when he'd return but promised he would. He'd left a note on the table: "Goodbye my dears. I love you all so much." Vona grabbed it and wanted to put it under her pillow. I said we should put it in a picture frame on our bedside table where we could read it every night before sleep. That morning we called Omi and while waiting for her to arrive, we served Mom breakfast in bed.

The next day Mom wrote Dad a letter, but never mailed it, hoping to deliver it in person. Years later, I found it stuffed in a shoebox along with some of the hundreds of his cards and letters she'd saved.

My poor darling, how it hurts me to see you suffer so. Don't worry one bit about us. We shall be all right even if the worst comes. Whatever you decide to do is right for me. You are a good man and no one can deny that, for what happened to you now could have happened to many others under the same circumstances.

The girls talk about you so much and miss you. Their affection for you will never change. I'll see to it that from now on, they only get the newspaper after I look it over.

I love you and miss you oh so much. Someday the sun shall shine warm on us and we will walk hand in hand again.

Helen

A long time ago, Mom had accepted Dad's desperate, near-frightening need for her unfaltering love and adoration. It was never more palpable than now. Her mission, she decided, was to be strong, brave and steadfast in her love, and thereby nurture the best of his complex and too often troubling nature.

Meanwhile, back in Elsa, Pike was now seriously agitated. An anxious man by nature, his arrogant dismissal of geologist Al Archer's advice to handle the super-rich ore like the treasure it was had set the stage for a record-setting silver heist. Leaving a fortune in the Bonanza Stope for months at a time was like hanging out a flashing "Help Yourself" sign. Now, it appeared, a few of his employees had done just that.

When his bosses in Toronto learned the details—and they would—Pike would pay. But not yet. Right now there were more important things to attend to: discovering exactly what those 671 sacks contained, and punching that cocksure Gerald Priest's cocka-mamie story full of holes. He'd hand-mined that ore on the Moon? Impossible. That ore belonged to UKHM, and Pike knew it.

In the 1960s, Canadian mining companies were riding a corporate high, and Falconbridge, the parent company of UKHM, was among the leaders of the pack. The company's Toronto headquarters put it within shouting distance of the nation's biggest banking and legal firms, and many of the company's senior executives had rock-solid connections with the federal government's Department of Mines and Technical Surveys in Ottawa.

Immediately after Pike relayed news of the suspicious shipment to his superiors, Falconbridge was on the phone to Roberts, Archibald, Seagram and Cole Barristers and Solicitors. Falconbridge's lawyers had pull. An injunction was quickly granted, preventing the ore from being smelted. But as the legal team, the Mounties and the Crown soon learned, building their case around the physical contents of those hundreds of ore sacks would prove daunting. There was no DNA test for rock. And unlike chemistry and physics, geology is not an exact science.

Nonetheless, much of the bagged ore was rigorously examined and painstakingly compared to other mine rock to see if a fragment of a match appeared. Even with ore microscopy, x-ray diffraction, chemical analysis and fire assay tests—performed by a team of scientists in the Mineral Sciences Division of the Department of Mines in Ottawa and by scientists at the University of British Columbia—no one could say with anything approaching certitude that the ore came from the UKHM mine.

"It should be pointed out that in complex mineralogy of this kind, it is very difficult to arrive at positive quantitative findings and that conclusions must be based on a broad overall assessment of characteristics such as mineral assemblages, textures and mutual relationships of the minerals, intergrowths and modes of occurrence along with the presence or absence of comparatively rare or unusual minerals," the government team reported in a technical paper pored over by Falconbridge's lawyers, as well as by Crown and defense counsels. In other words, pinning the ore to the inside of the Elsa mine couldn't be done.

Pike's diktat to leave the Bonanza motherlode lying on the mine tunnel floor was a gigantic miscue, as Falconbridge's legal team was reminded over and over for the better part of the next two years. With a growing awareness of how difficult it was to prove the ore came from the mine, attention began to shift to Gerald Priest's version of events. Just how credible was his story of hand-mining the ore from the Moon?

CHAPTER 12

Fool's Silver

Perhaps I am stark crazy, but there's none of you too sane;
It's just a little matter of degree.

IT IS LATE AUGUST 2011 AND I AM ON A MISSION. Nearly fifty years after Dad went on his Easter ore-hauling "holiday" with his snowmobile, I plan to retrace his steps, as best I can. Luckily, I've found someone to take me to the Moon. My guide lives in Keno, has a vehicle and is willing to spend the better part of the day getting me to and from, as well as show me around the mineral claims Dad once owned. Matthias Bindig is my man. Tall, tanned, with fair brown hair, in his mid-thirties and handsome as a husky, Bindig is the kind of man they invented the word "strapping" for. Better yet, he's a local history buff and is familiar—at least superficially—with Dad's saga, as related by Aaro Aho in his book *Hills of Silver*. The only chapter, curiously, where Aho names no names, including his own, is titled "The Mysterious Ore Shipment." A bonus is Bindig's partner, who'll join us—Lauren Blackburn is a gregarious, spirited, dark-haired woman who also happens to be a geologist.

Originally from Germany, Matthias Bindig has lived in the Keno area for about twelve years, doing odd jobs, but now works mainly as a prospector and dogsledder. We meet at noon on a cool, brilliantly clear day at the Keno City Snack Shop, the heart of what's left of Keno these days.

While waiting for Bindig and Blackburn over a cup of coffee, I do a double take. A plaque on a wall memorializes, of all people, Martin Swizinski, who lived many years in Keno. It says simply: "Martin Swizinski 1926–Jan. 5, 2003. Shift boss, mine captain (UKHM), mine superintendent, mine manager (Canada Tungsten), owner/operator Springmount Operating Company Ltd., Keno City."

Everything has changed since Swizinski and Dad's time in the Yukon. The day before, Jennika Bergren had graciously escorted me on a truck tour of what was left of Elsa. A perky twenty-something, Bergren exuded optimism and energy, about the opposite of how I felt. She worked for Alexco Resource Corp., the company that now owns the Elsa townsite and a whole lot more since UKHM went bust more than two decades ago. Committed to life in the north, Bergren hopes to have a daughter one day, and name her Elsa.

Why, though, is beyond me. All that remains of my hometown is an Atco trailer camp surrounded by encroaching bush and the remains of a few forlorn buildings—including, remarkably, the school. Anyone seeing this sight would never guess that, in its day, the Elsa–Keno mines gave up more than 213 million ounces of silver, 710 million pounds of lead, and 436 million pounds of zinc. Or that for nearly seventy years, thousands of people worked hard, played hard, raised children and forged eternal friendships here. Or that in 1985, Elsa became the first official hamlet in Yukon history.

Only a few years later, UKHM's owners decided the good times were gone. On January 9, 1989, the company operated its last shift and 170 people lost their jobs. United Keno Hill Mines was then the second-largest employer in the territory. Overnight the lights of Elsa went *pfft*. The town was rapidly abandoned. And after that, what was left fell into oblivion. In 1994 Elsa's prized Panabodes were sold, disassembled and shipped off to points west and south. Tourists and collectors scavenged a few retro items they found but what remained was largely left to rot. In 2003, when silver prices rose to profitable levels, Alexco Resources Corp., a Vancouver-based junior mining company, became interested in the old UKHM mines. Three years later the territorial and federal governments—who rightly viewed the poisoned valley UKHM had left behind as a $65-million liability—sold the assets to Alexco for the bargain sum of $410,000. Included in the deal was a promise that Alexco would spend an estimated $50 million to reclaim the horror in the McQuesten River Valley, where more than four million tons of tailings had been dumped for more than half a century. All told, the government sold the entire Elsa townsite and surrounding land, plus thirty-five former UKHM mine sites, to Alexco—a total area of 23,350 hectares.

In January 2011, Alexco began operating one Keno Hill mine and built their mill and crusher within the Keno community even though the original mill had been in Elsa. The move divided Keno's residents into two camps: those who see their town primarily as a tourist destination—the end of the Silver Trail—and others who view it as a mine site above all. A few managed to sell their homes and leave, shrinking the already tiny permanent population to a mere handful. Some just walked away from their homes. In 2012, the Yukon Environmental and Socio-Economic Assessment Board gave Alexco permission to further industrialize Keno. The company now has the green light to develop the Lucky Queen and Onek mines, both located near Keno. However, the way of the world may not allow that. Due to low silver prices, Alexco closed its one and only operating mine, Bellekeno, in September 2013. The company said it would reopen the mine someday, but only if silver prices improved.

In Elsa, Alexco dismantled and destroyed many buildings that remained, including the Catholic church, the market and the coffee shop. They saved the school to be used as a geological office. What once was a community with a capital C is now a dry workstation where employees fly in for two-week shifts of twelve-hour days from across Canada. And with that, Elsa has joined a ghostly assortment of Canadian mining towns that exist in memory only.

As I look out the café window at the empty dirt streets, it seems inevitable to me that Keno will one day join them. I mourn the loss of my hometown and realize that I can never show my family the special places of my childhood. Shortly, Matthias and Lauren arrive and we head off for the Moon, boarding an open-cab red Polaris six-wheel ATV. Besides extra jackets, the rig's loaded with water, snacks, mosquito repellent, a chainsaw and an assortment of picks, axes, shovels and other prospecting tools. I cling to the passenger seat beside Matthias. Lauren jumps on. Matthias turns the key. We rumble and bump uphill on a dirt road pointing northeast. The Moon claims, now called the Try Again claims, beckon about 8 miles away.

As we skirt the eastern edge of Minto Hill, the road narrows to become a stone-scattered track. Minto's summit is 5,026 feet in elevation and by now we are flirting with the treeline. We pass what's left of the old townsite, where Dad took us overnight camping so long ago. A haphazard collection of rotting boards, rusted hulks of machinery and coiled wire, one leaning shack and the skeleton of an old tramline bakes in the thin August air. Matthias and Lauren say they are urging the Yukon government to declare the area a heritage site and to honour Livingston Wernecke as the Yukon mining legend he was. Now at over 4,000 feet in elevation, we look down at the glimmer of Hanson Lakes and Ladue Lake at the base of the McQuesten River. Deep valleys encroach on three sides. In winter the McQuesten Valley becomes a sheet of ice and snow, making the Moon claims more accessible by snowmobile, as Dad knew. Still, whatever the season, the claims are over yonder—in the hinterland of the hinterland.

We turn northeast toward Faro Gulch on a washed-out mining road called the Silver Basin Trail and enter an alpine jungle of dense, overgrown willow and aspen as thick as the forest surrounding Sleeping Beauty's castle. Above the roar of the Polaris, I ask Matthias if there really was a trail beneath us. I see no evidence that man, machine or beast ever trespassed here. He assures me there was a trail some years ago. For the next hour and a half, I keep my head down, clutching the windshield while Matthias and Lauren swing their machetes, axes, arms and legs, hacking, chopping, pushing and shoving at the aggressive scrub blocking our path. The Polaris jerks forward, stops, starts only to stop, stuck in mud, and start again. At one point a ricocheting sapling whacks Lauren out of the vehicle. Luckily, we're only going about 2 miles an hour and she hops back in, rubbing her shoulder. Around another bend Matthias points at an outhouse perched precariously on the edge of a precipice. The facility's back half is gone but the seat and front frame are hanging by a sliver. "Anyone need to go?" he asks.

Eventually we reach a high open vista, where a sparsely treed burnt orange and dark green wetland spreads below while above, ridge upon ridge of purple—the Yukon Plateau—rolls northwest forever. I take a breath, and a rush of spicy, cool air fills my lungs. Down we motor onto a genuine trail that emerges and flattens out. We've landed on the Moon. It's taken more than two hours to travel 8 miles.

Relatively even expanses of land, the Moon claims are four 1,500-foot × 1,500-foot adjoining squares of ground partially cleared of bush and boulders. According to the Yukon Geological Survey, the claims contain deposits of lead, silver, gold and zinc. After slathering on mosquito repellent, we amble over a small rise and into a bowl-shaped clearing. It's like entering some archaic arena. Signs of humans are everywhere, but except for sporadic birdsong, silence reigns. There's been no real mining here for about a decade and nature has wasted no time in re-staking her claim. On one rock wall a collapsed adit gapes, its blackness half obscured by rotting wooden boards. Years ago a prospector's brother was crushed and killed in this same tunnel when the roof collapsed. Opposite the adit, a small, stagnant pool shimmers below rusted fuel drums and discarded beer cans. Bulldozer ruts trail off into the bush, ending in a push-pile of jumbled, irregular-shaped rubble. Matthias says the push-pile is a good place to look for ore. We let him go at it while Lauren and I hunt for traces of the cabin Dad stayed in. Scraping aside the moss, buckbrush (dwarf birch) and young aspen covering one flattish area, we find the cabin's worn foundation—long wooden boards shallowly embedded in the ground and marking a small rectangle. Not far below, the earth is permanently frozen. How many winter nights had Dad brooded, dreamed and schemed here, and what "hand-mining" had he actually done?

While Matthias believes the claims contain valued ore, he dismisses Dad's story of a massive boulder rolling down from Keno Summit and onto the Moon. "A 60-ton boulder?" he says. "That's huge, like Ayers Rock!" He's exaggerating, of course, but I get his point.

Lauren and I return to the rock pile, above and to the right of the adit where Matthias is chipping chunks off loose rock with the blunt end of his pick. "There's amazing quality here," he says. Giving me a quick and dirty geology refresher, Lauren reminds me that the earth produces three kinds of basic rock: sedimentary, metamorphic and igneous. The host rock found here, she continues, is an "igneous intrusion" largely made of fine-grained aplite, consisting of quartz and other rock. These rocks may hold minerals like zinc, lead and silver, but in such minute form they require smelting to be released.

Matthias continues picking up rocks and breaking them into fist-sized hunks. He calls me over, and with one precise smack cracks one open like an egg. I gasp. A galaxy of silver sparkle spills out from between two rusty crusts. Who knew? It's like opening a kiwi for the first time. Before I get too excited, Matthias cautions me that all that glitters isn't silver. We saw shiny galena, and the sample could contain variable amounts of different minerals including lead, zinc, antimony, arsenic or silver. But only a rigorous assay can reveal what and how much. Often, Matthias explains, dull interiors hold more promise. He retrieves another rock and chips it as well. No celestial fireworks here, just a thick strip of flat grey-yellow. It could be pyrite, also known as fool's gold, Matthias says. "There's the exposed quartz vein here," he adds, pointing at a stripe in the rock wall above us, "but is it dead or alive?" Meaning does it hold valuable minerals or not.

Suddenly we notice a chill in the air and lowering light. We need to hit the road—another rough and rocky 8 miles. And another two hours. This time we tramp up a short ridge toward the Polaris, the ground littered with scraps of wood, plastic and metal detritus.

"This is one of the most distant claims from Keno," Matthias says. "In terms of access, it's damn far."

Via the southern route, Dad had allegedly made up to seven round trips a day on his newfangled snow machine, pulling hundreds of pounds of ore behind him on a tow toboggan. "Totally ridiculous" was how Strathdee had characterized Dad's story. I get his point but desperados have accomplished far more foolish feats in their pursuit of fortune. And as I leave the Moon after my first and only visit, I realize that fifty years ago, Dad had indeed become a desperate man.

Back in Keno, we stop in front of the Keno City Mining Museum as evening begins to blush. Before I get into my own rented vehicle, Matthias allows me to choose from his selection of samples. I select four Moon rocks—two shiny and two dull.

Now that I've seen Dad's Moon claims and refreshed my Elsa memories, the troubles of the past take on a new stark clarity. Even before the ore had arrived at the Helena smelter, curious geologists and mine officials were crawling all over the Moon claims, the Duncan

Creek loading site and the Elsa mine. Among the first there, were chief and assistant mine engineers Bob Cathro and Bob Shank.

Gentle and tall, with turquoise eyes flashing behind wire-rim glasses, Cathro had been relatively new to the job when word of the heist broke. Archer's advice to Dad about the Moon claims was based on an erroneous report that said the Moon group had a lot of quartzite, the most important host rock for silver. "Turns out they didn't," Cathro told me years later. "They only had rhyolite."

Rhyolite. Right. I got what Cathro was saying: the Moon had the wrong kind of rock. After consulting the oracle, Wikipedia, I was better informed about quartzite and rhyolite. And more confused. Quartzite, it read, is "a hard, non-foliated metamorphic rock which was originally pure quartz sandstone... Sandstone is converted into quartzite through heating and pressure relating to tectonic compression within orogenic belts." My mind was spinning, and even more dazzling was the oracle's definition of rhyolite as "an igneous, volcanic rock, of felsic (silica-rich) composition (typically greater than 69% SiO_2—see the Total Alkali Silica classification). It may have any texture from glassy to aphanitic to porphyritic."

This jumble of geological jargon led me to wonder how a pre-Google juror—even a Yukon juror—would have handled such information as it related to Dad's contested ore.

For several months following Dad's arrest, page after page of such gibble-gabble accumulated in the Mounties' files as one field report or geological assessment after another rolled in, all aimed at either showing that the ore originated from the Elsa mine or, increasingly, that it did not come from the Moon. And more geological abstruseness would emerge from eminent geologists back in Ottawa. As police and Crown counsel wrestled with translating scientific opinion into something that was semi-comprehensible, Dad and his lawyer built a reasonable counterargument based on the testimony of their own experts.

Apart from some of the more arcane aspects of the geological investigation, it was already clear to Bob Cathro and Bob Shank that Dad's story of hand-mining ore from the Moon didn't wash. In late June 1963 the two UKHM engineers tramped across the claims looking for signs of recent mining. What they found was evidence of a decidedly curious nature. For one, the effects of recent blasting appeared totally inconsequential. There was a small exposed rock slide surrounded by a carpet of moss and stunted conifers, but the rocks had been blasted upslope with the aim of rolling them down-hill onto the surrounding moss. Virtually all the rock on the surface of the slide consisted of small boulders of white rhyolite (worthless). After digging just below the surface, the two men retrieved the odd 2-inch chunk of galena. Below that, they encountered the bane of every placer miner's existence: barren bedrock.

Galena—found in abundance in the Elsa mine—is the most important lead ore mineral and often contains significant amounts of silver. As the two men looked closer, they spotted another fifteen to twenty similarly sized chunks of galena, all sitting conspicuously on the moss. More small lumps of galena were discovered in the nearby cabin, lying in full view on a dusty wooden table.

The two were struck by the same thought: someone had purposely placed chunks of galena in prominent places—places where they'd surely be seen. In the mining world, such subterfuge has a name: salting. Usually salting involves scattering enough valuable ore in the right spots to lure a would-be investor into paying for mineral claims that may have little worth. On the Moon, the intended message appeared to be the opposite: something valuable *had been* there. But except for a few spilled leftovers, it was gone.

A month later, geologist Al Archer arrived for his own inspection of the Moon. Archer gathered ore samples too, but they were few. Since Cathro and Shank's visit, someone had gone onto the claims with a tractor—likely Bobcik, as he owned a BobCat—and chewed up a considerable piece of turf.

"Looks like whoever did it had one thing in mind—to obliterate any previous workings on the property," Archer told Strathdee upon his return.

Less than a month later, Archer was back. This time leading a group of eleven geology students who combed the entire four claims in a slow, coordinated march. With the outer edge of the first two claims established by compass, the men spaced themselves out and at Archer's signal began a steady walk at right angles from the outer line, using compasses to maintain their direction.

To the uninitiated, the scene had the grisly appearance of a methodical hunt for a missing body. But the men were looking for any unusual occurrences of ore and/or signs of work. Once they reached the end of their first pass, a quarter-mile walk, they turned, shifted to the right and walked back again. The pattern was repeated until they'd scrutinized the entire surface of the Moon. At the end of that long, hot and tiring day, Archer reported back to Pike: "No trails of recent origin were found. No workings or pits of any age were found. The only rock types seen outcropping were graphite schist and greenstone."

Falconbridge geologist Alexander Smith was at the Vancouver airport awaiting a flight to Whitehorse when he first learned about the strange ore shipment. The next day, after journeying from Whitehorse to Elsa, Smith was greeted by Pike, who told him the whole story—or at least as much as he knew and suspected.

That same day, Pike, Smith and Shank drove to the Duncan Creek loading site, where they found shredded fragments of old sack liners with traces of silver-rich galena clinging to their edges. There were also chips of galena on the ground, many showing signs of oxidization. In other words, they'd been above ground for a year or more.

In a cabin they found a few new jute sacks with what looked like concentrates from the UKHM mill rubbed into their rough exteriors as well as a cookie tin containing about 2 tablespoons of the same concentrate matter. And on the banks of the loading site, where the ore had been sacked and loaded onto the trucks, they discovered more traces of concentrates.

Smith told Pike that the concentrates found at Duncan Creek were "identical" to those produced at UKHM's mill. "We need to get this stuff examined by a metallurgist," Smith said. That's when Pike notified UKHM brass in Toronto and under their orders flew to Helena, where he helped himself to more samples from Dad's shipment. Two days later, eight of those samples were under the microscope at the University of British Columbia's Department of Mining and Geological Engineering. Six of the eight contained what looked like lead concentrates and precipitates from the Elsa mill. Before that could be confirmed, however, a massive sampling and ore analysis exercise lay ahead.

On August 12, Falconbridge's lawyers asked the RCMP if they could review "on a confidential basis" the contents of Dad's statement to FBI agent Bruce Lanthorn. Their wish was granted. At the same time, they also learned that the Mounties had chosen an independent expert to examine the shipment. Kenneth J. Christie, chief mining engineer for the Resources Division of Canada's Department of Northern Affairs and National Resources (DNANR), was ordered to scrap any remaining plans for summer fieldwork and give "top priority" to the case. The next day Falconbridge's lawyers told the Mounties that UKHM would pay for two additional geological specialists to rendezvous with Christie in Helena—two company-paid experts working alongside the Crown's chosen expert.

"We understand that this sampling is not of a nature of an ordinary mineral shipment," the Falconbridge letter read. "That fact has been made abundantly clear by the examination by Mr. A.E. Pike, the Mine Manager, very experienced in these minerals. One is left with the conclusion that the shipper has intermixed solid ores, well oxidized, brittle pieces and fines, high-grade pieces, lead concentrates, zinc concentrates and possibly precipitates in such manner as to confuse an examiner and make qualitative as well as quantitative analysis as difficult as possible. This deduction is in part confirmed by Priest's statement [to Lanthorn] that he had dumped bags of concentrates and other fine materials over the ore pile."

Joining Christie would be Falconbridge geologist Alexander Smith and a consulting metallurgist, John Mortimer, also paid by Falconbridge. Meeting at the Montana smelter, they quickly realized the enormity of their challenge. After they examined the 7 bags Pike had previously rummaged through, another 10 bags were opened. After examining the contents of all 17 bags, Christie, Smith and Mortimer confronted the ugly truth: each bag contained such great variations that they needed to open, dump and examine the entire shipment –all 671 bags.

Three smelter employees were assigned to help with the project. Every sack of ore in the two railcars was offloaded, cut open and its contents spread out and examined. After probing everything, the three experts decided that the entire shipment could be roughly broken down into twelve different categories. Their descriptions ranged from the technical "high siderite ore with tetrahedrite and galena" to the more pedestrian "gravel boulders." The men took a representative sampling of these twelve types from each sack and then bagged, numbered and tagged the hundreds of samples. The samples were boxed and delivered to chemists and metallurgists at DNANR in Ottawa, to Falconbridge Nickel Mines in Toronto and to Christie, who would carry them to his next point of call: the Yukon.

But more than ore was selected. As the men worked their way through the mountain of material, they turned up odd bits of metal: metal sack ties that probably originated from the mine; metal cable that looked like part of the pulley system in the mine; and bolts and other odd metal pieces that might be linked to the mine. After all visible extraneous material was sorted, a giant electromagnet, commonly used for unloading scrap metal, was attached to a crane and swept slowly over the unloaded ore to pick up any undetected metal bits. This complement of retrieved metal objects was duly bagged by Christie—in sample bag number 13653.

The team noted other odd items in their inventory: a half-eaten meat sandwich and a stray Doublemint chewing gum wrapper, with its distinct green bar and two arrowheads aiming in opposite directions. For Christie it was a fitting image as he left Montana for the long car journey to Calgary and the even longer trip to the Yukon. Would the amassed evidence point to the Moon as the source of the ore, or to the Elsa mine?

From Calgary, Christie caught a flight to Edmonton, where he overnighted before boarding a plane for Whitehorse. Included in his luggage were two large canvas bags full of heavy ore samples. In Whitehorse, Christie borrowed the local mining inspector's pickup, purchased a padlock and locked the two bags in the rear cab. After a long day's drive to Elsa, he delivered the samples into the waiting hands of Corporal Strathdee.

Two days later, Christie, Strathdee, Swizinski and Archer entered the Elsa mine to collect new samples they hoped would tie the shipment to the mine. Strathdee, by this point, had learned one thing about going underground. He hated it. It "was the dampest, darkest, dankest, most filthy place on earth." The mine also turned out to be bereft of anything worth sampling. But Christie and company chipped at some rock anyway, with the slim hope that it would yield a promising result.

That done, it was time for yet another visit to the Duncan Creek loading site. But when Christie arrived, he discovered the site had been recently bulldozed, just as the Moon claims had a few weeks earlier. The bulldozer operator hadn't, however, done a thorough job and Christie spotted traces of lead concentrates clinging to a bank. On the northerly cut of the recently bulldozed track, he eyed a lonely piece of galena. Both specimens were immediately bagged for analysis in Ottawa. Christie also found more Doublemint chewing gum wrappers.

Next stop, the Moon. By then, Christie knew that Dad said he'd hand-mined the ore on the Moon from a very large boulder that, once upon a time, had rolled down the mountain. A celestial gift, he insisted, that just happened to be loaded with silver-laden tetrahedrite and galena. Like Cathro, Shank and Archer before him, Christie dismissed Dad's story. He left the Moon that day convinced that nothing of value had been mined there in a long, long time.

"My examination of the geological formations found on the Moon mineral claims, where I could find no high grade galena or tetrahedrite in siderite, thoroughly convinced me that the ore in the shipment was never mined from rock in place on the Moon mineral claims... The wall rock found in the shipment was quartzite, similar to that found at the Elsa Mine."

This statement by the Crown's leading expert was the strongest indication yet that the Mounties not only had their man, but had the facts to establish his guilt. Little did they know that nearly all their sleuthing—which ate up much of the $300,000 spent on the case—would prove largely useless. Like that alluring yet ultimately worthless chunk of galena that Matthias Bindig cracked open on our trip to the Moon, Christie's and Falconbridge's conclusion looked impressive on paper but mattered little in a court of law.

CHAPTER 13

Fourteen Days
at the Northern Lights Lodge

How strange two "irresponsibles" should chum away up here!

IT WAS A CHILLY NOVEMBER even by Yukon standards. But in one of the coldest countries on earth, in a village known for its weather extremes, visitors and locals could expect nothing less. In fact, in the central Yukon, which Mayo middles, the mercury climbs higher and falls lower in any given year than in any other populated spot in North America. Still, few were prepared for day after day of minus 45 degrees Fahrenheit—and lower—so early in the season.

Least prepared was a twenty-four-year-old Vancouver lawyer named John Molson. Yes, his roots were tangled in that heady dynasty that founded what is now the oldest brewery in North America. Molson had arrived in this far-flung settlement at this insufferable time of year along with several other outsiders from as far away as Ottawa, Toronto and Montana to attend the longest and most expensive preliminary hearing in Yukon history. So long in fact that *Whitehorse Star* court reporter Al Godolphin filled more than a dozen shorthand notebooks covering the event, and transcripts ran to more than 48,000 typewritten lines—"the average length of a paperback novelette," as the *Star* put it. The hearing would determine if the evidence against Dad and Poncho warranted a criminal trial.

Only days before, John Molson didn't have a clue that Mayo was anything more than the creamy stuff you spread on Wonder Bread before you slapped on a piece of bologna. But at the eleventh hour and fifty-ninth minute, his Vancouver firm—Bull, Housser & Tupper—had thrust him into the proceedings and forced him to get up to speed on his new client, my father. Two days before the hearing started, Molson was summoned to the office of senior lawyer Bae Wallis, who supervised Molson's assignments. Wallis had just received a call from Henry Regehr, who outlined the general nature of the charges that Dad and Poncho faced. Regehr had reluctantly concluded that he could no longer represent both men. The charges they faced were complex and there was a good possibility that as the proceedings moved forward Poncho and Dad would find themselves in conflict.

"Henry Regehr's asking us to represent Gerald Priest, and he'll continue to represent the other guy, Anthony Bobcik," Wallis said. "I need you packed and ready to fly to Whitehorse the day after tomorrow. Regehr will meet you and drive you up to Mayo."

At the time, neither Wallis nor Molson appreciated just where Mayo was, or how the assignment would nearly cost Molson his life.

"I didn't know that Mayo was in the middle of nowhere," Molson later said with a rueful chuckle. "White socks, loafers, a white shirt and suit: that was about all I had; that, and a raincoat like you wear around Vancouver."

For Molson, Mayo was colder than Mars. In the sub-zero temperatures of a dull midday, Molson checked into the Chateau Mayo, a stark, two-storey wood-frame box with a flat roof and small rectangular windows. He soon learned that if you didn't smother your face when you went outdoors your nose would fall off. Parked outside the hotel and haphazardly everywhere else were cars and trucks with their motors idling. Any vehicle not up on blocks with its motor fluids drained risked a cracked engine, rendering it more useless than a dogsled without dogs.

In fact, the two policemen on the case had such trouble starting their new unmarked, black 1963 Pontiac Grand Prix that once they did turn it over they never turned it off. For three weeks, day and night, the car either idled or was on the move. (Within a year, it was deemed junk.) Adding to the clouds of exhaust, people's exhalations hung in the air as they scuttled between buildings like two-legged cocoons. On most days, Mayo was a soupy monochromatic haze of white, dirty black and grey.

Mounties Strathdee and McKiel also roomed at the Chateau Mayo. Every night, between November 19 and December 6, its bar and restaurant swarmed with over-lubricated men, and no doubt some companionable women, eager to dissect the day's revelations.

Apart from one Canadian Press story, the proceedings received little national attention, being understandably eclipsed by the November 22 assassination of John F. Kennedy. One key witness—FBI agent Bruce Lanthorn—sped home immediately upon hearing the news. Fortunately, he had just completed his testimony.

Held at Mayo's Northern Lights Lodge No.157, the Freemasons' gathering place, the hearing featured 248 separate pieces of evidence. A long-standing Mason himself, Al Pike was familiar with the lodge's membership. Under his direction, some fellow Masons had likely stolen samples of the disputed ore from one of the White Pass and Yukon Route trucks while the driver was lunching at the Mayo café. Indeed, WP&YR driver Peter McAleer testified that after his midday meal he "found a whole group of people climbing over my truck, some with samples in their hands." He couldn't name the men and, curiously, the incident—along with two others involving pilfered specimens from what the Mounties now referred to as the "Priest shipment"—were not pursued by police. In the two other cases, the men were Pike and consulting Vancouver-based geologist Aaro Aho. But the Mounties, the presiding police magistrate, Bill Trainor, and Crown counsel Vic Wylie apparently had bigger fish to fry. Molson and Regehr also raised no concerns about the illicit sampling. If their clients were committed to trial, however, evidence tampering was one possible line of questioning.

There was never any doubt that Dad and Bobcik, charged with theft, conspiracy and illegal sale of silver ore and concentrates, would have their day in court. The Mounties had amassed cartons of evidence, much of it packed in the trunk of their ever-idling Pontiac, including sacks of ore, maps, photographs, letters, cancelled cheques and bank statements.

The strongest indications of mischief, however, were raised by the thirty-one Crown witnesses, who ranged from the manager of the Elsa branch of the Royal Bank of Canada to three WP&YR truck drivers, to ASARCO smelter manager Stanley Lane, to a Toronto lawyer and mining company investor, to former UKHM mine employees and other associates of the accused, to the mine's most senior executives. Last, but certainly not least, was a phalanx of esteemed geological and mineralogical experts.

"They had a huge number of geologists ready to testify," Molson recalled. "They just kept pouring in—UKHM spared no expense."

Dad's defense, at least its bare bones, was by now well known. Thanks to his lengthy interview with Lanthorn, the Crown knew that Dad maintained his ore came from the Moon claims, which he and Poncho had "hand-mined" from a giant boulder of silver-rich rock. As far as the precipitates and concentrates were concerned, Dad's story was that as chief assayer he simply followed a long-standing custom that allowed assayers to take them.

For the most part, Molson believed Dad's story and thought he came across well. "I liked him. He didn't look like a thief. He was almost a spiritual kind of guy… Bobcik was rough. Priest wasn't. But he was very intense sometimes, and I wondered why."

Early on in his letters home, Dad made an effort to be upbeat and optimistic. In the sixties, long distance phone calls were expensive and used for emergencies only.

"Things don't look bad yet, but the evidence is not all in and I believe the worst is yet to come," Dad wrote on November 26. "But my spirits are good and people here are on our side to a great degree." He added that he planned to "fight this out for the opportunity to get home again" and ended with a romantic sentiment: "Your hand in mine, your face before me, always."

Mill worker Siegfried Haina's testimony was especially damaging to Poncho. With help from a German translator, a nervous Haina spoke of stealing precipitates from the mill and selling them to Poncho over a period of several months, as he had admitted to Strathdee after his intense interrogation. In exchange for his testimony, Haina had received a suspended sentence. Regehr tried to persuade Haina to say the police had pressured him to identify Poncho as the purchaser and that UKHM had even paid him to do so. But that strategy went nowhere.

When Pike took the stand, he refuted Dad's claim that, as chief assayer, he was entitled to keep "rejects" from the assaying process. UKHM policy dictated that any precipitates or concentrates either delivered to or produced in the assay office were the property of the company, Pike insisted. "No one was entitled to keep anything from the mine mill."

Another strike against Dad was the amount of precipitate material in the shipment, somewhere between 400 and 1,000 pounds. Such large volumes, explained mill superintendent Arthur Wall, could only have come from the mill because the assay office took only tiny portions of mill precipitates. Furthermore, he said, assay office precipitates were ground up, screened and weighed before delivery, making them extremely pure. Yet intermixed with the precipitates in the Priest shipment were numerous shreds or whole pieces of filter paper that could only have come from the mill. Then Wall delivered what for Dad and Poncho must have been a bit of a bombshell. "UKHM shipped all its precipitates to a smelter in Silbey, California," Wall said. "The smelter in Helena was not equipped to handle that product."

At the heart of the hearing, though, was the question of where the bulk of the shipment—the 70 tons of raw ore—originated. Mineral experts and geologists had a field day contesting Dad and Poncho's assertion that the ore came from the Moon. Federal government geologist Kenneth Christie thought that 90 percent could not have originated on the Moon. However, the defense counsels discredited his statement that it could not possibly have come from some other place on Keno Hill. Falconbridge geologist Alexander Smith believed as much as 80 percent likely came from the Bonanza Stope, although some may have originated in other parts of the same vein.

On December 3 the star of the show took the stand. A senior scientist in the Mineral Sciences Division of the Department of Mines in Ottawa and an internationally recognized expert in mineralogy and microscopy, Maurice Haycock was a true Renaissance man. Aside from his professional accomplishments, he was a consummate classical musician (French horn) and a highly regarded *plein-air* painter and a colleague of A.Y. Jackson. With a passion for Canada's north, Haycock was fondly known as "The Arctic Artist."

Employing state-of-the-art visual display technology—a slide projector and 35 mm colour slides—Haycock presented the hearing with a glimpse into the mysterious microscopic world of ore. Attendees were shown strangely beautiful Kodachrome images of glinting red, black, blue and silver.

Haycock's photos illuminated his conclusion that 90 percent of the ore samples "could have come from the Elsa Mine" and that only a tiny fraction of the shipment, under 5 percent, could have come from elsewhere. "Practically none of the shipment could have come from the Moon claims," Haycock said.

With the completion of Haycock's testimony, a trio of geologists had—or so Crown counsel Wylie hoped—firmly established that the ore came from the Elsa mine, and if it did not, that it most certainly did not come from the Moon. If the defendants were ordered to stand trial, their case would focus on evidence or expert testimony of the opposite. With the crackerjack team of rock jocks he'd amassed, Wylie felt that Priest and Bobcik were going to have a devil of a time. Still, the prosecutor admitted privately that his case was also going to be a tough slog.

Despite hundreds of ore samples analyzed up the yingyang by some of the brightest minds in the business, not a single piece of silver-rich rock could be directly linked to UKHM's Elsa mine, or the famed Bonanza Stope. Opining that the rock *looked* like it could come from something that didn't exist anymore was hardly the stuff of a successful prosecution. Worse yet, Wylie could not produce a single witness who saw Priest and Bobcik steal ore from the Elsa mine.

However, Wylie had an advantage most prosecutors today do not. Under the criminal code of the day, Dad and Bobcik were charged with an unusual crime that placed the onus on them to prove their innocence. Normally, the accused are presumed innocent until the prosecution proves them guilty. But because of a "reverse onus" provision in the criminal statute that dated back to petty mining thefts in early twentieth-century Ontario, Dad and Poncho were presumed guilty. The onus was on them to prove they were the rightful owners of the ore. No such charge exists today, as it would violate the 1982 Charter of Rights and Freedoms. Even back then, it was cause for consternation in other jurisdictions, as Dad would discover—to his advantage—years later.

Shortly after Haycock testified, the hearing ended for the day and another weekend began. It was a weekend John Molson will never forget. By then, he had become familiar with a few people and was actually on good terms with Strathdee. Earlier in the week, Strathdee had ambled up to Molson and Trainor and asked if they'd like to see the Moon claims.

On Saturday, off the men went in Strathdee's well-travelled Grand Prix. It was an excruciatingly slow, long drive on a snow-covered gravel road from one patch of nowhere to another: past Elsa, past Keno and past the old Wernecke ghost town. When the three men reached their destination, a narrow bench that offered a view down a steep gulch to the claim area below, Molson wondered what the heck they'd come there for. Snow, silence and an infinite emptiness engulfed the threesome. "It was just a sea of white," Molson recalls. "Christ, we couldn't see anything and we were cold as hell on top of this mountain, practically."

Perhaps the field trip had been Strathdee's attempt to emphasize what a friggin' long way the Moon claims were from anywhere, and that hauling 70 tons of ore out would be near impossible. But with the cold shooting through the soles of his black dress shoes like ice arrows, Molson didn't care. All he wanted was to curl up in the cozy confines of the Chateau Mayo, no doubt with a glass of his namesake's ale. In a second they were back in the car, making ready their escape. Strathdee stuck the key in the ignition and turned it. Nothing stirred. No sound of the engine even attempting to grip. The men looked at each other. No one spoke. Strathdee tried again. No response. And again. The stillness was deafening. Maybe the engine was flooded. They waited an eternal moment as the Ice Queen stroked each man's neck. Another thirty seconds and Strathdee cranked a fourth time. Sputter, cough and *vroom*. "We saw where the Moon claims were," Molson said. "But so what? Going downhill back to Mayo, the magistrate and I just looked at each other. We'd almost died in the middle of nowhere."

Consulting geologist Aaro Aho was the last person to testify. An ambitious and intellectually formidable geological engineer, Aho added his voice to the chorus discounting the Moon claims as the source of the ore. The idea of a massive boulder breaking away from a silver-rich vein up a mountain, rolling down and coming to rest on the Moon was preposterous, he told the hearing. "Such a piece of float would, by then, be no larger than a pea."

Unlike other experts, however, Aho had to perform some verbal gymnastics on the stand to explain why he had entered into various business agreements with Bobcik. Exactly when and how those questionable arrangements played out remains a mystery. As previously mentioned, Aho names no names—including his own—in the chapter called "The Mysterious Ore Shipment" in *Hills of Silver*, and died back in 1977. But a careful reader with some knowledge of the events can confidently decipher the code. The "shipper—a quiet brooding introvert" is clearly Dad. The "miner—a happy go lucky irrepressible extrovert" is Poncho. And "a consulting geological engineer" is Aho himself. Why Aho became involved with a slippery character like Poncho and with the Moon claims is obvious: he wanted a share in the riches.

According to Aho, Poncho flew to Vancouver in the fall of 1961 to tell the geologist about what he described as a fantastic find of between 50 and 60 tons of extremely rich silver ore. The only other thing he revealed, Aho said, was that it came from somewhere east of Mayo Lake. Perhaps Poncho intended only to plant a seed of interest with Aho because nothing more happened until the following year, when Poncho brought Aho beads of silver and ore samples, plus a plea for money and equipment to continue "mining." And this time he said the samples came from the Moon claims. Aho did not go north and inspect the claims, however. Instead, he and the directors of his two companies, Peso Silver Mines Ltd. and Silver Titan Mines Ltd., gave Bobcik $25,000 in equipment and another $25,000 for expenses. Aho and friends must have been smitten with the ore samples because Poncho also convinced Peso to do an intense amount of claim staking near the Moon. Soon after, Peso purchased twenty claims in the area for $150,000.

Then, in July 1963, Aho got wind that some 70 tons of high-grade ore had arrived in Vancouver and was being offloaded at the North Vancouver dock. The ore belonged to Alpine Gold and Silver Ltd. with Dad as the registered shipper. Aho had had no dealings with Dad, and no right to touch the ore. But he knew Poncho was associated with Alpine and, disgruntled with the deal they had struck a year earlier—Aho had so far seen no return on his investment—he arranged for a few samples to be snitched. Comparing them to the samples Poncho had shown him earlier, he saw that they matched. Finally Aho was motivated to travel to the Yukon and meet Poncho on the Moon claims. Almost as soon as he arrived, Aho told the hearing, he saw that the Moon could not possibly have yielded such rich ore. He pressed Poncho on that point, and Poncho admitted the ore was stolen.

As more evidence came to light, Bobcik's dealings took on an increasingly shadowy tone. Toronto lawyer Richard Irwin Martin— "a conservative Toronto solicitor, embarrassed at being involved," as Aho describes him—testified that Alpine was in effect Bobcik's company, with Martin nominally in charge as president. Martin would later tell police that Bobcik tried to have him structure a deal that would have done Dad out of his share of the proceeds. Under this agreement Dad's cash share would have automatically been converted to shares in a worthless company, leaving Bobcik to take the booty. But Martin and another Alpine director scuttled Bobcik's plans and Martin resigned as president just prior to arriving in Mayo for the hearing.

Why the Toronto lawyer got mixed up with a character like Bobcik and uncertain claims in the Yukon in the first place remains another unanswered question. In a review of hundreds of pages of RCMP files I later obtained from Library and Archives Canada, I discovered the rough outline of Poncho's plans to cheat Dad. However, because the files are heavily redacted, many details of these arrangements and others remain a mystery.

On cross-examination, defence lawyers Molson and Regehr asked Aho why he hadn't alerted police immediately upon learning the ore was stolen. Aho had a quick retort: if he notified police, he was sure the ore (which he had not seen and could not verify the origins of) would stay hidden. Instead, he had chosen to wait it out and see what happened. His explanation raised many questions. Why, knowing that Bobcik was behaving so suspiciously, had Aho continued to have anything to do with him? Aho's response was again less than satisfying and close to nonsensical: it had been "strictly against his will and advice" that Peso and Titan (of which he was president) had continued to deal with Bobcik. For some reason, he said, the company directors forced his hand.

At the end of the day, Strathdee was pleased with how the hearing unfolded. Still, he knew getting a conviction before a judge and jury was another matter—especially if jury members came from Mayo.

"The unpopularity of big mining companies is well justified," Strathdee later told me. Mines are generally dangerous and unpleasant places to work and when miners go below ground to risk life and limb for the supervisors above, they often feel they deserve a share of the wealth. The little guy making rich is a powerful myth in the mining fraternity, and Strathdee suspected that deep and longstanding resentment by workers and their families against UKHM could spell trouble.

"Barring the possibility of a prejudiced jury, which is a very real possibility should the trial be held in Mayo, I have every reason to expect convictions on all charges," Strathdee wrote in his summary of the hearing. He would no doubt have concurred with Dad's letter to Mom sent five days before the hearing ended:

> *The preliminary drags on—it will be the longest held in the Yukon. So be it. I'm doing fine, just letting it go in one ear and out the other. The talk around town is that if our trial is held in Mayo, we will get off. I'm just going day by day, knowing that some day all this will be just a bad dream and we'll all be together again.*

The Crown would win their argument for the trial to be held in Whitehorse, not Mayo. But Strathdee's hope that a change in venue would guarantee victory in court was just that: a hope.

Preparing to head home, John Molson knew his connection with the case was over. His firm was already out of pocket and Dad would unlikely offer anything more than a promise to share in the proceeds of his ore, once the case was resolved in his favour. That, Molson knew, would not be enough to keep Bull, Housser & Tupper in the game.

Which was too bad, because Molson was fascinated with the case. Priest's story seemed true. Yet Molson had seen where the ore allegedly came from and had to admit it would have taken a Hercules to hand-mine that much rock, break it up into manageable pieces, bag it and load it onto the bed of a toboggan, then make dozens of trips up and out of a steep gulch using a snow machine, before transferring the loads to a pickup truck.

On his last day in Mayo, Molson was flagged down by Strathdee, who wanted to show him one more thing before he left the Yukon. Amidst the stack of documents the RCMP investigator had accumulated was a scrapbook seized during a search of Dad's papers. "This would never be admissible in court, mind you. But I thought you should see it," Strathdee said. Molson opened the book and began flipping the pages, pausing briefly to examine one neatly pasted newspaper or magazine article after another. Each story chronicled a mine heist somewhere in the world.

"Interesting, eh," Strathdee said.

Molson closed the book, grunted in reply and walked away.

CHAPTER 14

A Home Again, of Sorts

A father's pride I used to know,
A mother's love was mine.

B Y DECEMBER 1963, fantasies of escaping to Elsa still fogged my slipping-to-sleep mind and shadowed my daydreams. Schooldays defined dull, my classmates were distant and I wasn't close to caring. When not in school, I walked Pierre and taught him tricks like rollover, dance and "bang, you're dead," none of which Caesar would consider even if you'd tempted him with a live rat. Vona and I played Chinese skip, double dutch, hopscotch, hide-and-seek and Simon Says outdoors, or twenty questions and pick-up sticks indoors, but she always won so I often played alone with my few toy farm animals. Neither of us was into dolls. Mostly, Vona and I were into one library book after another.

On Sunday mornings we reluctantly attended Sunday school at Omi's Mennonite Brethren church at Prince Edward Street and Forty-third Avenue. Most of the congregation was made up of urbanized Mennonites from the Fraser Valley, many from Russian Mennonite communities, giving Omi a tight group of comrades. After half an hour of Sunday school, which Vona and I rolled our eyes at, we joined the adults upstairs. Married couples bunched in the centre pew, single women—mostly widows—sat primly in the left pews, and a sprinkling of single men—mostly widowers—occupied a few pews on the right. Sermons were in German, as were most hymns and almost all the prayers. But there was one hymn sung in English that gripped me like a fist—"How Great Thou Art." Popularized by American gospel baritone George Beverly Shea during his sixty years with the Billy Graham Crusade, the words and music sent shivers down my spine. Mennonites could sing. When the soloist intoned, "I see the stars, I hear the rolling thunder, Thy power throughout the universe displayed," and the congregation soared in response, "Then sings my soooooul, my Saviour God, to Thee," some superpower rippled through every molecule of my being.

Those moments, however, were rare. Most of the time I tried not to nod off. The room was warm, the bodies close and comfortable, and the German language lulled me into a state of deep peace and relaxation. That is, until prayer time. Prayers were a peculiar, and for me dangerous, ritual. Everyone stood, heads bowed and eyes closed, and then spontaneously someone in the congregation who felt so moved told God their troubles. Out loud. Whatever they shared with the Almighty, they shared with all present. When one had finished with the recitation "In Jesus's name, Amen," another began. Sometimes two people started simultaneously and one had to yield. Sometimes men and women broke down while praying and couldn't go on. All of this continued for what seemed like hours. On at least two occasions, I stood so long I became dizzy and fainted, but strong arms picked me up and rushed me outside, where I regained consciousness. Truth is, we attended church just in case not attending was seen as slamming our heart-doors to the Lord. If that happened, Omi said, we'd burn in hell.

One Sunday morning, we woke to find Dad had come home in the middle of the night. Once again, we were all together as an ordinary family (except with one member missing, Caesar). But normal things weren't. Dad paced and stared out the window. His hairline was in rapid retreat. He was out a lot, supposedly to find work. Mom and Dad held hands even in the house and conferred long into the night. Dad proclaimed we weren't the country girls he raised, but had become "citified and sissy-fied." We vehemently denied it and wrestled him to the ground to prove it. To show us what real women were made of, he treated us to a movie at the Orpheum Theatre called *How the West Was Won*. It was a special event: our first movie outing in Vancouver, and far removed from the casual evenings in the Elsa recreation hall where Dad sometimes ran the projector. Vona and I dressed for the occasion, wearing identical black felt skirts ringed with white appliqué poodles and white rabbit fur jackets (all made by Omi and Mom). Mom, arm in arm with Dad, was wrapped in a full-length muskrat coat, and Dad wore a white shirt and tie, a long overcoat and a fedora. These details remain vivid because on the way to the theatre, renowned Vancouver street photographer Foncie Pulice snapped a picture of us. But after the show, which we thought the most rousing, romantic and action-packed epic ever created, we returned to our basement, where Dad had to duck his head whenever he negotiated a doorway and where the dampness of the winter rains seeped through the walls and a constant chill permeated the air.

"Darling, we must move to a real house," I overheard Mom say that night. "One nearby so the girls won't have to change schools and where we can have Caesar.

"Yes, yes," Dad said. "But first I need to find work."

The next week my father announced we were spending our first non-Yukon Christmas with his parents in Revelstoke. No one jumped for joy.

"For Christ's sake, can't I take my family to my folks' without everyone pulling a long face?" was Dad's response.

Visiting my paternal grandparents was a routinely unpleasant duty. No matter where they lived, their rented house was well worn, thin-walled and cramped. This one had only one spare room where Mom and Dad shared a twin bed. Vona and I squeezed into a single cot. I know they loved us because they said so but other than a peck on the cheek, they were stiff and taciturn. Everyone pretended our lives were the same but there were overflowing glances, petty conversations and canyons of silence. Granny was her coolly affectionate and sharply critical self. When we were all together Granddad barely said boo and reddened and sputtered when he managed to utter a few words. I knew he could speak in full sentences and even laugh because I heard him when he and Dad retired to the living room after dinner for smokes, drinks and cowboy records. Granny and Mom, meanwhile, mutely did the kitchen cleanup while Vona and I escaped outdoors to play in the snow and cold with Caesar. He'd turned himself inside out when we arrived. We'd been apart since we left the Yukon, six months earlier.

On the long journey home, without Caesar, it was a new year and while Vona and I whined and pouted in the back seat, Mom predicted 1964 would bring changes for the better. Like all decent fortune tellers, she was half right. Vona and I continued trading stomach flu, fevers, coughs and sore throats back and forth like a pair of caged mice. My grades wavered and dipped and on my mid-term report card the school principal, Mr. W.E. Whatmough, wrote, "With your ability, I feel that Ds should not be a part of your report."

But by the end of January, my parents had found a new home: a good-sized, wood-sided, two-storey gablefront house at 485 East Forty-fourth Avenue, one block west of Fraser Street. With a large front porch and a fresh coat of white paint with red trim, the property's winning features were its three bedrooms and fenced backyard. I could have my own room, in the partially finished basement, and we could bring Caesar home.

But not before there was more cause for celebration. Dad came home one day from his daily forays and proclaimed that he'd found a job paying $500 a month through the BC and Yukon Chamber of Mines. Our rent was $100 so that left plenty to live on. Dad must have thought so, anyway. While Mom shopped in second-hand stores for beds, a kitchen table and chairs, Dad arrived home one day in February driving a shiny red Jaguar Mark II. He said he traded in our former car—an older model black Rover—for the Jag. We all went for a drive that evening, after Vona and I stroked the silver leaping jaguar suspended on the hood. We revelled in the double takes coming our way as we cruised westward toward Jericho Beach.

"See, we are the fox," Dad said as he zigzagged from lane to lane, passing one car after another, "and the others are chickens. Watch how we outfox them."

Dad had a penchant for foreign cars, especially British models, and swore he'd never buy an American car because he hated American "politics." In the Yukon, his first car was an aquamarine Sunbeam-Talbot that spent most of its life up on blocks.

The next day Dad snapped a photo of his three "females," bedecked in matching red dresses, leaning against the Jag. It's the only picture we have of our flirtation with luxury. The following week Dad took the Jag out on the highway "to see what it could do" and rolled it in a ditch. The car was totalled but he walked away without a scratch. "Born to be hanged and won't be drowned," he said when the dust had settled. A yellow Morris Minor convertible that started only when it felt like it replaced the Jag. This was the clunker Mom first attempted to learn how to drive in. After three humiliating lessons from Dad, however, she gave up until a later date. And a new teacher.

Dad took up with a new friend through his work and suddenly we were socializing with a family that was very different from ours—the Fawleys. Of English extraction, Allan Fawley was a consulting mining engineer and geologist who had lived and worked in Tanganyika with his family until four years earlier. His wife Barbara was upper-crust English. With dark hair and a penchant for pearls, she dressed and talked like the Queen. They lived at 1947 West King Edward Avenue, behind a colossal cedar hedge, in a rambling rancher decorated with fine furniture and East African exotica, and had two daughters our age and a much older son whom we seldom saw. The family was friendly in a formal, frosty way, terribly proper and well groomed, and was obviously a class or two above us. But the Fawleys would play crucial roles in Dad and Mom's lives—Allan Fawley would testify in Dad's defense and believe in his innocence until he died, and Barbara Fawley would become and remain Mom's steadfast friend until her own death decades later.

The other family we saw frequently was of another sort entirely. The Klassens lived in semi-rural Abbotsford. Helene Klassen was the daughter of the Rempel family who had given Omi and Mom their first Canadian home some sixteen years earlier. Her sister Katie's family—the Willimses—were buddies also. Both families were large, boisterous and big-hearted broods that we viewed as being fun but far too devout. However, that didn't stop us from spending many days and evenings with them, playing games, eating good, plain food and feeling sort of like we belonged to a group even if their rules—no movies, no dancing, no rock and roll music, no makeup and no fashion—didn't jibe with our sensibilities. Back home, Vona and I were on the cusp of discovering what the sixties had to offer.

In May, Dad returned Caesar to his rightful home and our family was finally complete. Caesar, who had never been neutered, had been known to engage in the occasional, and savage, dogfight, as did most Yukon dogs. We had our trepidations about how he would handle Pierre's presence in his territory. Mercifully, he instinctively acknow-ledged Pierre as part of the pack. Although appalled by the miniature poodle's obsequious behaviour—he'd envelop Pierre's entire head in his open mouth as a warning—he never so much as snapped at him.

When school ended in June, Mom, Vona and I picked strawberries in Richmond so we could buy new clothes for the coming school year. We rose before dawn and caught the city bus to the bottom of Fraser Street, where we jammed into a flatbed truck with rickety sides along with dozens of others and rode to the fields. Most pickers were recent Chinese or East Indian immigrants and attempts at chit-chat on the ride out proved fruitless. We picked rain or shine, paid by the number of flats we filled. Anyone caught eating berries was docked pay. Mom didn't earn that much as she had to take frequent breaks because the bending and squatting hurt her heart, as she put it. But after two weeks of work, I stuffed thirty dollars into my pocket and spent the summer conjuring up images of the fashionable outfits I would buy.

I didn't and still don't know exactly what Dad's work entailed but it frequently took him to Vancouver Island, Terrace and the Yukon for short periods, often accompanied by Allan Fawley. In July, he took Vona with him but instead of taking her with him to Terrace, as he said he would, he boarded her at the Beaverdam 3-Bar Guest Ranch near Clinton in the Cariboo. Vona was in raptures: she slept in a barn, swam in mountain lakes and was given her own horse, a Welsh pony named Bucky that she had to saddle, bridle and feed. It was the closet she ever came to Dad's promise of a horseback trip through the Rockies. When she returned, she was more horse crazy than ever. Vona and I now received an allowance of ten cents a week and even had a TV, which we enjoyed on weekends. For the first while there were only two shows we watched: *The Wonderful World of Disney* and *The Ed Sullivan Show*.

On the last day of August, something happened that no one could have predicted and that would shape our future in ways we'd never imagined. At the age of sixty-one, Omi received a proposal. As her face turned into a beet, she told us a Mr. Wilhelm Teichroeb—a widower at church she'd barely spoken to—had asked for her hand in marriage. Mom beamed, and Vona urged her to accept so that she wouldn't be lonely, but my first reaction was total disgust. At eleven years old, I knew marriage meant intimacy beyond words and I couldn't comprehend my old Omi and some old man engaged in that unspeakable state of affairs.

After receiving the go-ahead from God, Omi accepted and on a sunny October Saturday, Maria Werle and Wilhelm Teichroeb wed. It was a joyous affair, and in the typical Mennonite way, understated. Vona and I, adorned in matching home-sewn turquoise brocade dresses, were the bridesmaids. The reception, prepared by the church ladies, was held in the church basement. "Grandpa," as we quickly came to know him, was a man of few words but non-stop smiles and hugs. One of his few rules was that the greatest sin next to not loving God was wasting food. He owned a house not far from us at 6380 Sophia Street. Gentle, devout and generous, Grandpa had five grown children and fourteen grandchildren and counting. Suddenly, we were part of an enormous and greatly varied family. But four days later we were short one member. Dad was gone. Again. I remember the day. It was October 7, 1964. The next day, in Whitehorse, Dad's first trial began.

CHAPTER 15

"In Geology, Anything Is Possible"

You can thumb your nose at fear,
Wish the horde in hell.
With the haughty you can be
Insolent and bold.

WHAT A DIFFERENCE ELEVEN MONTHS MADE. That was the length of time Dad had between his preliminary hearing and his trial to turn our lives around. With Omi's happy marriage as a good omen, we felt the stirrings of our formerly extinguished hopes—for a true home first, and then the adventures we'd been promised. Dad was doing the best he could. Not only had he secured a decent job, moved us into a real house and retrieved Caesar, he'd found geologists to act as expert witnesses on his behalf while managing to sway a very wealthy someone into bankrolling his legal fees.

But back then all I knew was that Dad was hard at work. Our fledgling Vancouver existence was slowly improving even if it was far removed from the life we'd known or the dream life he'd dangled before us like a candy apple at a fair. Dad's employment had something to do with mining, that much I understood, but what really mattered was that it drew him away for regular three- or four-day stretches, making Mom a more than occasional single parent and us fatherless girls. Today, with the benefit of RCMP files, I figure he was using that time either to stake claims or assay ore samples for his new employer, who became his legal sugar daddy. Now I know that in exchange for footing Dad's legal fees, Dad gave this man several Yukon mineral claims. As it turned out, the claims weren't worth the airfare from Vancouver to Whitehorse.

All of this became clear when Library and Archives Canada sent me the voluminous files amassed by the Mounties during their two-year investigation. Even with numerous pages withheld and many names blacked out, enough information survives to sketch out the essential facts. The money man Dad worked for was Robert Campbell, a wealthy Vancouver businessman who owned Campbell-Bennett Construction. But Campbell also dabbled in mining properties and had formed a second company called Colonial Mines Ltd.

Smooth and savvy discourse was Dad's forte and he must have spoken like Shakespeare to court Campbell, because after showing ore samples from his shipment to Campbell's geologist, Allan Fawley, Dad and Campbell struck a remarkable deal. Besides paying him a working wage of $500 a month, even during the trial, Campbell covered all of Dad's legal costs. In exchange, Dad would give Campbell the Moon claims as well as $50,000 cash, even though on another document he'd promised the Moon to Poncho. With one proviso, of course: that Dad be found not guilty and his ownership of the ore be beyond dispute.

Dad's tales of treasure proved irresistible to Campbell. He soon flew Dad to the Yukon to stake more claims close to the Moon. But while Dad may have been an adept assayer, he was no geologist. As an amateur prospector, his luck was no better than that of the tens of thousands of grubstakers who arrived during the Klondike

Gold Rush, most of whom returned home ruined. The Mounties learned of Dad's new flurry of prospecting from Gordon McIntyre, who as Mayo Mining District's mine recorder had met Dad when he originally purchased the Moon claims, two years earlier "Priest has staked, along with two native men—Tommy Moses and Jimmy Lucas of Mayo—a total of 20 claims which he recorded on 15 June 1964 in the Mayo Mining District office," Constable Lauren McKiel wrote in an RCMP memo.

As Dad coordinated the staking and registering of likely worthless claims in Campbell's name, he also pursued geological experts to testify on his behalf. He already had Allan Fawley, who accompanied Dad to the American Smelting and Refining Co. (ASARCO) in Montana in January 1964 to collect samples for Fawley to analyze in preparation for his testimony. It would be the last time that Dad, Fawley or anyone else would lay eyes on the shipment.

The following month, ASARCO processed the ore, which was registered to Alpine Gold and Silver Ltd. The smelting company did not inform Dad or anyone from Alpine before or after the operation. Instead, they notified UKHM and wrote the company a cheque for $125,322.17. Years later, that move would come back to bite both ASARCO and UKHM. Before receiving the cash, UKHM signed a letter of indemnity that essentially absolved the smelter of any responsibility in the event someone later laid claim to the money.

Dad would find out about the smelting some time later and be furious when he did. For the time being, however, he was focused on amassing the best geological experts he could find for his trial. I suspect one was our family friend Angus MacDonald, who had worked extensively in the Keno area and who declined. The other was Charles Jewell Brown, a geologist and adviser to the White Pass and Yukon Route Company, who agreed to testify on Dad's behalf. But it was Fawley who would emerge as the most impressive of Dad's expert witnesses. Dad's letters to these people reveal a man itching for a fight—someone who not only felt he could beat the charges but who drooled at the prospect of humiliating Al Pike and UKHM in the process.

> *My case is going good as hell! Stick around and watch me lick the ass off of United Keno Hill. There's a guy here with 3 million bucks that's going to back me up to beat those bastards, and by golly, I think we are going to make it.*
>
> *Was just wondering what your expenses would be to come up to Mayo and testify for me? With the kind of money behind me now, I'm sure I could cover them...*

In a second letter Dad spelled out just what an expert witness could expect to receive in compensation for his time.

> *I am receiving the full weight of Mr. Campbell's support. He's the head of Canada's second largest construction company, a millionaire three times over, and it's on the advice of his geologist who has examined the ore, that he is backing me.*
>
> *As of last week he has deposited $50,000 with my lawyer and if you have any doubt that your expenses will be covered, I suggest you drop him a line.*
>
> *So that's what it'll be, [name withheld], one hundred dollars per day plus all expenses, and a guarantee of a minimum of five days, or 500 dollars, even if you are only one day away from your business.*

Dad's offer amounted to about $700 per day in today's dollars. He ended his letter saying with the "backing of a man who can buy out United Keno Hill twice a week and once on Sunday," he was not only going to win his case, but would one day see a mine operating on the Moon.

In early October, Dad entered the courtroom in Whitehorse for the first day of what would be a trial lasting more than five weeks. It was a cool, turquoise-sky day and the first snowfall of autumn was just over a week away. A crescent smile flitted across his full lips. Dressed in a white shirt, royal blue tie and soft grey business suit, tailored to flatter his lanky frame, he was the essence of respectability and composure.

By then, he had a new lawyer to replace Molson. Patrick Hogan specialized in corporate law, particularly in the mining sector, and had a solid reputation in Vancouver legal circles. He was not an accomplished litigator but that hadn't prevented Dad and Campbell from hiring him.

Dad and Poncho pled not guilty to four charges: conspiracy to sell stolen silver ore; unlawfully selling silver ore; theft of ore concentrates; and theft of silver precipitates.

By the third day of the Crown's case, which closely paralleled the evidence presented at the preliminary hearing, Dad wrote home that the prosecution looked "far more worried than anyone else." Crown counsel Vic Wylie had good reason to fret. With the trial poised to drag on for weeks, and jurors up against hundreds of pages of geotechnical reports and arcane arguments from duelling experts, Wylie feared jurors might become so mired in methodological quicksand, they wouldn't know a crime if it bit them on the ass. Underscoring the point was Justice Parker's decree that due to the case's unusual complexity, the jury would sit for only four and a half hours a day.

Meanwhile, public sentiment was mounting in Dad and Poncho's favour. One story circulating in northern homes, hotels and bars was that a predecessor of UKHM, Treadwell Yukon Ltd., had waylaid a cartload of valuable ore that Dad happened to stumble upon. And now greedy and powerful UKHM aimed to do Dad and Poncho out of what was rightfully theirs. "There has been a considerable change in thinking amongst the mining inspectors and geologists," Dad wrote

Mom. "The opinion around town is that the ore was obtained over 40 years ago from another property on Keno Hill and dumped on the Moon claims."

One week later, Dad wrote Mom from his room at the Capital Hotel—"kind of expensive, but it keeps me in a good frame of mind"—that he was holding up well as the Crown case dragged interminably on: "I'm not nervous or upset, but cold as a cucumber! It's nowhere near as bad as I thought it would be. The jury is bored and they smile at me when I meet them."

True to form, in the seven letters Dad penned during the course of the trial, not once did he touch on the Crown's case. Mentioning the slew of expert witnesses who swore the ore came from the Elsa mine, or the disturbing volume of mill concentrates and precipitates in the shipment, or the former mill worker who confessed to stealing and selling precipitates to Poncho would have acknowledged that all was not exactly as Dad portrayed.

But he had an exceptional expert witness on his side. Allan Fawley was a founding member of the Geochemical Society, a member of the Canadian Institute of Mining and Metallurgy, and a lifetime member of the Society of Economic Geologists. He had a PhD in geology from Berkeley and a long list of work experience as a consulting mining engineer to augment his academic accomplishments. From his early student days working for the Geological Survey of Canada in Saskatchewan and the Northwest Territories, to employment with various Canadian mining companies including Pioneer Gold Mines, the International Nickel Company and the Freud and Lavaque Mines, to stints overseas working for the Marshall Plan and doing survey work in Africa for the Tanganyika Geological Survey, to various silver, gold and iron mine projects in South America, Fawley had covered an immense range of geographical and geological territory.

Under questioning by Hogan, Fawley told the court how surprised he was when he first saw the ore in question. "I was expecting it to look like underground ore and instead it looked like surface ore," he said. And there were few if any signs of powder burns indicating that the rock had been blasted from the walls of an underground tunnel, he added.

By the end of Fawley's first half-day testimony, Dad wrote, "The jury just love him! The Crown's case has finished on a sour note— both Regehr and Hogan are sure of the outcome… I'm going to make it!!"

Back home, Mom celebrated these exuberant missives, jotting in her Hilroy notebook, "His letters sound very good!"

The next day Fawley told the court that he had briefly inspected both the Elsa mine and the Moon claims and concluded that the presence of silver-rich ore on the Moon could certainly be explained. It could have happened in one of three ways. First, someone decades ago could have mined the rock elsewhere and then for whatever reasons dumped it at the site. Perhaps the miners intended to return one day but didn't. Maybe they didn't realize the value of what they had. Second, thousands of years earlier during the last ice age a glacier could have "rafted" the ore into position. Slowly, as the glacier retreated and its massive icy walls melted, the boulder could have come to rest on the Moon. This phenomenon was well known, Fawley said. Glaciers can carry giant pieces of rock, called "float," some 70 miles. The one problem with this scenario was that—as Crown witness Alexander Smith later rebutted—the northwestern part of the Yukon had not been glaciated.

Fawley's third theory was that the rock could have fallen on the Moon. This scenario would involve ice as well. But the timelines would have been shorter and the events far more dramatic. Instead of the 70-ton chunk rafting or floating into position it would have tumbled into place in a sudden, violent burst of gravitational energy.

Fawley explained, in the simplest terms possible, how this might have happened. The Moon claims lay at the base of a narrow, steep-sided ravine known as Faro Gulch. The ravine's rock walls were pockmarked with crevices. In the spring and summer, accumulated ice and snow in the crevices would melt and be augmented with rainfall. Then in the fall and winter, the water would freeze. This freezing action would exert tremendous pressure on the surrounding rock, widening the crevices ever so slightly, Fawley said. Over time, with repeated thawing and freezing cycles, a portion of the rock wall could have given way and fallen onto the land below. If the rock gave way in the summer when it was soft, Fawley said, it would have shattered into a million pieces. But if the break occurred in winter or early spring when the rock's pores were crammed with ice, making the mass heavy and hard, events would have unfolded very differently.

"That big block could skid down on the snow... without being broken up... particularly if you realize how hard a combination rock and ice is," Fawley said. Voila! Once fallen, the colossal chunk of silver-rich ore would lie there for eons until a sharp and lucky prospector came along. The treasure was there for the taking and, of course, was very, very different geologically from rock surrounding it.

In his cross-examination, Wylie couldn't poke many holes in Fawley's theories. He did, however, cast some doubt on the geologist's integrity. First, Fawley was forced to admit to having a small financial interest in proving Dad had title to the ore. Curiously, Fawley had advised Campbell to purchase the Moon claims before even visiting the site. This raised the possibility that Fawley made his recommendation solely on the ore from the shipment. Fawley conceded that he'd never set foot in the Elsa mine when the Bonanza Stope was being excavated. Therefore, Wylie's questioning implied, the geologist was in a poor position to infer that the bulk of the shipment could not have come from underground but was, instead, surface rock. Fawley also confessed to taking only a cursory look around the Moon, not a detailed geological survey. Finally, Fawley acknowledged that underground rock, in depths of up to 500 feet, could show signs of oxidization. In other words, underground rock could resemble float or surface rock.

Despite these and other admissions, Fawley's testimony stood up remarkably well. As Strathdee later wrote, he gave the court "the impression that in geology anything is possible."

Dad's second expert witness, geologist Charles Jewell Brown, echoed Fawley's theories and bolstered the defense's argument that while the occurrence of a 70-ton lump of rich ore on the Moon claims was improbable, highly unusual and even "unique," it was not impossible.

Finally, it was Dad's turn to speak. He would be on the stand for four days. For Strathdee, who took copious notes during the trial, this was the first time he'd heard Dad's story straight from his mouth. After preliminary questions—When had he started with United Keno Hill Mines? What did he do for the company?—Hogan led the alleged mastermind into the central matters at hand. First, he asked Dad to explain how he acquired the concentrates and precipitates.

In 1951, when Dad began at UKHM, it was common practice for all material left over from assays to be considered "rejects." Dad, however, knew that much of this material had value. So he wrote assistant mine manager Nicholas Gritzak a memo proposing that all material delivered by the mill be returned to the mill when assays were completed. In the same memo, Dad proposed other changes to how the assay office was run, including hiring more staff. Gritzak rejected Dad's requests. From then on, as far as Dad was concerned, everything he'd raised was off the table, including his suggestion that materials delivered to the assay office from the mill be returned.

For the next nine years, a growing pile of concentrates and precipitates accumulated at the assay office dump, a dirt-like pile outside the back window. Then, in 1960, a new directive came from mill superintendent Arthur Wall saying the office should place all materials left over from assays into buckets that would periodically be picked up and returned to the mill. But after a full year passed without any pickup, Dad added a ton of accumulated rejects to the stack outside. These, Dad said, comprised what he later gathered up and added to the ore shipment.

Defense witnesses Jerry Pope and Erik Nielsen, both garbage truck swampers for UKHM, testified that they took many reject samples off to Elsa's general garbage dump, bolstering Dad's point that UKHM couldn't care less about them.

Then Dad told the court how he'd discovered ore on the Moon. He first met the owner of the Moon claims in 1958 or 1959, when John Strebchuk brought him ore samples to analyze. The ore assayed at a low 2 to 20 ounces of silver per ton, but its composition of siderite, tetrahedrite and galena piqued Dad's curiosity. In June 1961, Dad happened to be near the Moon claims and decided to take a brief look. He discovered an old pile of ore behind Strebchuk's cabin and pocketed a few pieces for analysis. To his gleeful astonishment, the assays ranged between 150 and 6,000 ounces of silver per ton.

When Dad told Poncho what he'd found, the two made a verbal agreement to split whatever they mined on the Moon. The two men returned to the claims and after a thorough inspection came upon a massive clod of silver-rich rock in one confined space. They decided then that they would buy the claims from Strebchuk but not immediately. Over the rest of the summer of 1961, the two broke up the rock with sledgehammers, picks and crowbars and covered the mound of broken pieces with moss and brush. The claims were so remote no one saw them and no one reported this activity to Strebchuk. Later that same year, Dad told Strebchuk, who had evidently not been on his claims for a while, that he wanted to buy them. Strebchuk's price was $5,000. Dad held off. In June the following year, Strebchuk sold Dad the Moon claims for $1,000.

By then, Dad testified, he and Poncho had amassed 70 tons of ore averaging 2,230 ounces of silver per ton. And Poncho had targeted the Duncan Creek Road loading site as the closest unstaked ground where the ore could be stored.

But as Dad later learned, Poncho had ideas of his own. That July, Dad testified, Poncho flew to Vancouver to ask Aaro Aho for money to buy equipment and build a road out to the Moon so the ore could be trucked to the Duncan Creek site. Previously, Aho had staked a number of new claims close to the Moon group. Later, against Dad's explicit instructions, Poncho took Aho to the Moon claims. When Dad found out that Aho had been on the Moon, he demanded that Poncho sever all business ties with him.

Poncho failed to build the road, so Dad considered other ways to get the ore out. He settled on a Ski-Doo and tow toboggan. The tow toboggan, he added, had a protective coating of red fibreglass on its underside to avoid abrasion under the weight of all that rock. Dad moved the ore over numerous trips during his holidays in April 1963, leaving it at a temporary spot on nearby Hanson Lake Road. During the following month, after the roads were plowed, Dad and Poncho moved the ore by truck to the Duncan Creek site, where it sat until it was shipped to the smelter. In all, the two men made 130 trips to transport the ore.

That same month, Dad said, he and Poncho formed a new company—Alpine Gold and Silver Mines Ltd.—in order to avoid paying a large amount of income tax on the shipment. Just prior to shipping, he drove to the assay office and loaded twenty-seven sacks of rejects, concentrates and precipitates from the dump into his truck. Then he drove the load back to the Duncan Creek site and chucked the contents onto the ore.

But Poncho hit Dad with another unwelcome surprise. In the assay office attic, he showed Dad ten bags filled with precipitates from the mill. "I came up here to store some storm windows and found this," Dad recalled Poncho saying. "Don't know where it came from. How be we ship it with the rest of the ore?" Dad said he refused. He told Poncho to return the bags to the mill and throw the contents in with raw ore so it would be fed back to the mill and recovered. He watched Poncho drive to the mill and throw a sack or two into the bin. Then Dad turned around and left. The inference from Dad's testimony was that if Poncho had not dumped all the bags into the bin but instead added the rest to the ore shipment, he'd done so against Dad's will.

Throughout the last stages of waiting for the pickup, Dad said he kept talk of the shipment as quiet as possible. By doing so, he believed that Aho would let his claims near the Moon lapse and Dad could then scoop them up.

With that, Hogan sat down and Wylie stood up. Dad remained calm through much of the early cross-examination—When exactly did he start saving assay precipitates? Who had known about the ore shipment, and when? But he got decidedly agitated when Wylie suggested the ore could not possibly have come from the Moon. As Strathdee recalled, "He became very excited at this point and said it was his opinion that the RCMP and UKHM were in a conspiracy to take his ore."

Dad also became angry when Wylie asked about Aho's testimony concerning his business arrangements with Poncho. Dad called Aho's testimony "a pack of lies" and said Aho and his associates were after his ore.

Wylie then asked Dad how the precipitates happened to be in the ore. At first, Dad said, he believed Poncho had followed his instructions and returned all the precipitates to the mill, adding that he even saw evidence of this the next day when the assays of mill samples showed a spike in silver. The spike was consistent with silver-rich precipitates being mixed in with the ore. Only much later, Dad said, did he learn that Siegfried Haina was stealing precipitate material and storing it in the attic, and that Poncho intended to steal from Haina what Haina had stolen from the mill. These were damning words that Henry Regehr did nothing to counter, as he and Poncho had decided Poncho would not speak in his own defense.

As for the mysterious letter "M" in the documents, Dad said the P stood for Poncho (Bobcik's nickname) and the G for Gerry. The M, Dad explained, stood for Toronto lawyer Richard Irwin Martin. But why would Bobcik, who had written the notations and was known as a "definite first name user," use first initials in two cases and a last initial in another? Dad could not explain. This was the only reference to M in the trial and the only attempt by Wylie to draw Martin Swizinski into the crime. If Swizinski had been involved, Dad wasn't saying.

After Dad's testimony—the highlight of the lengthy trial—Hogan rose to give his closing arguments. Dad, he said, had established that the ore came from the Moon claims. If anyone's actions should be questioned it was those of the RCMP, UKHM and ASARCO. During their watch, Hogan pointed out, the prime exhibit in the case—the ore shipment—had been smelted and may as well have disappeared.

Dad's demeanour in the witness stand, Hogan continued, was one of "candor, forthrightness and fearlessness—that of a man who is telling the truth. He stood for four and a half hours giving evidence almost without prompting or questioning from me. And searching cross-examination for two and half days did not weaken him."

Judge John Parker, the man who tried and sentenced my father, took a classist and colonial approach to justice. Born in Essex, England, and educated at the Law Society of Upper Canada's Osgoode Hall, he answered the call of the north and spent fourteen years in the Northwest Territories as a criminal lawyer before being appointed to the Yukon judiciary in 1958. Coincidentally, he'd lost his first prosecution case early in his career to Vancouver lawyer Angelo Branca, who would go on to briefly represent Dad.

After five weeks of complex, conflicting testimony, Judge Parker instructed jurors on the difficult questions before them. Had Dad and Bobcik conspired to sell a substance containing silver, which they failed to prove they owned? Had they conspired to sell precipitates that Haina had admitted stealing? Had the two conspired to sell precipitates "unlawfully taken" by Priest during his assaying duties? Had they done the same with any concentrates Dad kept? Lastly, and this went to the heart of the criminal proceedings that pitted a Canadian mining giant against two former employees, was the ore from the Elsa mine or from the Moon?

With that, the six jurors retired to deliberate. Twenty-eight hours ticked by before the jury returned unable to agree on the first charge of conspiring to sell silver. On the second charge, that the accused had stolen mill concentrates, the jury found Dad and Poncho not guilty. Both men, they concluded, had "an honest belief" that an assay office custom allowed them to keep concentrates from the assay process. On the third charge, that the two men had stolen mill precipitates, the jury found Bobcik guilty and Dad not guilty. The last charge, whether the two had attempted to sell stolen silver ore to the smelter, turned on the same issue as the first. The jury had to determine where the ore originated. Sent away for further deliberation, they returned more than two hours later, still deadlocked.

The longest criminal proceeding in the Yukon to date had ended in a hung jury. Bobcik returned to jail to await sentencing for his conviction. Dad was free. He phoned Mom that night—damn the expense!—his relief giving way to relish. When she put down the phone, Mom scribbled at the bottom of her notebook "Hurrah! Victory!" Turn the page over though and there's an addendum—"But not quite."

As he boarded the Canadian Pacific Douglas DC-6B home, Dad knew his war was far from won. The RCMP and the Crown would never give up now, not after the time and money they'd invested, and with Falconbridge breathing down their necks. At best, Dad had gained—for himself and for us—some precious free time.

CHAPTER 16

One Slippery Slope

Was I not born to walk in scorn where others walk in pride?

Not a single charge against my father had stuck. After more than a year of exhaustive legwork on the part of the Mounties, a record-setting preliminary hearing plus one of the lengthiest criminal trials in Yukon history, Dad was once again out on bail. The Crown was not amused.

On an early Monday morning, in January 1965, an exasperated George Strathdee placed a fresh sheet of paper between the rollers of his Underwood typewriter and with a few slaps of the return bar began hammering away at the black keys. "It would be advantageous if a conference were held as soon as possible between Crown Counsel Wylie, Constable McKiel and myself with a view to reviewing the evidence produced at the recent trial in an attempt to eliminate all absolutely non-essential witnesses and also to strengthen any weak points in the Crown's case," Strathdee wrote.

As lead on the file, Strathdee realized how confounding the evidence and testimony had been. If another jury had to grapple with the same snakepit of perplexing postulations about the composition of ore and the finer points of underground versus above ground oxidization, Dad would surely walk, and hundreds of thousands of dollars in taxpayer-funded investigation and trial costs would swirl down the drain. The costs were already nearing double what the damn shipment was worth.

Strathdee and McKiel had wanted to show how ore from the Elsa mine was stolen and by whom. But without a single eyewitness to corroborate the theft, they'd failed. Too many mineworkers (and jurors for that matter) disdained UKHM and its parent company, Falconbridge. Then the Crown's efforts to prove that such rich ore could not have come from the Moon had also failed. The Crown's only victory was that Bobcik was found guilty of one charge pertaining not to the raw ore, but to the precipitates stolen from the mill.

Particularly galling to Strathdee, who'd always viewed Dad's tale of hand-mining and hauling the ore off the Moon claims as an audacious lie, was that the jury had thought his fabrication plausible. Somehow a new jury had to be convinced that his story was about as real as Santa's ninth reindeer. But how? After knocking their heads together, Strathdee, McKiel and Wylie decided that while the defense was certain to follow a similar script during the retrial, the Crown's strategy would differ.

In a land of ice, snow, rock and few roads, transportation has always been troublesome. The Eskimo, as the Inuit were then called, used dogs to pull sleds with runners made of whalebones or even frozen fish or caribou skins. Friction was reduced further by spitting on the runners, coating them in a thin sheen of ice. With the arrival of the Ski-Doo in 1959, the power of a gas-fired engine changed everything. Originally, the Quebec invention was called a Ski-Dog but a typo at the patent office was never corrected. Quaintly, it was also dubbed an "autoboggan" for a time. Despite its remarkable ability to whiz people and goods over deep snow, relying on such a machine to haul 70 tons of raw ore over multiple trips was another matter. The rock would need to be loaded on something strong and secure and dragged behind. Dad attached a toboggan behind his Ski-Doo. But not just any wooden toboggan. Anticipating extreme wear on the toboggan's undersurface from the weight of the ore, Dad had told the court he'd ordered a fibreglass coating be applied to the bottom. It sounded impressive, as fibreglass was a relatively new product that was beginning to gain widespread use in the 1950s for boat hull and sports car construction. As a result, the toboggan had held up well. But after all that hauling, Dad explained, the red fibreglass coating had completely worn off.

The Devil, they say, is in the details. And so for several weeks in the between-trial period Strathdee became obsessed with what had or had not been on the bottom of Dad's specially ordered toboggan. Did he indeed have the bottom coated with fibreglass? Could every bit of the coating have totally worn off after repeated ore hauls, as Dad claimed? It was a humbling conclusion to come to, but the final outcome of the case could very well hinge on the particulars of a toboggan, rather than on the expertise of some of the brightest minds in Canadian geological and mineral sciences.

Strathdee also realized they somehow had to disprove Dad's claim that it was customary for assayers to keep concentrates and precipitates brought to the assay office from the mill. The jury had concluded that Dad and Poncho had done nothing wrong by including hundreds of pounds of such material in their ore shipment.

While Dad had gained only a reprieve, it was hard to tell when he arrived home after the first trial that the prospect of a second one loomed over his head. "To the victor go the spoils," Dad said teasingly between forkfuls of homemade chocolate cake. Still children more focused on dreams than plans, we longed for what we had previously taken for granted: a permanent home with a contented mother and father. That I was loved was never in doubt. I can't speak for Vona, though, who frequently appeared miffed at my mere existence, especially when Dad was around.

That evening after the dishes were done, Dad allowed Vona and me to watch two hours of TV while he and Mom took Caesar for a long walk. They weren't home by bedtime and the next morning we knew the troubles that had struck our small family like a Biblical plague ever since we left Elsa were far from over. Mom had little to say and Dad spent hours ruminating at the kitchen table, nursing a cup of cold coffee and rolling one smoke after another, each one burning itself out in the ashtray. A heaviness settled on our household like suffocating layers of snow and Mom grew ever more withdrawn. Over the coming years, the silent treatment would become her main coping strategy, to the point where, with tears running down her face, she would deny anything was wrong.

Dad's sombre mood didn't last long and in the afternoon he said that since our piano was still in storage, we could choose another instrument to learn. One block away, on Fraser Street, was a small music studio where we could take lessons. I chose the acoustic guitar and Vona chose a full-sized piano accordion with thirty-seven treble keys and ninety-six bass keys. The monstrous squeezebox was so heavy she had to sit down to play, but being strong and already proficient on the piano, she mastered it within six months and impressed us with her finger-whizzing rendition of "Flight of the Bumble Bee." My apprenticeship on the guitar went slower but within a few months I could strum several chords well enough to accompany myself on songs such as "If I Had a Hammer" and "500 Miles." My performances, though, stayed between me and Caesar down in my basement bedroom. Not one to be left out, Mom found a fine bowl-backed mandolin in a pawnshop, took out a library book and taught herself to play Russian folk songs such as "Kalinka" and "Little Birch Tree."

Later, Dad asked about our grades and if we'd made any friends. By grade six, I'd eliminated all Ds and my marks were a mix of C-pluses and Bs. No one bothered to mention, however, that Vona and I were still regularly missing class due to chronic colds, sore throats and stomach flu. I was a short, skinny pipsqueak with shadows under my eyes and two long chestnut-brown braids drooping down my back. Vona was short too, but muscular, and had straight dark brown hair cut in a bob just below her ears. She bit her nails and suffered from persistent eczema. Neither of us had friends worth mentioning, certainly no one we brought home.

However, we did have a new cousin whom we were anxious for Dad to meet. While he'd been away, we'd spent a lot of time over at Omi and Grandpa's and met several members of our new extended family. We would get to know a few quite well over the coming years. Many of Grandpa's grown children and their families were a collection of sullen, serious and boring religious devotees, people Dad referred to as "brainwashed dullards." While they were perfectly polite, some broadcast low-level waves of resentment at our parachute entree into their family. Who were we to call their father "Dad" and their Granddad "Grandpa" and to drop into his home whenever we pleased? Uncle Johnny, Grandpa's youngest son, and his wife, Aunt Maxine, were the exception. Kind, funny and welcoming, they treated us like family from day one. Fortunately, most of the others lived out of town.

Cousin Ricky Nelson was also made from different matter. The only child of Auntie Ann (Grandpa's youngest daughter) and her husband, Uncle Ken, Ricky was thrilled to have two slightly younger "sisters" in his life. His family lived in a small, square stucco house across the lane from Omi and Grandpa's craftsman bungalow. Tall, blonde, winsome Ann was the looker in the Teichroeb family and her husband was a handsome contrasting match. Dark-eyed, dark-haired and a natural charmer, Uncle Ken worked as a Brown Bros. real estate agent. Ricky was a dreamy blend of the two. Only better. With his dark hair, dark eyes and square jaw, he could easily have doubled for his namesake, pop singer and teen idol Ricky Nelson.

Within a month, we were spending nearly every weekend together, playing board games indoors and chase games outside, often at our house or Omi's. Sadly, Ricky's mom had multiple sclerosis and craved rest, peace and quiet, so we rarely played at his house. Relentlessly good-natured and easygoing, Ricky was the antidote to Vona's and my increasingly divergent and occasionally bristly dealings. Vona craved Dad's roughhouse play, and Ricky was someone she could tease, play practical jokes on and "fight" with. When Dad met Ricky, he liked him as much as we did and enchanted him with legends of the north and outdoor survival stories such as a city kid had never heard. Ricky's presence lightened what was becoming an oppressive home atmosphere. He also loved being with us and especially admired Mom, whom he viewed as a cultured and exotic European lady.

In February, Mom and Dad went to help Granny and Granddad move, this time from Revelstoke to Kimberley. Meanwhile, we stayed with Omi and Grandpa, which meant we were extremely well fed and saw Ricky nearly every day. But they were gone only a week and when they returned Dad prepared to return to the Yukon. Again. We were told this trip north would be Dad's last. On March 1, 1965, Mom wrote in her notebook: "Gerry left to fly to Whitehorse. Another 'Battle'—this time I hope there will be a decision!"

Blue skies and warm weather marked the beginning of the trial but one week later the rain left puddles that turned to ice. A day later snow was falling. As Vic Wylie led the Crown witnesses through their testimony for the second time, George Strathdee sensed a change. Wylie had eliminated nine Crown witnesses—five who worked for the White Pass trucking company, three police investigators on the periphery of the case and one expert geological witness. Paring down the number of witnesses meant a speedier trial. Wylie also took a different tack in his questioning, placing more emphasis on the damning materials in the shipment—the concentrates and precipitates.

As the last of the Crown witnesses' testimonies drew near, Strathdee wrote: "The case appears to be reaching the jury in a much cleaner manner, making the Crown's case appear stronger than before."

If Dad saw things that way, he wasn't saying. A few days into the case, he wrote home, "There's been no new evidence entered and there will be 5 or 6 fewer Crown witnesses. The lawyers feel the case is won and the Crown is just going through the motions to save face. So!! Keep your spirit's up!! The chances are all for us!!"

On the eve of taking the stand in his own defense, Dad expressed surprise at the shortened Crown case, which had "come to a close rather suddenly. Our standing with the jury is high and will climb from now on in. This won't last more than 10 days at most and then I'll be home."

Three days later, he was under cross-examination. "Wylie is going at me hammer and tongs—but getting nowhere," Dad wrote. "They try to twist and turn my evidence every which way but it still comes out the same as before."

But Wylie's cross-examination was calculated precisely to prompt Dad to reveal more than he'd divulged in the first trial. The more details Dad provided on precisely how he'd hauled that ore off the Moon claims the better. The more details he volunteered on the customary practices of the UKHM assay office the better too.

The Crown's list of rebuttal witnesses differed from the first time around too, and showed how much Wylie and the police had learned from their past mistakes. In the first trial, the prosecution had placed great importance on the testimony and credentials of expert witnesses. To counter Fawley's testimony, for example, Wylie had called no fewer than three mineralogical experts. Yet the seemingly authoritative words of Alexander Smith, Len H. Green and Maurice Haycock, each one a PhD, had meant little to jury members, who were either not impressed or so confused they couldn't render a verdict.

This time round, Wylie didn't call one geologist or mineralogist to rebut Fawley's testimony. Instead, he kept the jury focused squarely on Dad's story. If jury members entered their deliberations with Dad's flawed character foremost in their minds as opposed to the conflicting statements of experts, Wylie predicted a guilty verdict was certain.

From the moment he began at UKHM, Dad said, he was aware that valuable concentrates and precipitates brought to the assay office from the mill were later sent to the dump as rejects. He described how he had asked UKHM general manager Brodie Hicks whether he could keep these rejects and he was told yes. Later, assistant mine manager Nicholas Gritzak refused to endorse the new set of assay office instructions Dad had prepared and shown him. The instructions allegedly included a recommendation that assay rejects go back to the mill. Dad repeated what he said at the first trial: that he took Gritzak's refusal as a tacit "yes" that he could hold onto anything delivered to the assay office.

Then former UKHM general manager Brodie Hicks was called to the stand. By 1965, Hicks had long left the Yukon to work for Faraday Uranium Mines in Ontario. "The normal procedure with respect to assay office rejects is that they are collected from time to time... by the surface maintenance department and returned to the normal mill circuit," Hicks testified. "I have no recollection whatsoever of having discussed the matter with Mr. Priest at any time. Should I have done so, I consider it most unlikely that I would have authorized any departure from this standard procedure."

Next Nicholas Gritzak took the stand. Strathdee and McKiel had tracked down Gritzak in Ontario, as they had Hicks. Neither man had testified in the first trial. "I cannot recall Priest ever coming to me with a set of assay office instructions for authorization. He would have no reason to do this, since he had complete authority in the internal organization and operation of his department," Gritzak said.

"It was normal practice that the assay rejects were returned to the mill bin. However, there were no formal instructions to this effect."

Years later, when discussing Dad's case with his former assay office assistant, George Duerksen, I learned that it was indeed common for concentrates and precipitates used in the assay process to simply be dumped outside. No one from the mill ever picked them up. In other words, security was shoddy at best. But shoddy or not, Dad had testified that it was "accepted practice" for him to keep the concentrates and precipitates, which it was not.

The final two rebuttal witnesses flew to Whitehorse from Winnipeg. Neither man had testified in the first trial either. Donald Goodman worked for Bendik Industries Ltd., the company that had made Dad's tow toboggan. Karl Robinson was president and manager of Sydney I. Robinson Ltd., the company that sold Dad his toboggan. Robinson produced receipts showing Dad's purchase of the toboggan, along with a pair of Ojibway snowshoes and snowshoe harnesses, for a total of $146. Goodman identified the 12-foot long oak toboggan made by his shop. Because of oak's oily surface, any fibreglass applied would "not likely remain," Goodman said. For that reason, no toboggans made by the company had fibreglass applications. Earlier, Strathdee and McKiel, who had thoroughly inspected the toboggan, had testified that it "was little worn and showed no signs of ever being fibreglassed."

In the legal world, testifying on one's own behalf is risky. While a defendant may feel in control when questioned by his own lawyer, when the prosecutor gets his go, he may feel otherwise. The testimony from the rebuttal witnesses had gouged a big hole in Dad's account of hauling 70 tons of raw ore over rugged terrain on the deck of a smoothly gliding toboggan.

No testimony, however, could erode Dad's confidence, which seemed impervious to selected parts of reality. Shortly before the end of the trial, Bob Cathro ducked into the Taku Hotel to have a drink with Al Archer. The two men were chatting over beers at the crowded bar when a patron beside them downed the last of his whiskey, dropped some change on the counter and left. Just then Dad walked in. As he approached the two UKHM employees, he stopped in his tracks.

"Hey," Dad said, pointing at the loose change, "I don't like to see this. Silver, just lying around? Not good."

On March 26, Dad wrote home for the second last time during the trial, which was fast approaching its conclusion. "We are confident it will be no less than a hung jury again, with every chance of a not guilty verdict," he began. "Wylie and UKHM have fought this case in the dirtiest fashion possible—Parker is showing his prejudice now and no doubt will give a convicting summation again, but the jury isn't going to buy it."

The following week, Judge Parker delivered his instructions to the five-man, one-woman jury. The charges against both men had been reduced to three: conspiring to sell stolen goods—in this case a "precious metal" containing silver; selling precipitates; and unlawfully selling ore containing silver. After nearly three hours of deliberation, the jurors found both men guilty on the first count. Sent back to consider the other two, the jurors returned late in the afternoon to pronounce Dad and Poncho both guilty.

That evening, long after we were in bed, Dad phoned Mom. In her notebook, she jotted: "He lost! After all this—found guilty!"

The next morning, April 1, a now shaken convict wrote his last letter home. "My Darling, in a couple of hours I will appear in court to be sentenced. It will not be a heavy sentence, as the Crown does not want me to appeal. We don't know what happened here—our case was stronger than before. But at the end, the judge directed the jury to convict."

In a bid for mercy, Hogan asked Judge Parker to consider his client's clean record and that he was the sole supporter of an invalid wife and two young children. He also pointed out that Dad had suffered nearly two years of "apprehensive concern" during the lengthy hearing and two trials and asked for a suspended sentence. Parker was unmoved. "I do not make light of the burden of a prison sentence, it could weigh heavily on these two men," the judge responded. "In Priest's case the burden will be on his wife and two children who will inevitably suffer. Unfortunately, this is frequently the case.

"However, I cannot overlook the fact that the amount involved here was very substantial. It is true that the accused have not, in fact, benefitted at all as a result. Priest held a position of some responsibility with United Keno Hill Mines… his obligations were higher than Bobcik's… Mr. Priest took an extraordinary attitude toward life and toward people… a bitter, cynical attitude which I hope he will be able to put behind him."

And then Judge Parker sentenced Dad, aged thirty six, to four years imprisonment. Bobcik, thirty-two, received three years less the four months he'd already served. Dad would begin doing time at Oakalla Prison Farm, one of British Columbia's roughest jails.

With the swift return of a guilty verdict, Mounties McKiel and Strathdee sensed that public sentiment had shifted against the two criminals. With that change, they felt that maybe someone somewhere would finger the third man they knew existed.

"I do not feel that we should relent in our efforts toward definitely establishing the third party," McKiel wrote in a memo following the convictions. "Many persons interviewed stated that they knew nothing about the activities of Priest and Bobcik, but appeared to be concealing the truth of their actual knowledge. It is hoped to re-interview these persons and gain further information toward definitively ascertaining the third party involved… neither Priest or Bobcik have any intention of implicating anyone else in this case."

But McKiel's hopes were never realized. No one but Poncho and Dad would ever do time for the crime.

CHAPTER 17

In the Jailhouse Now

Fate has written a tragedy;
its name is "The Human Heart."
The Theatre is the House of Life;
Woman plays the mummer's part;
The Devil enters the prompter's box
and the play is ready to start.

WHETHER OR NOT HE KNOWS, is prepared or cares a whit, a father holds his daughters' hearts in his hands. Dad, like many men, had steady, strong and tender hands when we were young, but as Vona stampeded and I tiptoed toward womanhood, his hands trembled, became rough and, at times—there is no other word for it—cruel. It didn't help that we were raised in a remote northern hamlet in the fifties—an era of gullibility, tranquility and family-focused cohesion. And that we came of age in a west coast city at the height of the sixties—*the* decade of sex, drugs and rock and roll. And rebellion. Another knock against us was that the year Vona and I turned thirteen and twelve respectively, Dad was in the slammer.

And what a slam dunk of a slammer it was. Oakalla Prison Farm, built in 1912, achieved notoriety as a full-service penal colony. Full-service meant nearly anyone could be incarcerated there: innocent men and women awaiting trial, convicted murderers and child molesters, pimps, rapists, armed robbers, petty thieves and white-collar criminals. (In the scheme of things, my father was a blue-collar criminal.) A monstrous brick Dickensian gaol, Oakalla boasted a reputation for inmate brutality and prison escapes. Originally built to house a maximum of 484 prisoners, its population bulged to nearly 1,300 by the mid-sixties. As former Oakalla guard Earl Andersen wrote in his book *A Hard Place to Do Time: The Story of Oakalla Prison, 1912–1991*, despite sweeping reforms in the fifties, Oakalla continued to be "vastly overcrowded and infested with misery. Destruction of prison property was equaled only by the destruction of human lives."

Life in a 6 × 8 concrete cell was not living but existing for Dad, as it was for many. For someone whose elbows felt grazed when he walked down a city street and whose signature anthem was "Don't Fence Me In," it must have been hell. His finely penned dispatches of witticisms, hopes and extravagant promises were squeezed between rivers of rancour and worry. His main complaint was oppressive boredom and loneliness. Other inmates were "a bunch of up turned glasses" and deliberately kept to themselves, as he did, especially avoiding his former "bosom buddy" and accomplice Poncho.

April 9, 1965

Please excuse this novel stationery! As with everything else in my new life, I find there are regulations for things I never dreamed of! How are you and the children? Not taking it too hard?...
Am still getting a kick out of Parker's words when he sentenced

me—said that due to some incident in my early life or marriage, I had become a bitter and cynical person and that I needed to establish a happier outlook on my fellow man!! Just wait and see how a few years in prison will improve my outlook!

One outgoing, single-page letter a week, on narrow-ruled penitentiary stationery with Oakalla's communication regulations on the back, was all prisoners were allowed. They could receive unlimited incoming mail—all if it, of course, censored. And write him Vona and I did, every week, as we were not permitted to visit, being under the age of eighteen. He wrote almost every weekly letter to Mom, occasionally reserving part of the page for notes to Vona and me. He was also allowed only one visit a month, but Dad discouraged Mom from seeing him. "I don't want you coming out to this grubby hole again." When she did visit, they communicated by speakerphone through a thick plate-glass window.

By now, Vona and I knew the truth. At least the version circulating at the time: Dad had lost his trial but he "didn't steal anything, hurt anyone or threaten anyone." So while he was behind bars now, he'd be freed when his appeal bail was granted and then a new trial would right all the former wrongs and he'd subsequently receive tons of money, allowing us to finally move to that paradisiacal home in the country. But not before he and Vona crossed the Rockies on horseback, and he and I explored Disneyland, although I sensed a definite waning of enthusiasm for the Magic Kingdom. In one letter, he asked if I wouldn't rather canoe down the Stewart and Yukon Rivers instead: "The same canoe trip I took while you were being born!" I immediately changed my mind and wanted to cross the Rockies too. When he responded that he'd take us both, Vona declared that first he'd have to take her *alone* as he'd originally promised. In yet another letter, he said we'd buy a boat and cruise the world's oceans—"that should please your mother!"

Competing for Dad's love and approval became a full-time job. Good marks were always prime ammunition. Getting a C in anything was unacceptable. But the real zingers were recurrent avowals that, at heart, we were still his country-loving, bush-savvy girls and hadn't been tainted by "that miserable city." In April, I sent him a three-page letter peppered with endearments, a few *Mad* magazine jokes (such as "Support Mental Illness: Join the Klu Klux Klan" and "Save Water– Shower with your Steady") and a bucolic drawing of our future home: a two-storey log house, Mom parting the curtains at the window, cows in the corral, chickens and goats running free with Caesar and Pierre, Dad and I holding hands in the front garden and Vona riding her horse high on a hill.

In May, Vona launched a formidable salvo.

Dear Pal,
I really love you and every time I think of you behind bars I nearly cry. But I stop myself because a girl who wants to go out in the Rockies with the best horseman in the world shouldn't cry like a baby. But it's pretty hard not to, because I love you so much.

A month later I dispatched the following volley:

Dear Pappy,
At school they had sports day and I came third in running! Vona didn't win anything. Ha-Ha!

Then Vona delivered the final and winning shot.

Dear Pal,
I still sleep with your picture and your two letters under my pillow. I love you more than all the horses in the world and you know how much I love horses!

As Judge Parker had poignantly predicted, Dad wasn't suffering solo. Like a stone plopped in a pond, his misery rippled out and collided with his parents, his younger brother Ronnie, and Omi and Grandpa. Most grievously, it threatened to drown his daughters—and his wife, who, with a scared and faltering heart, had to manage a house, two dogs and two antsy teenage girls, and deal with disapproving in-laws, a new level of poverty and a husband in the hoosegow. The immediate effect was the bottoming out of our bottom line. Within two weeks of his sentencing, the cheques from Campbell ceased. Within four weeks, Judge Parker denied his application for appeal bail. Increasingly dissatisfied with his lawyer, Patrick Hogan, Dad raged and attempted to console us from his cage:

May 4, 1965

I don't know what's become of this case of mine—I've come to the conclusion that I can't believe much of what Hogan says. I don't think that Hogan or any other lawyer can really do anything. They'll do exactly what they want.

Please honey, watch your health and don't work. You didn't look too well when you came to see me the other week. I know you won't have much money but enough to scrape by on. You know I'm still sure I'll win in the long run and we'll come out way ahead! The children are on the right road now and won't be affected to any great extent by this whole business. We'll lick this wicked world yet!

I'm sure you are enjoying this in a rather perverse fashion. Now you can sit in the evenings with your mandolin and sing those sad, melancholy Russian songs!

Enjoyment was not on Mom's menu. Macaroni and cheese was. At least it wasn't Kraft dinner, but start-from-scratch white sauce with orange cheddar, the only kind available. On a good week we mixed in a can of tuna or cut up a couple of wieners. We'd already received our first visit from a social worker and overnight we slid from lower middle class to welfare class. Mom's cheeks flamed as she explained why she couldn't go out and get a job. She tired easily, slept only with the aid of pills and suffered shortness of breath with little exertion. As she would say more and more, "My heart hurts." In more ways than one. For Vona and I being on welfare meant monotonous weekday meals, more weekend feasts at Omi's and, if we wanted new clothes, more strawberry picking, bean picking and babysitting. Our choice retailers were the downtown Army and Navy outlet or Honest Nat's Department Store at Forty-eighth and Fraser. Another source of income for me was my hair. I had been growing it since we left Elsa and by 1965 it touched the small of my back. Later that year Mom cut it just above my shoulders and I sold my brown strands to a wig maker for ten dollars.

Behind bars, Dad made ineffectual attempts to decrease our expenses and increase our income: "Send Caesar to my brother and save on dog food." (Unthinkable.) "Pawn my two gold wristwatches and one pocket watch I inherited from my grandfather." (Never.) And, most intriguing, "Get me Martin Swizinski's address in Elsa." Mom followed through on that one. A month later, she received an envelope from Elsa with no return address. Inside was fifty dollars cash. Finally, Dad ordered, "since you still don't have a driver's license, let my Dad take the car and he'll send $200 for it." She did that too, but the money never came. Relations with Mom's in-laws, my grandparents, were more strained than ever, with Granny writing Mom missives such as "How are your English classes coming? Can I look for an improvement in your letters?" They got worse after what happened next—the one fortuitous outcome of Dad's enforced absence.

Saint Paul had his epiphany on the road to Damascus. Mom had hers on Main Street. While he was being tried, she'd told her husband she held a single thought before her, and turned to it like the North Star whenever she felt lost and discouraged—he would come back to her. Although she would always, she vowed, stand by her man, her man couldn't or wouldn't always stand by her. In fact, chances were he'd be elsewhere for a long time. Despite her faltering heart, she had two promising girls and two dogs depending on her and she wasn't about to hook their futures to the whims of a landlord. Even the birds didn't rent, Mom used to say, which irked Dad no end given that his parents viewed a mortgage as a capitalist ball and chain.

The same month Dad was locked up, Mom revealed that Uncle Ken, Ricky's realtor father, had found us an affordable home—a house to own, not rent! But Omi would pay the down payment. Unbeknownst to us, years before Omi had bought a small plot of Fraser Valley farmland in Clearbrook. She would use the $1,000 from its sale for a down payment for our new $8,000 property at 6136 Main Street, between Forty-fifth and Forty-sixth Avenues. The rectangular, flat-roofed, two-bedroom, one-level cottage was painted white with bright blue trim, blue awnings and cherry red front steps, giving it a Mediterranean flair. Two white faux-Grecian urns bookended the front entrance. Perfect for life in a rainforest. The cottage sat far back from Main Street traffic on a long, narrow lot with a small tool shed and a cement pad for a backyard. Our home was, by Omi and Mom's mutual agreement, registered in Omi's name to ensure that Dad never got his hands on it.

On a rainy Friday in late May of 1965, with help from Uncle Ken, Ricky, Angus MacDonald and other friends, we moved once again. This time we had our piano and a number of treasures from our Elsa home resurrected from storage: Mom's Italian vase and Queen Anne bone china Yukon tea set; precious books, photos and pictures; our phonograph and records; Dad's three hunting rifles and his twenty-nine-volume collection of the 1911 *Encyclopedia Britannica*. Dad was so proud of the dark brown suede-covered set, he'd demonstrate its superior binding by dangling an entire volume by a single tissue-thin page. Our new home was small—about 800 square feet of living space—with no grassy backyard, so Caesar had to be walked four times a day. But it was ours and Mom's eyes glittered with the pride of homeownership. After all, welfare cheques made out to Helen Priest paid the sixty-dollar monthly mortgage and Maria Teichroeb's name on the registration was only a formality. Mom didn't have money to decorate her "cottage" or even buy a washing machine, but trundling our dirty linen to the laundromat at Main and Forty-eighth was a small price to pay for some stability and security: the first Mom had since the uprooting from Elsa.

Now, if only her girls would settle down. A small home with two tiny bedrooms became smaller still due to their dreary interactions. I viewed my sister as a bossy bully and an arrogant know-it-all. She saw me as a whiny tattletale tangled in Mom's apron strings. How could we be expected to share a bed? Mom solved the problem, at least temporarily, by giving Vona her own room while I slept with Mom. When Dad came home, of course, Vona and I would be stuck with each other. Other disruptions arose too. Vona quit accordion but continued with piano, although lessons were skipped. I quit both piano and guitar lessons. We complained about the entire dog walking/dish washing/laundry hauling/bathroom cleaning chore routine. Our school marks were rising but not as quickly as our hormones. And that meant arguments, subterfuge and amazingly creative excuses. My big sister was not only a year older but endowed with a wildly different temperament. And we both felt surges of a force and yearning that alternately pulled us out of ourselves to some unknown place and then drew us deeper within.

Whatever it was, we were bound for a head-on collision, not only with Omi's Mennonite creed, in which dancing and popular music were considered tools of the Devil, but with the traditional values of Mom and Dad, which, if closely examined, were not all that different from those of the Anabaptists. There was a boy at school I'd been making eyes with, and he with me, but that's as far as my romantic forays went, other than strolling by his house occasionally to quicken my pulse. We listened to C-FUN radio every spare moment, and the sounds blaring from our black transistor stirred our souls like Jericho trumpets. They blew the roof off and the walls down and home was never the same. The top ten hit me like an A-bomb—lyrics broadcasting how wrong the world was, melodies that melted my innards and rhythms that rattled my bones. Not dance? I'd rather sign up to roast in that very warm place.

The Beatles sang "Help," The Four Tops crooned "I Can't Help Myself (Sugar Pie, Honey Bunch)" and The Beach Boys chimed "Help Me, Rhonda," but Mom was the one who needed assistance. As an old German aphorism goes, "Little children, little problems. Big children, big problems." *Cinderella* and *Gilligan's Island* didn't cut it anymore. Now in grade eight at John Oliver Secondary, Vona begged Mom to let her see a James Bond double bill: *Dr. No* and *From Russia with Love*, playing at the Fraser Street cinema. There could be no answer but "No." Vona went anyway. Tension between Mom and her first-born escalated. By mid-June, Mom shared her parental frustrations with Dad and one day we got a letter addressed to Thing One and Thing Two:

> *Daughters! Here's a letter to both of you so you can fight over who reads it first! Please!!! More consideration of your mother! I kid you not!! Remember, you have only one Mommy—there just ain't anymore to go around. And if you are not kind, thoughtful*

and helpful to this Mommy and you wear her out, then I shall marry an old witch who will be your stepmother and will beat, starve and make scullery maids out of you! So please—help her through these difficult times until I get home to look after her.

A week after that letter arrived, a local hound bit Mom while she tried to break up a fur-flying, Caesar-initiated, traffic-stopping dogfight in the middle of Main Street. Normally unruffled and obedient, Caesar had an inexplicable hatred for cocker spaniels. One second our shepherd was sleeping in a sunny spot and the next he was torpedoing across Main Street, where he grabbed an unleashed cocker spaniel and dragged the creature into the street. Cars from both directions braked as we joined the whirling mass of teeth and tails, the spaniel's owner's shrieks adding to the shouts, growls and barks. Caesar's jaws were clamped around his archenemy's throat and he shook him like a dead weasel.

A dogfight is an ugly thing to watch. And more ugly to try and stop. In the Yukon, where no respectable canines were spayed, neutered or leashed, such events were as common as a litter of puppies. I had been taught to step back, walk away and let the dogs finish what they started. But that wasn't Mom's approach. She reached into the melee in an attempt to grab Caesar's collar and met the teeth of the thrashing spaniel. Suddenly, a man stopped his car, and got out.

"Give me that shovel, lady," he said as he seized the trowel from Mom's hand and brought it down on Caesar's noggin, whereupon Caesar released the spaniel and staggered stupidly toward the oncoming traffic. I attached Caesar to a leash while our neighbour Art drove Mom to the hospital for a tetanus shot. When Dad found out he was beside himself, and in his usual hyperbolic style blamed everyone and everything from Caesar to the city to the TV to leaving the Yukon in the first place:

Vona comes home for lunch and that's all there's to it! I kid you not! I can hardly wait to get my long, sharp eyeteeth into the back of her neck. Not long now and I'll straighten her so straight they'll use her for a ruler at school! Hold out there honey, just a little bit longer… Yup—they are 12 and 13. Hate to see them getting started as teenagers in this town. What they'd have missed if we'd stayed in the Yukon!!

Away with the TV! I can see it is a destructive influence and must be eliminated—especially for Alice's sake!! And I underestimate her not! Take my hatchet and smash its evil tubes! Take it to the backyard and burn it at the stake—dancing around and chanting "Ho-Ho—The wicked TV is dead!" Or, now that you have my rifles, you could shoot it first and put it out of its misery!

Our lives were not completely wretched, however. Whether out of pity or graciousness or because they simply liked us, many people were good: our immediate neighbours—Art Hawkes to the north and Ed and Alma Romme to the south—our friends the Fawleys and the Nelsons, and especially the two large Mennonite families in Abbotsford, the Klassens and the Willimses, with whom we spent many glorious long summer days. They all treated us with kindness, love and immeasurable generosity. Art took us hiking up Mount Seymour and fishing in Indian Arm; the Rommes took us to the horse races and taught us how to bet (the two-dollar minimum); we had sleepovers and rode horses at the Klassens'; and the eldest Willims daughter, Elly, treated us to a trip across the border to Birch Bay for a whole weekend. Most exhilarating of all, we spent long carefree days at the Pacific National Exhibition (PNE), escorted by cousin Rick (no more Ricky) and the Klassens' eldest son, Neil.

Meanwhile, with no appeal date set let alone a chance of bail, Dad's disposition went from feisty to fed up to forlorn. Although he'd have moments of satisfaction too. In August he learned that Al Pike and UKHM assistant general manager Alex MacDonald had left both Elsa and UKHM after the trial."I really cleared a bunch out, didn't I!" he crowed.

In truth, UKHM was in disarray for many reasons, including declining ore reserves and a shortage of skilled labour. Nonetheless, Dad and Poncho's drawn-out criminal saga had played its part. "Several staff members resigned," Aaro Aho wrote in *Hills of Silver*, "their last years clouded by controversies, difficulties… and the court case on the mysterious ore shipment." One incompetency on Pike's part that came out during the trial was his sweetening of lower-grade ore with the more-valuable Bonanza Stope ore.

Still, Dad's glee in seeing his primary adversary, Al Pike, get his comeuppance for leaving all of that valuable Bonanza Stope ore lying around, just begging to be taken, was a bittersweet consolation. Christmas approached. He was behind bars. His family was living from one welfare cheque to another. His parents, who had moved again, this time to Williams Lake, were living in a motel until they found rental housing, and were virtually penniless, as was Uncle Ronnie. And he was quickly using up what few friends he had.

In October, he stooped to asking if Mr. Teichroeb, Omi's husband and our Grandpa, who was retired and owned his home, would consider signing his appeal bail if the need arose. His letter included a confession that "I'm a little sad but brave and optimistic… I'll come out smelling like a rose yet!!" December, however, was never a season for roses. While Patrick Hogan had promised the appeal would be heard before Christmas, chances at this late date were slim to non-existent. In his last missive of the year, Dad made it clear that he'd resigned himself to his first jailhouse Christmas: "Are you going to Omi's for Xmas dinner? I believe we'll have roast seagull here with caterpillar sauce!"

CHAPTER 18

A Strange Bird Flies the Coop

Some poet chap has labeled man the noblest work of God:
I see myself a charlatan, a humbug and a fraud.

O NE OF JUDGE PARKER'S BELIEFS was that company men on salary ought to be held to higher standards than workers paid hourly. Salaried men like Dad were in positions of authority, had more responsibilities and supervised others. In return for this status they enjoyed many perks: better housing, higher pay and commemorative gifts like gold watches. Consequently, if they abused the trust placed in them, they deserved to be punished. Hard.

That attitude partly explains why Parker sentenced Dad to four years and Poncho to two years and eight months, even though both were found guilty on all counts at the second trial, and Poncho had a previous conviction. If Dad had had a previous criminal record, Parker said he would have sentenced him to five years.

But there was likely a more personal reason why Parker treated Dad more harshly than his co-conspirator. Over the course of two trials, as he watched and listened to Dad testify for days on end, he formed a less than flattering opinion of the man. Indeed, Parker came to dislike Dad intensely.

"Priest is a strange bird," Parker wrote in a note to the parole board shortly after sentencing him. "He is a clever man but seems to have a grudge against society and… admitted no duty of loyalty to his employer. His general attitude seemed to be that the company had plenty of money and so long as he… performed his assaying duties properly it was up to the company to protect itself against any other activities in which he might engage." According to Parker, Gerald Priest's carefully worked out scheme treated his employer—and others—"in a shameful fashion."

Minimum security measures would likely suffice to prevent Priest from escaping, Parker continued. But he predicted that Dad would have no trouble convincing prison authorities to grant him parole. Priest will "pretend to be reformed and penitent with a view to securing early release and I would think that too early a release would only persuade him that he had played the Parole Board for a sucker. He is, in my experience, a very unusual person."

Less severe, by far, was Judge Parker's assessment of Anthony Bobcik, which undoubtedly was shaped by Bobcik's decision not to testify. Parker's impressions of the man were gleaned from watching Bobcik sit mutely in court. In his note, Parker opined that the twice-convicted thief appeared "relaxed" and that his behaviour in the courtroom was "quite correct." Meaning, it seems, that at no point did Bobcik utter a word.

"I see Bobcik as an amiable but shrewd fellow who is quite prepared to turn a fast corner to make a dollar. My own guess is that Bobcik would be cooperative as a prisoner."

After the conviction, Hogan had quickly filed an appeal with the Yukon Court of Appeal, also asking the court to release Dad on bail pending the outcome. The application included a statement from Dad attesting to his good behaviour while on bail on three previous occasions leading up to the preliminary hearing and two trials.

Early on, from behind bars, Dad was defiantly confident of being granted bail in a matter of weeks *and* winning the appeal in a matter of months. Less than two weeks into his sentence, he wrote Mom:

I'm well aware of the cheering going on in the UKHM, Parker & Wylie camp—but when the appeal court gets a hold of Parker's summation, I'm sure there'll be some fireworks! Parker took the prosecution from Wylie when it was failing and turned on us in absolute defiance of any precepts of law... at least I know that the only way we can have anything resembling a fair trial is to get it out of his hands. And that's been done now. It must go to a higher court. If I don't get out this week, this is the last letter I can write till next Sunday so stay cheerful, won't you?

However, as quick as a falling gavel, Parker had denied Dad's bid for bail. Instead of awaiting yet another trial as a free man, Dad watched a cherry-blossom spring drag into a high-sky summer and a grey autumn give way to a cold, rainy winter through the small window of his concrete cubicle. Discouraged with Hogan, who had repeatedly promised the appeal would be heard before Christmas, Dad no longer believed anything his lawyer said. Facing his first ever Christmas away from his family, he sent me a letter dated December 6 and enclosed a ten-dollar bill. In his flowing, finely crafted script, he wrote the entire dispatch in rhyming couplets:

So now on you I have to call, and beg from you a favour small, a present to come from me, for Mommy 'neath the Christmas tree! Perhaps she'd whisper in your ear, some hints on what her heart holds dear. Ten dollars I will send to you, and trust you know just what to do. A mink coat would be very slick, a Cadillac would do the trick, a diamond bracelet would be fine, and I think Mommy's eyes would shine, and she would really come alive,

*with a barrel of Chanel No. Five! But I'm very sad to say, ten
dollars won't go all that way! So I'll leave it up to you and trust
she will not be blue, nor look beneath the Christmas tree, and
say—"What, nothing here for me? Does my husband love me not,
and my present he forgot?"*

I eagerly accepted Dad's challenge. After much rummaging through
the Army and Navy bins, I found a white fake fur collar that Mom
could clip onto her black wool coat.

Shortly before the big day—which, in our family, trumped all
other celebrations—Dad wrote Mom:

*I've arranged to have a visit from you on the 23rd, okay? I'm
enclosing a form that shows what I can receive in a parcel.
Nope—no meat! Though I sure would enjoy some smoked
sausage… I'm very optimistic these days, more sure than ever
that we'll win—and it's a thousand dollars a day for every day
I'm in here!! There are much better Xmas's ahead for us, cross my
heart and hope to die!*

Dad may have been prepared for his first holiday away from loved
ones, but he was not primed for Mom's Christmas gift to him. Like
many men, Dad underestimated the power of a lonely woman. On
December 20, Mom phoned Dad's original lawyer, Angelo Branca,
who by then was a BC Supreme Court and BC Court of Appeal
judge. The next morning Mom—wearing a red wool dress with
double-breasted brass buttons and angled hip pockets, and with her
dark hair swept back and high—was ushered into Branca's office. No
record exists of what transpired next, other than a short entry in her
tiny coiled notebook observing simply that Branca "was very nice."
Evidently he was, because the following day Hogan told Mom that
Dad would be released the next morning, December 23. His surprise

homecoming was our best Christmas present, even if it meant Vona and I had to share a bed once more.

Surprisingly, Branca's get-out-of-jail card turned out to be more than just a Christmas reprieve. It marked the beginning of nearly five months of freedom. How sweet it was. For about two weeks. After the initial euphoria and family fun—this time with cousin Rick's frequent presence—Dad's restlessness and agitation resurfaced. Out of work and hating the cramped house and busy city his wife loved, he slumped into the brooding, cranky and unpredictable character we'd glimpsed before. I took the long way home from school each day, fearful of what mood he'd be in. Grey, blue or black, his disposition washed our world.

While Dad had complained about Hogan in his letters to Mom, the truth was that without money there was only so much unpaid work his lawyer could do. With Campbell gone, Dad earning nothing and our family on welfare, it fell to his supporters to fund Hogan so he could get papers filed and prepare for the appeal. Some highly placed people still believed Dad was innocent, and a few were certain he had been falsely tried.

By February 1, 1966, thanks to the largesse of Ray McKamey, Charles Brown, Allan Fawley and someone named A.H. Moisey, a total of $1,149.09 was raised for the Gerald H. Priest Appeal Fund. By then nearly half of that money was eaten up by payments for copies of court transcripts, and Hogan's time.

The bail conditions imposed on Dad were beyond me, but the terms seemed fairly loose. Easter holidays loomed and Vona and I were anxious to do something exciting and outdoorsy with Dad, who'd been so gone from our lives over the past three and a half years. One evening, out of the blue, he proclaimed he'd found some work staking mineral claims in northwestern BC. This time the mineral was copper. More shocking was his decision to take cousin Rick along. And that he would pay Rick ten dollars a day for his work, almost as much as we'd earn in five days of berry picking! Vona—a year younger than Rick, equally strong and a damn sight more bush smart—had been promised wilderness escapades with Dad since forever. Now, Dad was bound for a land of deep snow, forests and cold with a boy he barely knew and cared for less. Vona's blue eyes turned green. And wet.

"Don't fret, Pal," Dad said, trying to wrap his octopus-like arm around her broad shoulders. "Come summer, it's you, me and the Rockies! How many horses should we take—three? Four?"

But Vona slipped from under his grasp, went into our room and softly closed the door. All that mattered was that for the next two and a half weeks she'd be left behind while Dad showed off to a city boy in awe of her father as some kind of mountain man.

The British Columbia town of Smithers was their destination. From the town, Dad and Rick helicoptered into a remote wilderness where they were dropped off with supplies. For the next hour, they tramped down a wide circle of snow, then erected a large canvas US Army–issue, Korean War–vintage tent insulated with asbestos to accommodate the use of a wood stove and stovepipe. The next morning and every morning after, Dad and Rick ate a quick fried breakfast before heading out into the winter whiteness.

"We did a good ten hours' work each day," Rick recalled decades later. "We trekked around in snowshoes staking claims… It was great fun. It was very, very cold at night, but nice during the day. We saw all kinds of wildlife, wolves and coyotes. It was challenging work, up and down through ravines and crossing creeks. But for a young guy, it was fun."

Dad taught Rick how to shoot a rifle, start a fire and tell north by which side of a tree moss grows on. In the tent, with the wood stove radiating warmth, they played back-to-back chess games, which Dad won every time for the first several days, until Rick caught on and prevailed in the odd match. One day, Dad and Rick spotted wolverine tracks heading toward camp.

"That was a different era," says Rick. "We had no radios. We were a long ways in the middle of nowhere. If the wolverine had got our food we would have been in a lot of trouble." Luckily, as they got closer they saw the creature heading away from the camp, which looked undisturbed.

One night Dad related the story of how he'd landed in jail. "He and his partner were taking ore off their claims, but they had to cross United Keno Hill's property to do so," Rick said. "There was some kind of dispute, so they went at night and dragged the stuff out with a snowmobile. His partner took the assay samples that were garbage as far as United Keno Hill was concerned, and added them to the ore. And that's what they were convicted on. I believed him."

Despite the trouble Dad was in, Rick said, "He was not a bitter man. He was in good spirits."

Not so when the two returned to Vancouver, where Dad's spirits plummeted. Surrounded by his family, he grew quiet, almost morose. Anchored at the kitchen table, he'd oil his guns, time and time again, peeved about the lack of work in a city he detested, and anxious about the outcome of his long-postponed appeal. We crept around his dark moods and joyfully joined his less frequent sunny ones. One evening when Rick was over and Vona was out, we tackled another round of off-the-cuff poetry. The topic was "your country."

Her Russian blood astir, Mom wrote:

Stand up for your country
You miserable wretch!
March forward and hold your head high.
You slumbered enough doing nothing at all.
Now go! And don't mind if you die!

Patriotic young Rick wrote:

What does my country mean to me?
It means much more than a dogwood tree.
It means much more than a maple leaf,
Or selling stocks of surplus beef.
It means a land of liberty,
A land of free fraternity,
This is what it means to me.

I, forever courting Dad's favour, wrote:

The flag up there—it stinks
You dirty rotten finks
You give the rich more land,
The poor with empty hands.
You ruin our lakes
And poison our pancakes.
You push us from our house
And give it to the mouse.
You louse!

And Dad wrote:

Oh Canada, you wondrous land!
You take me by my little hand,
And throw me in a prison cell.
I say now, isn't that just swell?
Here's to beautiful Canada,
Fertile, free and rich.
Take back your jail—get me out on bail,
You miserable son of a b_ _ _ _ .

As the day of his last stab at a legal victory approached, Dad ran his fingers through his increasingly retreating hair, blew more smoke circles in the air and spent more evenings striding city streets with Caesar in tow.

Then, finally, for three days in May 1966, three years after the whole shemozzle began, Dad made his final court appearance. At the time, the court consisted of justices from the BC Court of Appeal and the case, like almost all others, was held in Vancouver. Hogan and Wylie both made lengthy submissions to the three appeal court justices but no records of their submissions survive. The press attended, and once again Mr. Priest was in the news. A *Vancouver Sun* story headlined "Yukon Friends Aid Appeal" stated, "The Yukon came to the B.C. Court of Appeal Tuesday when friends financed the appeal of a Vancouver man against conviction and a prison sentence in connection with a $140,000 lode of silver. Gerald Henry Priest, 38, of 6136 Main, was convicted in March of last year and sentenced to four years for conspiracy to sell a substance containing silver."

Whether in the Yukon or in British Columbia, however, the scales of justice were not tipped in Dad's direction. A tiny clipping of yellowed newsprint, its two columns running a couple of inches, sports the headline "Assayer Loses Appeal against 4-Year Term." Overlapping the headline in blue ink is Mom's handwritten *May 19/66*. She retained a lifelong habit of dating documents. That same day, in her coil notebook, she scribbled, "All hopes are lost!! Hogan phoned... I knew right away Gerry was not coming home for a long time—what a sad, empty feeling."

With his conviction now immutable, Dad would bounce back to Oakalla for nearly three months, then move to the BC Penitentiary for more months. He was a model prisoner, spending his time eating, sleeping, reading and playing chess.

With Dad's renewed absence, our home life got both better and worse. A lightness returned to the house, and daily existence resumed its calm, spontaneous and yet predictable nature. I was finishing grade seven and my grades grew stronger. I had made a few friends, girls I chummed with at school or walked to Oakridge Mall with on a Friday evening, but never would confide in or dare invite home. I'd joined the choir and the tumbling team and I nervously anticipated a fresh start at John Oliver Secondary School in the fall. "Jayo," as it was and is still called, was a massive multi-building institution at Forty-first and Fraser Street with an enrollment of almost 1,200 students—twice as many people as Elsa and Calumet combined. High school threatened to swallow me whole. But I had a sister there, and I had a passion for choral singing, which was a plus because under the directorship of Teo Repel, a renowned choral conductor of Polish descent, I had an opportunity to sing in a choir that was consistently among the best in the province, and that included many Mennonites. (Mennonites have a strong choral tradition that in Canada includes famed tenor Ben Heppner and soprano Edith Wiens.)

In September I enrolled in grade eight and Vona in grade nine. One day while changing classes, I spied my sister with her group of friends. "Hi Vona," I called out, waving with pride to be in high school just like her. Like any older sister that age, she rolled her eyes, turned her back and walked on without any response, obviously embarrassed to be singled out by her younger sibling. As normal a teenage reaction as that may have been, I was hurt, and it was a sign of a bigger problem. Vona was drifting away from us and spending more time out of the house than in. Between Mom and Dad, there was talk of Vona "running with the wrong crowd" and a proposal to take her out of Jayo and send her to the educational equivalent of prison as far as an adolescent girl was concerned: the Mennonite Educational Institute in Abbotsford. But that would mean boarding her away from the family and Mom vetoed the idea.

With prospects of triumph and retaliation gone, Dad's letters became harder to take. A humiliated man with an increasingly sarcastic sense of humour, Dad struggled to maintain a modicum of pride. When cousin Rick, the boy Dad had taken into the bush, wrote him a letter, he took offence: "Who twisted his arm? Tell him I'll stand up on my hind legs and wave to him too, when he walks by my cage. Come to think of it, I'm short of peanuts these days." And when Mom wrote that we both now had our periods and were maturing quickly, causing her to wonder if some basic sex education might be appropriate, he responded: "Well, there's nothing I can do about the girls from here—Go to the museum and get some medieval chastity belts for our daughters until I get home with my shot gun!" (Sex was a four-letter word in our home. The closest Mom came to "education" was leaving a thin paperback on the kitchen counter titled *What To Tell Your Children About Sex*. I didn't touch it.)

When Mom asked Dad one day if our neighbour Art could borrow his tent and cook stove, Dad acquiesced but added: "Ye Gods! I just thought—Dad has my car, Art's got my gear, U.K.H.M. has my ore, the jail has me—all I have to hear now is who has my wife!"

On that score, Dad had nothing to worry about. Mom had neither the energy nor the inclination for an affair despite several suitors, both married and not, knocking on our door. Every letter from her husband, however, reminded Mom that she was the only girl for him and that when they were reunited happiness would reign. One line captured his sentiments perfectly: "You'll never find anyone who loves you as much as me."

Unable to do anything except fantasize about future schemes and apply for early parole, Dad kept Mom scrambling. His demands included contacting the John Howard Society to see if they could help him find work once he was out, asking for a claims map of Keno and a map of the Queen Charlotte Islands (where he heard valuable opals were waiting to be discovered), repeated requests to phone Hogan, and requests that Mom attend to his mother when she came to Vancouver for medical tests.

Mom's biggest worry was what job Dad would get after prison and where we would live. If the only work Dad could find was in some remote locale south or north, she would have to, reluctantly, follow. In jail, his re-education proposals included everything from a course in geology to classes in gemology, to studies in refrigeration and air conditioning—none of which he seriously pursued as his time for release drew nearer.

Once again, Mom may have greased the wheels of the freedom chariot. In mid-October, a Mr. Sheppard from the National Parole Board visited her. And according to Mom's notebook, "We had a long chat." A week later, Dad was transferred to the minimum-security prison in Agassiz, where we visited him one memorable day—Saturday, October 22, 1966.

We packed a special lunch with his favourite foods, such as cold chicken, potato salad and pickles. Mom still couldn't drive so Grandpa drove us out in his true red 1963 Ford Comet with a "three in the tree" gearshift. We motored through a valley so green and wet it courted neon. I recall the day so sharply because it was the first time we'd seen Dad in more than six months. I sat back balancing a cocoa-cream-filled chocolate cake on my lap as a fine mist soaked the world—we passed flooded fields, cows shivering under trees and a few shuttered houses rimmed by rusting hulks of trashed metal. This was the same broad valley Mom and Omi emigrated to from Russia via postwar Germany some seventeen years earlier.

We arrived at a high, wire-fenced, flat-roofed concrete building and were ushered into a large, overheated room with benches and plywood tables crowded with other prisoners and their visitors. Omi and Grandpa stayed in the car. There was Dad. His face surrendered into Mom's shoulder for what seemed like forever and then he pulled back and hurriedly hugged and kissed us. But before we unpacked the feast, he recovered and began joking, ridiculing boyfriends we didn't have, daring us to get straight As, reciting "The Cremation of Sam McGee" or stanza after stanza of "The Highwayman": "The moon was a ghostly galleon, tossed upon cloudy seas." He was so clever, so witty—no matter what, we adored him.

After the meal, which he picked at, he rolled a cigarette and then brought out a surprise: three pieces of jewelry he had created in the prison workshop. My sister got a bracelet with glinting blue and green gems. I received a sparkly guitar-shaped brooch. Mom's gift was the prettiest: a multi-spiked chrysanthemum ornament festooned with amber stones. We were agog. Not only was Dad a superior craftsman but he had access to jewels—in jail. The only explanation that made any sense was that he received special treatment because people at the top knew he was innocent.

Three weeks later, Mom heard from Mr. Sheppard that Dad had been granted parole." Is this really the end of a long, long nightmare?" she jotted in her notebook. Five days later, Dad was free, retrieved in Abbotsford by Omi and Grandpa and delivered to his ecstatic family. Mom wrote, "What a relief—home to stay at last!"

Not everyone, however, greeted the news with jubilation. When Justice Parker heard that Gerald Priest was released on parole on November 15, 1966, he was incensed. In a letter to the National Parole Board, he noted that in his eight years as a judge he had never before complained about a decision to grant early release. "Your actions make the Court proceedings something of a joke," Parker wrote. "It may, of course, be that Priest is dying of some incurable disease and that is the reason you are releasing him. If this is the case, then I think I should have been told."

He continued: "What have you done about Bobcik? He was Priest's partner in the several crimes but was a much finer personality than Priest. Bobcik was a rather likeable fellow, while Priest was a most objectionable person. If you have not already released Bobcik, you should do so immediately because it would be a gross injustice to retain him after releasing the other man. The most agreeable thought which I can summon in connection with the matter is that it is most unlikely that Priest will return to the Yukon."

National Parole Board executive director F. P. Miller responded to Parker. Miller explained that Bobcik "was simply not interested in parole… Some first offenders are so independent that they prefer to serve out the sentence in the prison rather than to have any restraints or restrictions placed on them after their release."

Miller's next bit of news would make Parker's blood boil. Unbeknownst to the board, Dad had not even served the legal minimum time in jail, which was one third of his four-year sentence— sixteen months. Because of Dad's five months out on bail, he'd only served fifteen. How could this miscarriage of justice have transpired? For whatever reasons, one or more of the penitentiaries failed to inform the board of Dad's hiatus from prison, and so they released him under the false understanding that he'd done his due time.

Nonetheless, Miller felt comfortable in the decision, and taking a tip from Parker sketched his own psychological portrait of Dad. "This is the rigid type personality who feels he has been hard done-by, carries on for many years as the hard-working employee but concocts some elaborate scheme to get some of his employer's funds," Miller wrote. "We find that these people usually are so rigid that they cannot destroy their own self-image by even admitting guilt. However, their control again takes over and we find that they are unlikely to commit another offence of this nature or any other nature."

And so it was that a strange bird flew the coop early, much to the chagrin of the man who'd slammed the door and turned the key.

CHAPTER 19

Free Fall

And I know at the dawn she'll come reeling home
With the bottles, one, two, three;
One for herself to drown her shame, and two big
Bottles for me,
To make me forget the thing I am and the man
I used to be.

ONE NIGHTMARE ENDS AND ANOTHER BEGINS. Liberated at last, and home with his wife, daughters and dogs, Dad is different. Thin and pasty. His eyes are enormous, deep and piercing. When he furrows his brow and fixes his gaze, his face looks as intense and incontestable as a hawk's. Who is this man I love like no other? Who can roll a smoke while driving a car, sing all sixteen verses of "Strawberry Roan" by heart, who smells soothingly of tobacco, coffee and car grease, and whose long, strong arms still cradle me to bed. Who can play with a story, the truth and a lie so skillfully, it's anyone's guess what is where. Dad is as much a part of me as my arms and legs. Not home a month, however, he is itching to be elsewhere. I've never seen him squirm so, as if after existing in a cage, he can't cope with freedom.

One moment he proclaims his devotion to us and blusters about his determination to now, finally, restore our happy home. "No, I don't want to chase around the bush anymore," he says. "I plan on a job that keeps me with my family, even if that means not in Vancouver. It's a good thing we all agree to get away from this wicked coast country as soon as possible." Mom and I swap downward glances. The next moment, he turns as nasty as a fox in a leghold trap. When I tell him Vancouver is not so bad and that I am actually beginning to enjoy school, especially singing in the choir, he says, "Oh yeah, I've heard of that group—The Disgustables, right?"

When Vona asks if she can go to a Friday night school dance, he says, "Nope."

"Why not?"

"Because I said so."

His tyrannical responses used to be greeted with rolled eyes and bitten lips. Not anymore. At least as far as Vona is concerned. Sometime, during Dad's incarceration, she picked up the notion that a family is a democracy.

"Come on Pappy! Why not? The dance is supervised by teachers and all my friends are going and I'll be home by ten. I promise."

"Did you hear what I said?"

Vona is mum.

"Answer me or I'll clean the wax out of your ears!"

"You said No," Vona mumbles.

"Damn right I did—your days of fraternizing with a bunch of callow, blind, opinionated and hormone-crazed hoodlums are over!"

Steamed, Vona stomps out of the house equally determined to never let Dad see her cry and to somehow attend the dance. That will entail either saying she's at a girlfriend's house or sneaking out our bedroom window. Both tactics have been used successfully before.

Mom brightly suggests we celebrate Christmas with Omi and Grandpa and the Nelsons, who have done so much for all of us.

"I don't see why I have to put up with their Jesus chatter," Dad says. "Anyway, I've decided we're spending Christmas with my folks this year."

And so we journey to Williams Lake, where another dismal festive season awaits. Vona and I find comfort in the crystal cold sky and diamond whiteness, but Mom is unusually quiet and excuses herself after the dishes are done. That evening I overhear Dad and Granddad chatting.

"How's Helen? She seems rather poorly," Granddad says.

"Well, no doubt having a husband back is a bit of a shock," Dad replies. "She'll adjust. Or not. But if Shakespeare tamed the shrew, no reason the Priests can't do likewise. Eh?"

Two days after we return home, Mom is admitted to Vancouver General Hospital for a week. She undergoes numerous tests including a heart catheterization and a barium swallow. Dad visits her every day and brings her roses and halva. When she is discharged, she weighs 100 pounds, down 15 from her normal weight.

As 1967 unfolds, Dad's moods rule the roost. He can be affectionate, broody, taunting or teasing; his temper is spookily unpredictable. Petty things like how we spend our babysitting money on pop records make him furious. The Beatles are a bunch of squirming cockroaches. Stevie Wonder, a yowling jungle bunny. And The Beach Boys sound like a bunch of strangled cats. Why is Dad so contrary? Is it lack of work? He's always professed that idleness causes a black streak within him to bubble to the surface. Searching downtown for a job most days, he returns with unsavoury prospects that he throws out just to trigger our dismay. One day there is talk of an assaying position in Yellowknife, NWT, the next day one in Edmonton, another in Hermosillo, Mexico, which Dad says he'd jump at if skipping the country didn't violate his parole.

"A great opportunity for you girls to learn Spanish," he adds.

All go nowhere. The truth—unspoken but looming large—is

that after four years in Vancouver, we are adjusting and don't relish the thought of being uprooted again. But, of course, a fresh start is exactly what Dad wants, and I know part of Mom, the part that views her marriage as a job, agrees.

Equally iron-willed and increasingly sharp-tongued, Vona clashes with Dad in short ugly eruptions. In prison Dad wrote that he'd have "a good long talk with Vona and straighten her out a bit" but now he threatens to send her "on a free trip to the moon" or feed her "a knuckle sandwich." Meanwhile Mom's attempts to play the intermediary, disciplinarian or peacemaker are dismissed by both. The more brave and brash Vona becomes, the more mouse-like I am. Unable to hold my own in our increasingly hostile home, I withdraw into schoolwork and teen illusions about pursuing a career as a naturalist, an actress or an astronaut.

In March, Dad suddenly packs up his camping gear as if bush-bound and drives north. He tells Mom he's off to explore employment options in Williams Lake. In her notebook, she writes "Nothing! Nothing! Nothing!" Two weeks later he flies to Calgary and again she writes "Nothing! Nothing! Nothing!" The following month, she records this cryptic passage: "It was one of my unhappiest days ever about Gerry and Vona! Gerry asked me point blank about taking Vona the previous night and I said No!"

Taking Vona where? Back to some small town in the bush? To live with his parents? It didn't make sense if he so wanted to keep our family together.

Forgiving to a fault, Mom's faith in Dad quickly resurfaces a few days later when he secures a job as an assayer with Columbia River Mines Ltd. The job is in Golden, in southeastern BC, nestled in his beloved Rockies and close to the Alberta border. Dad explains that it isn't a permanent job but will tide us over until he finds something in a bigger town. But first he and Mom go used-car shopping and after parting with $1,000 they come home with a silver Citroën that looks like a squatting duck. A new-to-us car raises my parents' spirits for a short while, as it has in the past. But two days later Dad leaves for Golden.

Abandoned again, Mom puts on her bright and brave mask and tries to keep house, home, daughters and dogs in some semblance of contentment. She finally had her driver's license and when I win a C-FUN radio contest for two tickets to see the pop group The Monkees in Seattle, Mom drives us 120 miles south for the show. (I had a killer crush on Davy Jones.) She sleeps in the car while I squeal along with hundreds of others. Vona is mortified by my behaviour and lets me know. Of course, we have no money for a motel so when the hullabaloo is over Mom drives us the 120 miles back. I know she misses Dad but I, at least, am warming to his absence. "I guess the house is a lot more cheerful now with the grumpy old bear gone back to the bush where he belongs," Dad writes.

In late August—the week of Dad's and my birthday—he plans to come home for a visit and we prepare for a party, complete with a special dinner and a cake. When he doesn't show, Mom, who is almost allergic to anger, jots a letter so uncharacteristically outspoken that she doesn't have the guts to mail it.

> *What gives? Do I still have a husband? You don't turn up and don't even write or phone! This kind of marriage—I don't like! I protest. No really, that is not right. I don't like it when you are mad at me—it's so degrading. So, you think you can make it home next time? You better!*

Mom's feelings toward Dad are seriously conflicted. Justifiably furious, and not for the first or last time, she addresses him in the same letter as "Liebchen" and signs off with "Love, hugs and kisses." Thoughts of leaving him cross her mind. But for what? And with what? She's trapped and determined to bring out the best in her man.

Dad's job lasts six months, during which there are several family developments: his parents move again (this time to the tiny community of Haney, since swallowed up by the sprawl known as Maple Ridge), and I pass to grade nine, get elected to student council and make the honour roll. Things change for Vona too. At their wits' end with their rebellious and underachieving first-born, Mom and Dad transfer her to York House, a private girls' school in Vancouver's Shaughnessy neighbourhood. How they pay for it, I don't know. I suspect Omi is in on it. But the move does nothing to quell Vona's mutinous adventures. If anything, her after-dark forays and her arguments with Mom escalate.

Years later I will learn of something else that happened during 1967. Dad comes clean to Mom. He tells her the truth about his ore theft. At least he offers a version of the story in which he admits to some guilt. At the same time, he confides that he can never tell his parents, who believe him to be an innocent and gravely wronged man. He makes Mom vow that she will never tell them, and so in their presence live a lie. It is a promise she will always regret.

Home once more, Dad does temporary stints as a mining chemist while awaiting an offer of a permanent job. Mom's notebook around this time becomes increasingly sketchy. Pages are ripped out and the remainder filled with pseudo-philosophical scraps such as: "The past is a dream, The present a strife, The future a mystery, And such is life!"

In late September, Dad and I have a rare run-in—one that gets a rise out of me to this day. Our school choir is hosting another choir from Washington state for a few days and our choir members are billeting our American friends in their homes. We have no spare room and even if we did I wouldn't dare risk exposing anyone to our family dynamics. Nonetheless, we are expected to play host and show our guests the city. I meet a boy one year older than me who asks if I would be willing to go downtown with him. David is soft-spoken, terribly polite and cute in a fair-haired, blue-eyed and freckled way. The best part though is his offhand sense of humour. He makes me laugh. It is a sunny Saturday afternoon and with my parents' permission we take the bus downtown to Stanley Park. It isn't a date… but it is. We wander through the green and exchange stories and opinions and rent paddleboats on Lost Lagoon and splash each other and giggle and catch a bite to eat and oh who ever knew life could be so rich? Then he suggests we catch an early movie on Granville. He'll have me home before nine p.m. Why not? I want the day to last forever. We see *To Sir, with Love* and I sniffle when Lulu sings that song, and then David takes my hand in his. He holds it all the way home on the bus. We walk from the bus stop to our doorstep where David is about to knock when an ashen-faced Dad flings open the door.

"How dare you keep my daughter out this late? Who do you think you are?"

"I'm sorry sir, but we…" David begins, but Dad cuts him off.

"How do I know what your intentions are?"

"My what?" David asks.

"Don't be an ass. All you need to know is that you will never see my daughter again! Get it? Now, get going. You're trespassing!"

Humiliated and speechless, I can't meet David's eyes but I cast Dad one hate-filled glare before racing to my room. The next morning Dad tries to tease me about "my first date" but I'm not biting. For days, I don't speak to him unless I absolutely have to, and vow that David was the first and last boy I'll ever bring home.

In early December, Dad finds a good permanent job in Calgary with Core Laboratories. Come January, he states firmly, we're all moving there. We'll have a good house, near the foothills, and eventually we'll have horses and resurrect the family we once were. I beg him to let me finish grade nine at Jayo. My pleas provoke him. Escaping to the bathroom, I turn on the taps and fill the tub with the hottest water I can stand.

Dad leaves for Calgary soon after, then returns for Christmas and on January 2 heads back to Calgary, taking Vona with him. For now, Mom, the dogs and I stay put. Mom writes in her notebook: "Our dear Vona left her own family… the family is now broken up—once a nice respectable family." But that upset is a raindrop compared to the hurricane that lies ahead.

I focus on school, wrapping myself in self-absorbed denial of the fact that I will be forced once again to leave a place that feels right. I know Dad's choice of housing in Calgary will be cheap and dirty. I also suspect Vona won't be riding horses every weekend and acing grade ten. By then we lead vastly disparate lives, and despite being a solid letter-writing family, we never correspond. Years later Vona tells me their Calgary home was a hovel, a clapboard ground level basement apartment she was ashamed to live in let alone show to friends. She tries to go out at every opportunity and if she returns even five minutes past her curfew, Dad hits her. We've been raised with the threat of corporal punishment as the ultimate form of discipline, as were most children of our time. However, Dad seldom raises his hand, preferring to raise his voice. I recall only one spanking when I was five or six and Vona and I couldn't stop giggling when we should have been sleeping. But fifteen-year-olds aren't spanked. They're beaten.

Back in Vancouver, Mom and I struggle with an aging and ailing Caesar. Nearing ten, he's slowed down and is losing control of his bladder. Mom says it's because of all those Yukon winters he lay outside on ice and snow. In February, he collapses after a slow, short walk. Mom and I manage to coax him into the kitchen where he lies down on a thick blanket. That night I toss like a salad until I rise and snuggle down beside him. In the morning Mom phones Dad and asks what she should do.

"Take Caesar to the vet and have him put down."

"I can't do that, I can't. He's your dog—come and deal with him."

"Now you're being ridiculous. He's old. Have him put down and send me the bill."

I help Mom get Caesar into the back seat of the Citroën but don't have the guts to get in the car. For years, Mom has nightmares about that day. Her face is the last thing Caesar sees.

The inevitable draws near and, in late May, Mom flies to Calgary for a visit. Appalled at the filthy and derelict home, she immediately looks for a better house and finds a three-bedroom duplex at 207A Forty-second Avenue sw, near the Elbow River and traffic-heavy Macleod Trail. While she is away, I blithely try out for next year's cheerleading squad—the epitome of female high school popularity— and am accepted. Surely, they won't make me move now!

In early July, Mom and I say goodbye to Omi and Grandpa, pack the Citroën, grab Pierre and drive east. Mom rents out our little blue house, which remains in Omi's name. As with our move from the Yukon, I don't tell a soul, preferring to disappear into thin air. It is a miserable, hot and aborted trip. We limp as far as Kamloops before the fully loaded Citroën dies. We sit under a tree in a public park waiting for our car to be fixed only to learn the repair will cost more than the car is worth. Again, Mom phones Dad, and is told to get a motel for the night and he will collect us in the morning. By then Dad has acquired a weird little German car called a DKW 900—a *Dampf-Kraft-Wagen*. The two-door, snub-nosed black and tan putt-putt has a three-cylinder engine, front wheel drive and a three-speed manual transmission. It gets us to Calgary but our belongings are shipped by train.

We start anew, with a fresh beginning in our fifth home and third locale in five years. Before school starts, Vona turns sixteen and I fifteen. Vona attends Western Canada High School, where she is a cheerleader, fails all her courses and has a few good friends. I go to Henry Wise Wood where I am a mediocre student and have no friends, until late in the year when I hook up with a freckled and funny girl named Jane Moxon. A preppy school with fraternities and sororities and country club families who ski at Sunshine Village every winter weekend, Wise Wood is a far cry from working-class Jayo, where basketball reigns and drinking in the park comes a close second.

Dad is his misanthropic self, only worse, at times irritated with Mom for her household mismanagement, such as spending too much on groceries when all you need to make a good stew is an onion and a pack of chicken backs and necks. Most often though he is miffed at Vona—for doing poorly at school, for putting on too much makeup, for rolling up the waistband of her skirts, for talking back or a hundred other reasons. He spends a lot of time tinkering with his car, mending his outdoor gear or oiling his guns in the basement. Mom gets a part-time job in the ladies' sportswear section of the Woodward's department store to earn some house money but quits after she faints while fitting a customer with the perfect pantsuit. I walk Pierre or stay in my room, where I pick at my guitar, listen to melancholy Simon and Garfunkel tunes or read. Somehow, the days roll by. Until one day they don't.

It is a cool May evening, a Saturday, and Vona is going out to a cheerleader practice.

"Your curfew is eleven p.m., young lady."

"Okay."

"And when I say eleven, this is what that looks like. At precisely eleven o'clock, I will rise from my chair and lock all the doors. Then I will go to bed. Understand?"

"All right, already."

At 11:07 p.m. Vona knocks on the front door. She bangs on the door. She yells to be let in. I bury my head under the pillows but can still hear her, and Mom and Dad arguing in the next room. Above their voices, the knocking stops. Vona has gone. She does not come back. Instead she moves in with a girlfriend's family and later is fostered by another. She never comes home again.

After that, life spirals into the surreal. I sleepwalk through the days but don't want to wake up. Mom is quiet, worried and looks ill. Dad leaves for a Yukon "holiday" with his father in June. When he returns Mom confronts him with a spiteful letter she received from his mother, scolding her for not "standing by" her man, who is, after all, innocent. She begs him to tell them the truth.

"They're my parents and I'll tell them whatever I want!"

The next day she tells him about Vona. It is midday and they are in their bedroom with the door closed. I hear strange sounds coming from their room. I rush in to see Dad erupt in a spasm of shaking and shouting. His arms flail and his face shines with a terrible pink sheen. Mom's face is white and her lips are pressed together. Dad grabs our sacred red leather-bound Yukon photo album, and starts ripping pictures of our family in half, spitting on them as he grinds them on the floor with his foot. Mom is motionless and mute. Her whole body shakes.

"She's not my child anymore!" he sputters. "And if you don't make the right choice, you won't be my wife! You choose—it's either your husband or that... that... slut! It's up to you! Choose! Now!"

Suddenly they turn and realize I'm in the room. Mom moves to take my hand and put it in Dad's. He turns, sees me and snaps out of his trance. His eyes down, he leads me to the living room where he sits and guides me onto his lap. His fingers knead his thumb furiously. Hot tears run down my face and drip onto his hands and mine but I can't utter a sound. My throat feels like I've swallowed a shag rug. We sit semi-frozen like this for what seems like an hour.

"Have you nothing at all to say?" he asks abruptly.

I choke out a croak: "What is happening?" I still his frantically moving hand with mine.

"I love you and always will but you and your mother need to get out of this house. I cannot be responsible for my actions tonight."

In my mind I see his well-oiled rifles on a rack downstairs. Within the hour he phones Omi.

"Come and collect your daughter."

September 1969. My family—once as tight, warm and sheltered as a well-chinked log cabin—shatters in three different directions: Dad to a job in Yellowknife; Mom, Pierre and I to Omi and Grandpa's basement; and Vona to Calgary's Sprucecliff Home for Unwed Mothers.

CHAPTER 20

A Small Measure of Revenge

There was triumph, triumph, triumph
down the scarlet glittering street,
And you scarce could hear the music for the cheers.

A T ANOTHER TIME, THINGS MAY HAVE turned out very differently. In their day, the charges Dad and Poncho faced were highly unusual. If Section 337(1)(b) of the Criminal Code existed today, it would violate the Canadian Charter of Rights and Freedoms. That's because the 1963 charges placed the onus on the accused to prove their innocence—the reverse of the sacred legal tenet "innocent until proven guilty."

All that changed, however, in 1989, seven years after the Charter, when six men in the Timmins area of northern Ontario were charged with an offence virtually identical to Dad and Poncho's. The case known as *Regina v. Laba et al.* (Andrew Isadore Laba being one of the accused) is part of Canadian legal history for triggering a small but significant change to the Criminal Code.

Before Laba and crew's story could be revealed, their lawyers challenged the charge, saying it violated Section 11 of the Charter, which deals with the presumption of innocence. The Ontario court agreed. When the Crown pushed back by arguing that the government had a right to such a law because the Charter allowed for "reasonable limits" to be placed on constitutionally protected rights and freedoms of individuals, the court was unmoved. Two appeals and five years later, the case went before the Supreme Court of Canada, where the charge was indeed deemed contrary to the Charter. But the Supreme Court did not categorically reject the idea. Instead, a new requirement was written into the Criminal Code, whereby people accused of such crimes were now expected to come up with evidence that raised a "reasonable doubt" about their guilt. It was a fine but important distinction. If it had existed in 1963, and if Dad and Poncho had not added the concentrates and precipitates to the ore shipment, they may well have walked. They had their experts after all, to testify that the ore came from the Moon.

Speculation aside, in the first trial Dad convinced jurors he had some legitimate claim to the disputed ore. In the second trial, however, the more he pontificated about how he'd mined and transported his ore, the more the new jury believed otherwise.

With most people, that would have been the end of it. But not with Dad, even with his defeat before the BC Court of Appeal. In fact, that defeat left him more determined to exact some measure of revenge. In letters home from jail, he vowed to "sue the pants off" the smelter, which had processed the ore and paid the proceeds to UKHM before the first trial. (To this day, I can't fathom why UKHM got the goods, given that ownership of the ore was never proven in court; it was only proven that Dad and Poncho *didn't* own it. Perhaps the corporate bully got what it wanted, not only with the smelter but also with the law, which never batted an eye at the payout.)

Dad filed a civil action against the American Smelting and Refining Co. in BC Supreme Court in December 1966. But by March he had abandoned the effort, turning his attention south of the border. The next year notice was served on ASARCO that Gerald

H. Priest was suing the smelter for breach of contract. It was an audacious gambit but one that Dad's new lawyer in Seattle felt was worth pursuing.

Nelson Christensen was a Seattle lawyer working for a prestigious firm by the name of Howe, Davis, Riese & Jones. Dad explained how he had delivered nearly $200,000 worth of raw ore (with Dad, the value of the ore skyrocketed with every mention) to ASARCO in June 1963 and how two years later he had been convicted of theft. But well before he had been found guilty the smelter processed the disputed ore and cut UKHM a big cheque. "That's a violation of the contract I had with ASARCO," Dad told Christensen. "Isn't it?"

It was an intriguing question. By then, Dad barely had two spare nickels to rub together. Likely, Christensen agreed that his legal costs would be deferred in the event that the courts ruled in Dad's favour or the parties settled out of court.

The filing of the claim against ASARCO rang alarm bells at UKHM for obvious reasons. Before ASARCO paid UKHM, the smelter had required the company to agree that if Alpine or someone such as Gerald H. Priest recovered funds from the smelter, UKHM would pay it back.

Dad's next day in court was before the United States District Court for the Western District of Washington, with the hearing held either in Spokane or Seattle. David Wagoner, a Seattle lawyer working for another of the city's big firms—Holman, Marion, Perkins Coie & Stone—argued that Dad's previous criminal conviction in Canada prevented him from launching a civil action against the smelter. Like the presumption of innocence, it is also an accepted legal truism that anyone convicted of a crime cannot profit from it. Christensen argued that the smelter had breached the terms of the contract prior to Dad's criminal conviction by smelting the ore before Canadian courts issued any ruling. After considering both arguments, the court ruled in ASARCO's favor. But the fight wasn't finished. Dad appealed to the United States Court of Appeals, Ninth District. And there, finally, he was victorious—it was his first legal win since his troubles began six years earlier. On March 20, 1969, with his family unravelling and oblivious to his international legal forays, the appeals court overturned the lower court's decision.

Surely, the court stated, the manner in which Dad was convicted must be considered. Was the judgment trustworthy? If there was any doubt, then Dad should not be prevented from making his case before the us courts. The circuit court judges concluded that Dad's earlier conviction was tainted because of the peculiar reverse onus charge. With that, the door was opened for a full-fledged civil action in the us.

By August of that year, ukhm's lawyers were worried. If a trial in the us went ahead, weeks of court time would again be swallowed up at huge expense to the company. And at the end of the day, ukhm would likely be holding the bag if the court ordered a payout. Soon after, asarco's lawyers called Christensen with an offer for an out-of-court settlement. Dad took the money. How much? According to Mom, he received $80,000, half of which went to his lawyer. Once he'd paid his sugar daddy Robert Campbell the $16,000 he owed him for his legal fees, Dad was left with $24,000. Not long after, he bought a small wood-sided bungalow in Slocan City, a forgotten village in bc's West Kootenays.

The house would be the one tangible thing Dad would garner from his Moon claims. And it would come from ukhm, the company he'd devoted twelve years of his working life to; the company that created Elsa, where he spent the happiest years of his life; the company he stole from, and that did its utmost to ensure he was punished. It was a paltry and ironic victory.

What Really Happened?

I strolled up old Bonanza. The same old moon looked down;
The same old landmarks seemed to yearn to me;
But the cabins all were silent, and the flat, once like a town,
Was mighty still and lonesome-like to see.

I N THE SUMMER OF 1992, my husband Ben, our one-year-old daughter Charlotte and I visited Dad in Slocan City, where he lived with his second wife and his son Andrew, the boy he'd always wanted. On that late summer day, as we drove into the lush and verdant Slocan Valley, my excitement was diluted by a heavy dose of trepidation: our stopover would be the first time Dad would meet his son-in-law and his granddaughter, and it would be my peacemaking with a father I'd been largely estranged from for twenty-three years. I also anticipated meeting Andrew, my twenty-eight-year-old half-brother, whom I'd last encountered as a round-cheeked, saucer-eyed toddler.

When the family fractured back in 1969, Dad wrote me for the first two years or so, his envelopes occasionally stuffed with a five- or ten-dollar bill. "Treat your mother and yourself to a banana split on me," he'd write. That was the sum total of alimony and child support he offered. When Mom asked for a divorce three years after they split,

Dad sent her Vancouver lawyer Elspeth Munro Gardner a startling letter, every word a stinking lie.

> *Dear Madam:*
>
> *Before you proceed with an action by Mrs. Priest, I feel that you should be informed of the following:*
>
> *In 1969, Mrs. Priest did desert her home and did refuse to return to it.*
>
> *She was supported until 1970 when she refused an offer of a home. She did refuse, previous to our separation, the services of a marriage councilor [sic]. On written statement of her own doctor, she is or was in 1969, in an impaired mental condition.*
>
> *Last, but not least, is the fact that in 1971 I divested myself of all my properties and forwarded the sum of 327 thousand dollars via Switzerland and Poland to a Children's Aid Society in North Viet Nam [sic] and am now penniless, unemployed, and in possession of only the simplest necessities of life.*
>
> *I occupy a log cabin on the shore of Slocan Lake. A snowshoe trail of about one mile connects me with the nearest road. I have lived in the vicinity of Slocan since September 1970.*

Our correspondence halted after my parents' uncontested divorce one year later. The truth is that after working in Yellowknife for Terra Silver Mine for two years, Dad married a woman with a twelve-year-old daughter, and together they had a son and moved to Logan Lake near Kamloops, BC, where he worked for Lornex Copper Mine until his retirement in 1986. I could count the number of his letters since the divorce on one hand and the number of times we'd seen each other on two fingers. Depending on his mood, he addressed me as either Alice or Alicia and signed off as "Pappy," "Dad," "your father" or "G.H. Priest." He never forgave me for not asking him to "march me down the aisle" in 1989. "That's what fathers *do*," he later grumbled. But there are things I couldn't forgive him for, so I skipped the apology.

Our sorry history aside, Dad was all grins, hugs and brazen hospitality when we arrived in Slocan City. We were directed to come for lunch to his "second" house, not the bungalow he bought with the money from UKHM, which my grandparents once inhabited and where he now lived with his second family, but a three-room log cabin bathed in sunlight. Dad told us the dwelling was his alone—his sanctuary when his wife and son drove him "to distraction."

As we stepped out of the car, Dad rushed forward with a tight embrace for me, and a brief handshake for Ben. Taller and thinner than I remembered, he had a fringe of grey hair rimming the back of his head and was close to toothless. What few teeth remained were yellowed, worn-down stumps, except for an artificial bridge of four incisors. He was clean-shaven and wearing dark jeans cinched tightly above his waist, a freshly washed but permanently stained tan work shirt and crumpled cowboy boots. His pants stopped a good 3 inches above his ankles. Despite his joy at seeing us, his downcast eyebrows and intense glower gave him that avian predator expression I knew so well. All in all, the word "pathetic" comes to mind.

Margit, his wife, hugged me and kissed Charlotte. She was a short, plump woman with thinning dyed red hair, a high rounded forehead, large dark eyes, bright orange lips and long orange fingernails, and spoke with a heavy German accent. She was also a good twelve years Dad's junior. In a high-pitched, singsong voice, she began to ask about our trip but was summarily dismissed by Dad, who said he wanted us all to himself. Andrew would not be making an appearance, he added.

"Ben, bet you're glad to get your family out of that cesspool of a city, even for a few weeks. No place for a thinking person, let alone a place to raise a child!"

"Oh we love the Kootenays all right," Ben replied. "But we like Vancouver too."

Ushering us proudly in, Dad urged me to sit at the small kitchen table while he fixed lunch. Close by, a wood-burning stove threw out warmth and the smell of roasting fowl. As Dad set the table I looked around. The cabin was clean and cozy, with log walls sparsely decorated with retro northern kitsch. A flock of green ceramic ducks was in flight on one wall, rows of hardcover books with titles like *Quiet Flows the Don* and *Haji Baba of Ispahan* backed against another. An old glass kerosene lamp sat on a small wooden table. There was no electricity in the cabin.

We ate a remarkably good meal of juicy chicken, browned potatoes, boiled carrots and fresh bread. Throughout lunch, Dad conversed nervously, tickling Charlotte, throwing me backhanded compliments and recounting one outdoor adventure after another. Then out came a plate of store-bought chocolate chip cookies. Apparently, these were for the women and children, because at that point Dad pulled out a plastic bottle of red wine. Around the bottle's neck dangled a tiny black bull on a string.

"This'll put some hair on your chest, Ben," he said, getting out two short-stemmed goblets. "Sangre de Toro—Blood of the Bull. It's a man's drink."

"Yeah, that's pretty good stuff," said Ben. "Thanks."

Wine poured, Dad opened a door by the stove and signalled Ben into another room.

"I call this my den for men. No females allowed," he said, grinning in my direction. "I spend a lot of time here."

I smiled and said us "females" would rather be enjoying the sun anyway. But as Dad and Ben took their seats in threadbare chairs, I glanced through the open door. Staring back, from walls, desktops and side tables, were large framed photos of Mom in her resplendent prime, Vona and me as carefree cherubs, Omi beaming and leading one of us by the hand, and Caesar guarding his charges—all females except for the dog. A phonograph and turntable with our favourite vintage records waited in one corner. His now scuffed and scratched guitar and harmonica sat cradled in a stand. A standing brass ashtray brimmed with ash and cigarette butts. Even our old decorative rug with the exotic Persian camel market scene was there, though the pattern had become barely visible. And on one wall, a wooden rack displayed three gleaming hunting rifles. No direct sunlight entered the room and a dusty pall hovered over the artifacts. What was his den for men? A shrine to better days? A mausoleum of memories? His personal time machine?

Suddenly, I had to get out of that haunted house and into the sunshine. Grabbing Charlotte, I bolted outside into blinding light, letting the warmth wash over me like a balm. I wondered what cauldron of twisted thoughts Dad cooked up when he sat brooding hour after hour in that room. And how did Margit and Andrew view his obsession with a world they were so patently excluded from? Within twenty minutes, we had said our farewells and were back in the car.

"Don't be a stranger," Dad called out as we turned up the main road leading out of town.

It is spring 1998 when I find the courage to ask Dad for the truth about his thieving days so long ago. I've heard various versions over the decades since, and most of the time I pretend to forget it ever happened. But so many years have passed, and with a family of my own I need to hear his story from his own mouth. I write to him, hoping for the final and definitive word on the matter. We've been back in touch through letters and occasional short visits, but the six years since we've reconciled have been tumultuous, to put it politely. It's been twenty-nine years since we lived together as a family in Calgary, more than a generation ago. During that time, Mom had four open-heart operations that left her with three artificial valves and a pacemaker. She remarried in 1975—much to Omi's chagrin—and enjoyed fifteen years with a low-key, fun-loving Englishman until his death in 1990. In 1996 she travelled to Germany for a reunion with her brother who had travelled from his home in Siberia. They had not seen each other in 56 years. Tenacious Vona, in the meantime, single-handedly picked her broken self up and moved to Vancouver where she completed a high school diploma while working as a legal secretary. At UBC, she pursued a degree in zoology followed by medical school and a residency in psychiatry. She practices her profession in the BC Interior where she has a 10-acre hobby farm populated by horses and many other animals. She never married and never had another child.

At the time of my 1998 inquiry about what really happened, Dad is living alone with a small buck-toothed dog and a free-flying parakeet in the basement of a derelict house on a sad street in Castlegar, BC. Parakeet poop is everywhere, especially in the kitchen sink under the bird's wooden perch.

He quickly writes me back with his answer to my "what happened at the mine" question. Despite all we've been through and as well as I thought I knew my father, I am stunned by the long and convoluted fairy tale he sends me on four scrawled pages.

While working for UKHM, Dad writes, he chanced upon some records from an old assay office based in Keno that hadn't been in use for years. Reading them, he discovered that back in the thirties three "sleigh loads" of high-grade ore, 35 tons each, had been dumped over the far side of Keno Hill. The ore, the files explained, originated from what was called the Million Dollar Stope of the old Wernecke mine.

"I found them, and because I did, I wanted them," he writes. "The ore was supposed to go down to Mayo Landing (where you were born!), but either by theft or guile, those sleighs were dumped over the edge."

Enlisting Poncho's help, and that of his trusty snowmobile, Dad says he hauled two sleigh loads (70 tons) of ore to a pickup spot on Duncan Creek Road. The third sleigh load was hard to access but Dad agreed that if Poncho could retrieve it, the entire load was his. But Poncho got greedy, and demanded half of the two sleigh loads as well. When Dad refused, Poncho stole 700 pounds of precipitates from the mill and, unbeknownst to Dad, added it to the shipment. That's why Poncho was found guilty at the first trial and Dad wasn't. At the second trial, Dad didn't have a chance.

"The trial was one of 'reverse onus'—such laws have been knocked out by the Bill of Rights, and don't exist today," he writes. "UKHM… got $250,000 of taxpayers' money to prosecute me. I only had $5,000 in defense and as the Russian proverb says, 'When denim rubs against velvet, denim wears out.'"

Once he explained how he found the ore, Dad tackled the fun part of his story. Because ASARCO had smelted the ore before the first trial and had given the proceeds to UKHM, they were in a position to be sued. Prison guards smuggled a letter out for Dad to the Law Society of Seattle outlining his case. The letter landed in the hands of a young lawyer eager to take up the fight. So eager, in fact, once Dad was out of jail, he represented him for free.

"At the house on Main St. I got a phone call from some Colonel Blimp type at the defense's lawyers in Vancouver," Dad writes. "He was bursting a blood vessel with rage, and called me 'the most despicable character he had ever known' because of course he'd heard that the suit was going on in the States. Swine that I am!"

The suit proceeded, with Dad demanding $400,000 in damages. Of course the smelter hired the "most expensive Jewish law firm in New York" and after "two days and two nights" of bargaining, the case was settled out of court "for a large sum."

Dad's lawyer cautioned him against bringing such a large amount back to Canada as the government could seize it on the grounds that no one can profit from a criminal act. "No criminal act had been committed in the States so the money was safe there," Dad adds. But not safe enough. Dad's lawyer urged him to move the money even farther away, so after bringing back $20,000 to buy the house in Slocan, Dad flew to Liechtenstein, where he invested his hundreds of thousands at "a very high rate."

"Oh yes, I could have gone to live in Europe or South America," he writes. "I never touched the money for 25 years during which it nearly tripled."

And then? Spurred by a rumour that Canada would require all citizens to declare their foreign assets, Dad jetted to New York and directed that all the money be deposited in an American bank in Mexico City.

"I had, for a number of years, sent support to a little girl in Mexico. Hah! And at about the same time, a revolution had begun down in southern Mexico. VIVA Zapata!"

He then travelled to southern Mexico but the military had sealed off the border. After meetings with the Catholic Church, in particular a group of Jesuits—"a rock hard bunch"—Dad drew up an agreement that his money would be used to set up and support an orphanage in southern Mexico.

With his mission accomplished, he ends his tale. "There's the family history you wanted. I don't want to own anything any more. All I've got is a suitcase and a few clothes. Suits me, everything is off my neck now."

Fast-forward a year and a half. Dad's slovenly living conditions have deteriorated to a point where public health authorities force him into what he calls "a filing cabinet": a Castlegar residential care facility. The day he is admitted is the last day he ever walks, although nothing is wrong with his legs. We journey from our home in Victoria to see him the following spring. We arrive in the early evening, and Ben and Charlotte check in to the Sandman Hotel while I drive to the care home for a quick visit before they lock the doors.

As I enter, I see that the lights have already been dimmed, and the halls are quiet and empty. Dad's room is the second on the left, near the nurses' station. His door is slightly ajar. I find him on his back, eyes closed and his long body tightly tucked in. A warm amber glow emanates from his overhead bed light. Several days' worth of stubble darkens his lower face, and his cheeks cave in like dented fenders. I kiss him on the lips. "Hi Pappy." His eyes spring open and as I fumble for a nearby chair he pulls out his left arm and tightly grasps my right hand, bringing it to his chest and cupping his other hand over mine. His hand feels massive and warm. Like a bear paw. I inch my chair closer.

"I was a very bad boy," he says, looking directly into my eyes.

"Uh-huh," I say, giving his hand a squeeze and hoping for more.

"I didn't want to be. I really didn't. But I was."

"Yes?" I prompt.

"A very bad boy."

Turning his head away, he rolls over, closes his eyes and releases my hand. That is it. I press my lips to his forehead, tell him I'll see him tomorrow and leave.

The next day when Ben, Charlotte and I visit he is gruff, haughty and monosyllabic. Ben shaves him, an act he begrudgingly permits. Charlotte draws him a picture of the mountains. He glances at it. The visit turns awkward and as I am saying we'll return tomorrow when he is feeling better, he raises his hand to silence me.

"Don't hang around on my account."

"What?" I reply, not sure I heard right.

"I said don't hang around on my account."

His voice is loud, monotonic, and his eyes stare at the wall ahead. I walk out, along with Ben and Charlotte.

Dad dies four years later in the early morning of January 7, 2006, at Mountain Lake Seniors Community in Nelson—toothless, penniless, diapered and demented. I am with him the day before. But that is not how I remember him.

Framed and backlit, a young fair-haired man bends beside a shallow, rocky mountain brook. Dressed in jeans, leather chaps and a fringed buckskin jacket, he is alone but for a tall, all-black horse standing beside him. In the background, sunshine warms a row of stunted black spruce and bunched scrub grass. Above, shadows and sun stream across a ragged snow-patched crag. Off scene, positioned at just the right spot, is a tripod mounted with a 35 mm single-lens reflex Pentax camera. The man lifts the water-filled brim of his Stetson to his mouth. And drinks. Click.

Forgiveness has nothing to do with love.

A Note on Sources

MANY YEARS AGO, complete transcripts of my Dad's first and second trials were stored in a heavy cardboard box in a dark corner of my Omi and Grandpa's basement in East Vancouver. My mom, in anger and shame, threw out the box and its contents long before I even considered tackling this story. Decades later, when I'd changed my mind and began research, I discovered, much to my dismay, that the Yukon Department of Justice had lost the complete court files. Someone had borrowed much of the official record and failed to return it. And that was that. What remained with the department, however, was of immense help and included testimonies from key witnesses such as FBI special agent Bruce Lanthorn and geologist Alan Fawley; correspondence between Justice John Parker and the National Parole Board; and some Yukon Court of Appeal documents.

Fortunately, the official RCMP file on the case that I obtained after sending an inquiry to Library and Archives Canada filled in significant gaps in the trial record. That request yielded more than nine hundred pages of RCMP notes and correspondence relating to the investigation, the preliminary hearing, the two trials and the appeal. Although many pages and names were blacked out, they revealed a more complete picture of what occurred than I ever imagined. Included in the pages were valuable summaries of the preliminary hearing and the first trial written by Corporal George Strathdee. Strathdee's summary of the actions taken by the prosecution between the first and second trials was invaluable in understanding how the Crown shifted its focus after the first, unsuccessful attempt to convict my father.

A number of people either involved in the investigation or the trials shared their stories with me. Without them it would have been impossible to reconstruct events of fifty years ago. They included George Strathdee and Lauren McKiel, both long-retired from the RCMP; professional geologists and former United Keno Hill Mines employees Bob Cathro and Al Archer; and retired Vancouver lawyer John Molson, who represented my father at the preliminary hearing. In the Acknowledgements I name other people who provided important insights and information.

A handful of writers have briefly sketched out versions of the robbery. They are Aaro Aho in *Hills of Silver: The Yukon's Mighty Keno Hill Mine* (Harbour Publishing, 2006), Jane Gaffin in *Cashing In* (Nortech Yukon, 1980) and Joe Riddell in the magazine *The Yukoner* (Issue 22, 2002). Bob Cathro also wrote an account of the caper, *The Keno Hill Ore Theft*, published in 2002 in *The Moccasin Telegraph*, a now defunct online newsletter. He gave me an unedited copy of his story. Of even greater benefit was Cathro's 2006 article "Great Mining Camps of Canada 1. The History and Geology of the Keno Hill Silver Camp, Yukon Territory," published in *Geoscience Canada* (Volume 33, No. 3).

Both Aho's and Gaffin's books also provided rich details on the history of Yukon mining and settlement. Other historical accounts I drew on included Christopher Burn's *Guidebook to the Surface Geology and Environmental History of the Silver Trail* (Silver Trail Tourism Association, 1985); Jack Hope and Paul Von Baich's *Yukon* (Prentice-Hall, 1976) and the Mayo Historical Society's *Gold and Galena* (1991).

The Yukon Archives in Whitehorse helped me access *Whitehorse Star* articles published in 1963, 1964 and 1965 editions, and copies of *The Tramline*, a weekly mimeographed newsletter published in Elsa. At the archives I also discovered a small booklet titled *Souvenir Brochure of the Yukon Territory*. It was filled with useful facts about and wonderful pictures of the Yukon and its mining history. The brochure was written by former United Keno Hill Mines general manager Al Pike, and published to commemorate the gathering of the Sixth Commonwealth Mining and Metallurgical Congress, held in September 1957.

For insights into Justice John Parker, I drew on Frank Wade's *Advocate for the North: Judge John Parker—His Life and Times in the Northwest Territories* (Trafford Publishing, 2005). As for learning about conditions in the first prison Judge Parker consigned Dad to, I turned to Earl Andersen's *Hard Place to Do Time: The Story of Oakalla Prison, 1912–1991* (Hillpoint Publishing, 1993).

The selected passages from the poems of Robert Service reprinted in this book are taken from two collections: *The Best of Robert Service* (McGraw-Hill Ryerson Ltd., 1953) and *Songs of a Sourdough* (McGraw-Hill Ryerson Ltd., 1957). Readers interested in learning more about the man, his poetry and his times would do well to read Enid Mallory's *Robert Service: Under the Spell of the Yukon* (Heritage House Publishing, 2008).

Finally, my great appreciation goes to my mother, who thanks to a healthy hoarding streak kept all my father's letters and all of my sister's and my letters to our father when he was imprisoned, as well as many of her journals and records of her early years. She died in 2011.

Acknowledgements

M<small>Y BOOK IS CONSIDERED TO BE A MEMOIR</small>, the narrative telling of my recollections. But it is much more. It is also: a true crime story, a record of an essential era in Yukon mining and social history, a tribute to a disappeared place and lost way of life, and an important instance of Canadian legal evolution. Without the contributions of so many, however, it would be none of those. I am indebted to everyone mentioned below.

In 2009 I was at Yukon Justice requesting copies of any transcripts of my dad's preliminary hearing and two trials. Initially told that there was nothing, employee Natalie Paquette later emailed me a smattering of transcripts from the first trial. Later, Karin Keeley-Eriksson sent me more helpful materials.

From there, my research spun out like a skein from a ball of yarn. Whitehorse author Jane Gaffin handed me the first thread that led to the unravelling of a great ball of hitherto unexplored information and adventure. When I told her I needed someone to help me retrace my dad's footsteps on his former Moon claims, Jane lined me up with Keno City prospector Matthias Bindig. Matthias and his partner, geologist Lauren Blackburn, spirited me off one late August day on a hair-raising trip to the Moon. The day before Alexco Resource Corp. permitted employee Jennika Bergren to escort me around the Elsa camp and Keno mining site in a pickup truck. My evenings and nights were spent in Mayo with friend and fan Tex Fosbery, who hosted me in perfect, understated Yukon style.

Once I was back home, Jane introduced me via email to former UKHM mining engineer Bob Cathro, who happened to live just on the other side of the Malahat Highway from me. Bob, who testified against my dad, has graciously shared his memories and his expertise ever since. Bob connected me with Al Archer, the sharp-minded former chief geologist at UKHM, who related his version of events and even gave me hand-sketched maps of the crime scene. Bob also put me in touch with the two prime investigators of my dad's case: retired RCMP officers George Strathdee and Lauren McKiel. I was astounded at how well they remembered the case and how forthcoming they were in sharing their memories. George told me the official police file must still exist somewhere so after turning over a few barren rocks, I luckily encountered Library and Archives Canada senior analyst Diane Simard. Simard unearthed my nugget of gold and sent it to me in the form of a nine-hundred-page official RCMP file. Even though a good third of the file was redacted, it revealed more information than I'd ever hoped to find.

Former Yukon-based friends-of-the-family George Duerkson, George Esterer and Virginia Grundmanis, who knew my dad, supplied invaluable details about Elsa life as did childhood Yukon buddy Darryl Andison and former Yukoners Don White and Joe and Louise Volf.

Obviously, all the memories are not mine alone. I thank my sister Vona Priest for sharing some of hers and dusting off some of my own. Ever generous, Vona also shared her Yukon mementos, scrapbooks and photos. My cousin Rick Nelson openly related his experiences with my family, as did Helene Klassen and Neil Klassen.

For legal matters, I turned to Vancouver lawyers Robert Bellows, Chris Johnson and Allan McDonell as well as to retired Vancouver lawyer John Molson, who briefly defended my dad, and to retired Seattle lawyer David Wagoner, who contested my dad's American lawsuit.

On the photo front, I first credit my dad, who was an exceptional photographer and who took most of the photos in the book. For sharing their photos I also thank Lauren McKiel, Bob Cathro, Valerie and Jane Fawley, Kathy Haycock and Grant MacKenzie. For their help in tracking down archival photographs I am grateful to Cheryl Charlie, of Yukon Archives, and Anne Doddington from the Vancouver Public Library. My appreciation also goes to professional photographer and friend Garth Lenz of Victoria, for his help in making good photos great.

Special thanks to my special friend Robin Fowler for her keen editing skills and enormous heart. And a deep bow to Dude Dave Marshall for building my book website like only a geezer of his stature can.

At Harbour Publishing, I thank publisher Howard White, who showed keen interest in my query letter from day one. It didn't hurt that Howard has spent time in the Mayo–Keno area and even had a distant recollection of my dad's trial. Thank you to Pam Robertson, my eagle-eyed and gentle editor, for her exacting skill, and to Heather Lohnes, Harbour publicist extraordinaire. Thanks too to Harbour Managing Editor Anna Comfort O'Keeffe who helped shepherd everyone together to complete the project, and to Peggy Issenman for her stellar work on the book cover.

For his faith in my ability to write this book no matter what, I thank long-time friend and author Tom Wayman. Tom was the first person who, many years ago, gave me the confidence to become a writer after years working as a nurse. I also thank author Richard Mackie, who taught me a course on historical writing and took my query letter to Harbour.

I would be nowhere without my emotional cheerleaders—Susan and Steve Fox, Robin Fowler, Marjie Cave, Mia Stainsby, Lise Johnson, Sara Darling and Annie Carrithers. And my rock of a daughter Charlotte Priest who intuitively knew when I needed a cuddle or a poem to keep on going.

Finally, my book would not exist at all without my husband, my best friend, my superman Ben Parfitt. His devotion to this book and to me is beyond description.

Index